St Kilda

St Kilda

The Last and Outmost Isle

Angela Gannon and George Geddes

edited by

Jill Harden and Adam Welfare

Published in 2015 by
Historic Environment Scotland

Historic Environment Scotland
John Sinclair House
16 Bernard Terrace
Edinburgh EH8 9NX

telephone +44 (0) 131 662 1456

Historic Environment Scotland
Scottish Charity No. SC045925

British Library Cataloguing-in-Publication Data.
A catalogue record for this book is available from
the British Library.

ISBN 978 1 902419 91 6

Design by Oliver Brookes, HES

Typeset in Garamond, Brunel and Gill Sans

Printed in Poland by Skleniarz

Front Cover

St Kilda is situated in the Atlantic Ocean over 160km from
Scotland's mainland and 65km from the Outer Hebrides. For
many it is Virgil's Ultima Thule – the furthest flung place in
the inhabited world.

2015 The Centre for Digital Documentation and Visualisation LLP

Back Cover

'Getting the fulmar, St Kilda'. Norman MacLeod captured a
series of iconic scenes on St Kilda during August 1886. Here,
three St Kildans pose with their catch on Stac an Armin,
which could only be reached after a five mile row and a
difficult climb.

Norman MacLeod 1886 University of Aberdeen C4252

Endpapers

Sir Thomas Dyke Acland's sketches of the 'Isle of Borera
& Rock of the Solan Geese [Stac Lì]' (front) and the 'Isle of
Soer' (back), the first of which was drawn 'in the morning,
July 17 1812'. In these drawings, he has exaggerated the
natural scene by introducing numerous boats at different
scales set in an unusually calm sea.

National Trust Collection, Devon Heritage Centre, 1812,
1148M/23/F19

Frontispiece

The islands of Dun, Hirta and Soay float on the horizon,
some four miles from Boreray. In the foreground is the rocky
knoll of Clagan na Ròsgachan and Stac Lì.

Ian Parker RCAHMS, 2010, DP099638

Contents

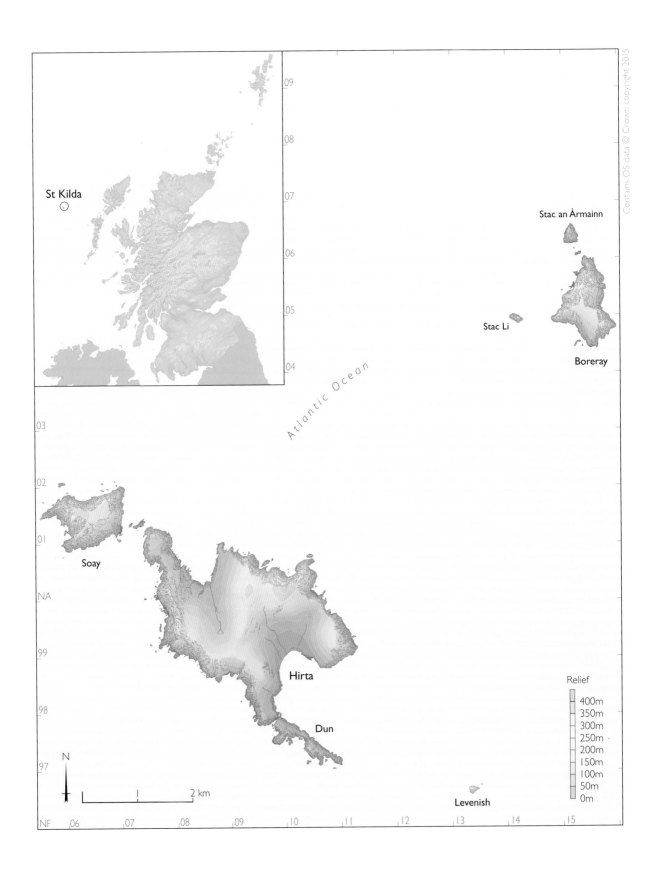

Contains OS data © Crown copyright 2015

St Kilda

Atlantic Ocean

Stac an Àrmainn

Stac Li

Boreray

Soay

Hirta

Dun

Levenish

N

| | 1 | | 2 km |

Relief

400m
350m
300m
250m
200m
150m
100m
50m
0m

Introduction

'The last and outmaist Ile', Hector Boece's description of St Kilda[1] – a brief, partly factual, partly mythic account – first brought these islands to the notice of a wider world in 1527. It sparked an interest in this remote archipelago that continues to the present day. Indeed, so powerful is the fascination of the *Island on the Edge of the World* that its allure has been translated into more than 700 books, articles and maps.[2] The majority of these accounts have been created by authors who have never set foot on St Kilda, or if they had it was only for a short time, with the result that they provide little more than a first impression. Very few have been penned in Gaelic or by native St Kildans.

The archipelago of St Kilda (Hiort) is situated in the Atlantic Ocean about 65km from Àird an Rùnair, the closest point on North Uist (Uibhist a Tuath), and 88km from the harbour at Leverburgh (An t-Òb) on Harris (Na Hearadh), both of which belong to the long chain of islands known as the Outer Hebrides (Na h-Eileanan Siar).[3] St Kilda forms an isolated part of the parish of Harris that has been administered by the Western Isles Council since 1975, but which was historically part of the County of Inverness. The archipelago comprises four islands, namely Hirta, Boreray, Soay and Dun (Hirte, Boraraigh, Sòthaigh, Dùn). In addition, there are three impressive sea stacks: the first, Levenish (Lìbhinis), guards the entrance to Village Bay on Hirta; while the others, Stac an Àrmainn and Stac Lì, are situated to the north-north-west and west of Boreray respectively. On a clear day Hirta and Boreray appear as dark silhouettes on the distant horizon from Harris and the Uists. Whilst the whole archipelago has been intensively exploited at one time or another, the focus of settlement appears to have always been in Village Bay on Hirta.

St Kilda is renowned for its dramatic landscape and scenery, its extensive sea bird colonies, its distinctive subspecies of woodmouse and wren and its two unique breeds of sheep. Above all, however, St Kilda's fame is as a lament for a lost way of life and the desertion of a landscape. The last 36 permanent inhabitants were evacuated on 29 August 1930, when they boarded HMS *Harebell* and set sail for new homes on the Scottish mainland.

St Kilda's most recent history is a story of recognition and protection at a time when an interest in natural history and the environment were very much at the forefront of social and political consciousness. Before his death in 1956, John Crichton-Stuart, the 5th Marquis of Bute, bequeathed the archipelago to the National Trust for Scotland (NTS); and the following year St Kilda was designated a National Nature Reserve by the Nature Conservancy – now Scottish Natural Heritage. Almost simultaneously, the United Kingdom Government established a military radar tracking station on Hirta

St Kilda – the archipelago and its location.
RCAHMS, 2015, GV005720

and the island remains part of a missile testing range operating from Benbecula. In 1986, recognition of the quality of St Kilda's dramatic landscape, its significant natural habitats and the species these support, resulted in it being inscribed by the United Nations Educational, Scientific and Cultural Organisation (UNESCO) as a World Heritage Site. This status was extended in 2004 to include the surrounding marine environment and again in 2005 to include its cultural heritage, establishing it at that time as one of only 24 sites in the world recognised for both natural and cultural criteria.[4]

The extension of St Kilda's status emphasised the need for a detailed historic environment record for the islands, fully integrated with a geographic information system. To address this, in 2006 the NTS invited the Royal Commission on the Ancient and Historical Monuments of Scotland (RCAHMS), in conjunction with colleagues from the NTS, to map systematically the archaeological features of the archipelago. This was carried out between 2007 and 2009 using a combination of satellite-derived survey positions and high definition rectified aerial photography. The results of the survey, together with a desire to place them in a wider Hebridean context, underpin this publication. In addition, the synthesis is supported by two large scale maps, one showing the archaeology of Village Bay, the other the archaeology of the archipelago, which draw on data produced during the RCAHMS surveys of 1983–6 and 2007–9, with additional information derived from surveys by Mary Harman and Glasgow University Archaeological Research Division (GUARD).

As the following chapter sets out, RCAHMS has a long history of involvement with the islands, which has been pieced together from unpublished material in its archive. Although of interest on its own account, this also provides an insight into how official attitudes and objectives have changed with time. The growing interest of RCAHMS in St Kilda over 100 years illustrates and reflects that of professional archaeologists more generally, and highlights St Kilda's developing place in the national consciousness.

Of course, there is a considerable amount of documentation from other sources on the history of the islands. By exploring this material we have charted the growing awareness and understanding of the archipelago's past from the earliest written accounts to the more modern programmes of research and investigation. There is clearly a bias in favour of St Kilda's later history and this too is played out in the archaeological record, as elements of the more recent past have swept aside those of earlier phases. Nevertheless, some evidence for these periods remains to permit an initial sketch. This book pieces together a continuous narrative of St Kilda from prehistory through to the present day, but continuing to improve the quality of the historical record will be a major challenge for the future.

In the process of writing this book, a wealth of historical and modern imagery has been unearthed. This material is showcased throughout the text, but is examined in detail in a special extended section. The photography covers various aspects of St Kilda, ranging from the landscape, the people, their seasonal activities, and the arrival and growth of tourism, to the evacuation of Hirta in 1930, the military occupation and, finally, the more recent expeditions undertaken by naturalists and historians. Many of these illustrations have never been published before and they include 19th and 20th century images from the collections of the NTS, the National Museum of Scotland and the School of Scottish Studies at the University of Edinburgh, together with modern ground and aerial photography produced by RCAHMS.

By rethinking the broader historical problems of St Kilda, we are challenging the romantic view of insularity and isolation that has characterised so much of the previous writing. There is no doubt that the archaeological remains of this archipelago are exceptional and in some cases represent unique responses to the local environment. Yet at the same time it seems clear that daily life could only have been sustained throughout much of the past if the islands were part of a more complex social and economic network. It is this narrative of *connection* that makes the history of 'the last and outmaist Ile' so remarkable.

The archaeology of St Kilda reflects the unfolding story of the
islanders over hundreds of years. Mrs Ann Gillies (née Ferguson),
pictured here walking down the Street with her knitting in her
hands, was born on Hirta in 1866. Ann was the daughter of the
senior St Kildan, Donald Ferguson.
National Trust for Scotland, c1930, 1002627

The Archaeology of
St Kilda

Chapter One

The Royal Commission and St Kilda

The establishment of the Royal Commission in 1908 created a national institution whose remit was 'to make an Inventory of the Ancient and Historical Monuments and Constructions connected with or illustrative of the contemporary culture, civilisation and conditions of life of the people in Scotland from the earliest times to the year 1707, and to specify those which seem most worthy of preservation'.[1] From the outset this has been undertaken through a programme of research, the investigation of sites in the field and the publication of the results either on an individual basis, or as part of regional and national syntheses.

At the heart of this process was the need to understand these 'Monuments and Constructions' in their wider context, whether topographical, historical or archaeological, in conjunction with a requirement to consider those that were 'most worthy of preservation and in need of protection'.[2] Since the 1990s, RCAHMS archaeological publications have departed from the traditional format of the Inventory and have instead offered a synthesis of landscape change and development. Both *Eastern Dumfriesshire: An Archaeological Landscape* (1997) and *In the Shadow of Bennachie: A Field Archaeology of Donside,*

Aberdeenshire (2007) present the results of this more holistic approach to archaeological survey, providing frameworks that allow the reader to appreciate the dynamic character of multi-period landscapes, rather than focusing upon a simple presentation of isolated monuments that survive within them.[3]

St Kilda was first considered by RCAHMS during their survey of the Outer Hebrides, Skye and the Small Isles for which fieldwork began in 1914. However, this did not conclude until 1926 and their *Ninth Report with Inventory of Monuments and Constructions in the Outer Hebrides, Skye and the Small Isles* followed only two years later.[4] Acknowledgement was made of the 'special circumstances' that necessarily prolonged the task, specifically the 'broken and difficult character of the area under investigation' and the weather, which was 'at once an influential and unstable factor'.[5] Progress had also been halted between 1916 and 1920 by the Great War, while it had been hindered both by a restrained budget and the lack of an archaeologist on the staff between 1919 and 1925.[6]

The Ninth Report included a list of monuments deemed most worthy of preservation, a historical and general introduction covering the archaeological remains, the secular and ecclesiastical structures, together with a list of relics – all of which preceded an inventory of 692 articles, illustrated by 314 plans and photographs. The introduction referred to St Kilda as the location of the discovery of two oval brooches assigned to the 'Viking Age' and also in a discussion

Known traditionally as Taigh an t-Sithiche (House of the Fairies), this Iron-Age souterrain, or underground chamber, is the highlight of St Kilda's prehistoric archaeology. First discovered by a crofter in 1844, 80 years later Captain Patrick Grant helpfully provided RCAHMS with notes and photographs for the Inventory.

Captain Patrick Grant, 1924, SC1467660

of 14th and 16th century charters.[7] In reviews of the report, Sir Cyril Fox noted that the lengthy introduction was 'an important contribution to the archaeology of Scotland', while Sir Mortimer Wheeler observed that 'the Commissioners show a praiseworthy reluctance to overestimate the antiquity of these [medieval and later buildings] merely on the grounds of their primitive appearance'.[8]

In the early discussions about the fieldwork for this report the Commissioners contemplated the hire of a steam yacht and debated a dedicated budget for this of some £200, although by 1914 it was considered inappropriate.[9] Instead, queries with regard to the problems of transportation were sent to both the Northern Lighthouse Board and the Board of Fishing. While RCAHMS staff had reached most of the Outer Hebrides, Skye and the Small Isles between 1914 and 1926, the investigation of the monuments on St Kilda came to depend upon the testament of a Captain Patrick Grant, late of the Indian Army, who happened to be visiting the island.[9] This must have been considered an acceptable response to the budgetary issues, especially as only the souterrain in Village Bay appeared to satisfy the terms of the Royal Warrant.

The entry for the souterrain, or 'earth-house' as it is termed, is dated 22 July 1924 and three photographs and one drawing credited to Grant survive in the

archive.[11] It was written with close reference to the writer John Sands' exploration of the structure in 1876 and draws specific attention, not only to the details of its architecture, but also to the finds, which included a 'large number of rude stone implements resembling hatchets and wedges', part of a lamp and some sherds of coarse pottery.[12] Unusually, the entry is followed by a note which shows that wider research had been undertaken, although none of the sites mentioned merited an individual inventory account. The list includes a reference to the subterranean structure on Mullach Sgar, the Amazon's House – which the authors were careful to describe as a beehive shieling – and the possible promontory fort on Dun.[13] In addition, the supposed stone circle and the settlement known as Taigh Stallair on Boreray are also cited, although there was nothing to record beyond a reference to an earlier account.[14]

It was not until 1956 that the advice of RCAHMS was again sought with regard to St Kilda, this time in response to a proposal to establish a military range in the Outer Hebrides. At that time the Ministry of Works was responsible for the protection of archaeological sites and this was a matter that had been raised in the parliamentary discussions that preceded consent.[15] Stewart Cruden, then Chief Inspector of Ancient Monuments for Scotland, directed his Regional Inspector, Roy Ritchie, to undertake preliminary surveys on the Outer Hebrides in 1955 and St Kilda in 1956.[16] The resultant programme of rescue excavation on South Uist in 1956 included the excavation of three sites by Richard Feachem, Alastair MacLaren and Kenneth Steer – all of whom were RCAHMS archaeologists.[17] These excavations were part of a two-year programme which, viewed in the light of contemporary work, has been described as the 'biggest archaeological project ever mounted in Scotland'.[18]

Despite newspaper articles to the contrary, there is no evidence that the staff of RCAHMS visited St Kilda in 1956.[19] However, in correspondence later that year between Stewart Cruden and Angus Graham, then Secretary of RCAHMS, Cruden noted that his Ministry had persuaded the Military 'to confine the disposition of their hutments and plant to the area outside the ruined village'.[20] RCAHMS was invited to undertake a survey on St Kilda at this time, but they concluded that 'emergency survey operations in St Kilda will not be necessary', continuing that 'there

Plans for the construction of the Hebrides Missile Range were addressed by a massive programme of survey and excavation led by the Ministry of Works. RCAHMS archaeologist Richard Feachem is pictured here (wearing a tie) with his wife Megan and a group of local workmen during excavations at Drimore on South Uist.

RCAHMS, 1956, SC1360474

is evidently an attractive field here for anyone wishing to make a detailed study of an old-standing village community, but this is not within the Commission's scope' – a pointed reference to the Royal Warrant which, although allowing for discretion, still required a focus on the period preceding 1707.[21] As a result, the scheme of recording on St Kilda was undertaken by the University of Edinburgh, led by Stuart Sanderson of the School of Scottish Studies.[22] However, in an undated memorandum, Alastair MacLaren of RCAHMS suggested that 'failing the completion of the record' by the School, 'an architectural expedition by the Commission, to make records of the bee-hives, the shielings, the well-heads and the cleits, and the other earlier and later medieval monuments, would serve a useful purpose'.[23] At that time, however, the two architectural staff were deeply engaged in the survey of buildings in Stirlingshire and Peebleshire; and the estimate that the trip would require four weeks may well have stifled any such plans.

In October 1964, Richard Feachem prepared a document summarising the known sites and monuments of St Kilda, probably because there was then a possibility that the Military might abandon the islands.[24] However, he concluded that 'at present there is no call whatever for excavation, indeed every reason

to abstain from it'. He also noted that if 'there was, as seems very likely, an Early Christian Settlement on St Kilda, then no addition to the knowledge already acquired would be worth the effort if it fell short of a complete survey of all the ruined structures and enclosures in both Village Glen and Gleann Mor'. This was a task that he estimated would take an entire field season, involving 'two, preferably four, architects and draughtsman for the whole period; an archaeologist for the initial exploration; and a photographer at the beginning and later on'. Although Roy Ritchie pursued this the next year, the logistical concerns of transport and the practical difficulties of obtaining food and accommodation contributed to the RCAHMS decision not to venture to the islands.[25]

In 1974, Mary Harman, an archaeologist and osteologist, began to gather information about St Kilda. This inspired her interest in the cleitean, which became the subject of a detailed study approved and supported by the NTS. Geoffrey Stell, an architectural historian with RCAHMS, was one of those from whom she sought advice and this subsequently helped inform her methodology.[26] Harman's familiarity with the islands was also instrumental in her later becoming part of RCAHMS survey team, which was formed in response to a request by Alexander Bennett to 'carry out a detailed survey … of all the remains, structures, dykes, cleits and drains to be found in the village area'.[27] Bennett was then a Building Surveyor with the NTS, with additional responsibility for St Kilda and Canna. That request to John Dunbar, the Secretary of RCAHMS, in 1982, had been preceded by exploratory discussions between Bennett and Stell[28] and by the next year it was understood that the main task would be 'the survey and analysis of the island's archaeological sites and historic buildings, with the resulting information being made available in an entirely disinterested way to all those who require it'.[29]

It is clear from the surviving administrative records that the project developed piecemeal over the following years with competition for RCAHMS resources casting doubt on the viability of each season's fieldwork; while the decision to publish came relatively late. Nevertheless, the results proved useful to the NTS and a programme of excavation by Durham University ensued in close association with the Inspectorate of Ancient Monuments, the University and RCAHMS.[30] This and the RCAHMS survey were also used in support of the nomination of St Kilda as a World

Heritage Site – for both cultural and natural values – in late 1985, although only the latter were inscribed.

Geoffrey Stell, writing of the survey almost a decade later, reflected upon its two main aims: the first was to illustrate the overall extent of occupation and the second was to present a selection of buildings in greater detail where phasing could be observed.[31] Three main areas had been surveyed between 1983 and 1984 – Village Bay, the east side of Gleann Mòr and An Lag Bhon Tuath – and more than 30 detailed surveys had been taken of individual structures or groups of structures by 1986.[32] The accompanying accounts followed the traditional format of a descriptive textual commentary and analysis, supported by interpretative drawings and photography, with a summary of the results published in 1988, two years after the fieldwork had been completed. Stell remarked: 'Given the extent and complexity of the areas involved, not to mention the logistical difficulties of all operations of this kind on St Kilda, it was clear from the outset that the execution of the first of the simple strategic objectives – the area surveys – would probably be the greatest technical and physical challenge which the Royal Commission had encountered to that date.'[33]

When *The Buildings of St Kilda* appeared in 1988 it was the first publication 'to be prepared and presented … almost in [its] entirety in word-processed form'.[34] This marked an important step forward for RCAHMS, but such changes were also being mirrored in methodologies employed in the field. The survey of Hirta was unusual in that it entailed detailed recording over large areas at a scale of 1:500 and the establishment of a network of stations to control accuracy. To this end the surveyors used an electronic distance measuring instrument mounted on a theodolite in all three areas, within each of which they created a series of divorced surveys using plane-tables and self-reducing alidades; and when finally completed the survey drawings covering the crofting township and the adjacent area of An Lag Bhon Tuath measured some 5m in extent.[35] A summary of the RCAHMS 1983 to 1986 survey was published as a broadsheet in 1998.[36]

This introduction of more accurate and rapid mapping techniques meant that RCAHMS surveys throughout Scotland were no longer constrained by the range of optical instruments and instead the context and relationships of sites could be plotted over much greater distances. Complex multi-period landscapes could now be readily illustrated and the potential was explored in mapping the medieval and later remains of Waternish (Bhatarnais) on Skye.[37] Moreover, entire Hebridean islands could now to be mapped effectively by combining the readings from electronic distance measuring equipment with positions derived from satellites.[38]

RCAHMS staff visited St Kilda in 2004 and in 2006, just a year after the inclusion of the cultural landscape in the inscription of the World Heritage Status of St Kilda, RCAHMS and the NTS began to plan a new survey, in order to satisfy the request from UNESCO 'that a survey and record of the cultural landscape of St Kilda [should be] undertaken so that appropriate management regimes can be delivered'.[39]

Following a reconnaissance of Hirta in April 2007, the survey was divided into two ten-day trips each year between 2007 and 2009 – with RCAHMS staff working alongside NTS personnel. The poet and essayist Kathleen Jamie joined the team for one trip in 2007[40] and Mary Harman for another in 2008. The sketch maps and photographs resulting from Harman's previous work, which had been developed into a database by the NTS, provided the foundation for the accurate survey of the cleitean that were to be mapped and described throughout the islands. At the same time, the NTS was able to gather information about the condition of the numerous structures encountered, which would in future allow them to monitor their condition. Inevitably, new features were discovered and some of those that were already known were reinterpreted. High-resolution vertical aerial photographs were used wherever possible and the surveys of the 1980s were digitised and thoroughly checked on the ground to facilitate their use in a geographic information system. Where time allowed, detailed plans of selected sites were also taken, but the written descriptions of every structure that were made at the time were only summarised in Canmore – the RCAHMS online database of Scotland's archaeological, architectural and maritime heritage.

Although the RCAHMS survey of 2007 to 2009 concentrated largely on Hirta, a brief foray to Dun took place in the final year, allowing the known features there to be reviewed. The rich archaeological landscape on Boreray was recorded during a ten day research expedition in 2010 in partnership with the NTS and a short description of this was published in 2012.[41] Aerial sorties were flown over the archipelago in 2012 and 2013, while a failed attempt to land on Stac an Àrmainn in 2013 was countered by a return to Dun. In addition, a final field trip to Hirta in 2014 led to the completion of RCAHMS portfolio of blackhouse plans and a study of the remains of the pre-Improvement settlement. An analysis of the field system of Village Bay was included in a reflexive discussion of field-survey techniques in 2013.[42]

During this period, the opportunity has also been taken to re-evaluate a number of the shieling sites in Lewis (Leòdhas) and Harris that were studied by Captain Frederick Thomas in the middle of the 19th century.[43] These played an important part in the interpretation of St Kilda's antiquities at the time. Field trips have also been made to the islands of Pabbay (Pabaigh), Ensay (Easaigh) and Killegray (Ceileagraigh), in order to review the archaeological records for those islands. RCAHMS has also reviewed the Neolithic monuments on the main Hebridean islands north of Barra (Barraigh) and has also undertaken archaeological surveys of Barra Head (Beàrnaraigh), North Rona (Rònaigh a Tuath), the Flannan Islands (Na h-Eileannan Flanach), the Monach Isles (Heisgeir), and two portions of North and South Uist.[44] These, together with RCAHMS longer history of work across the Western Isles, actively shape and inform the current understanding of St Kilda.

The survey of St Kilda relied upon information provided by a GPS system collecting data from a base station and from mobile units carried by the staff. The lead surveyor Ian Parker is shown here setting up the base station, which beamed a signal to these units throughout the rugged island landscapes.

taken by Angela Gannon RCAHMS, 2007, DP212657

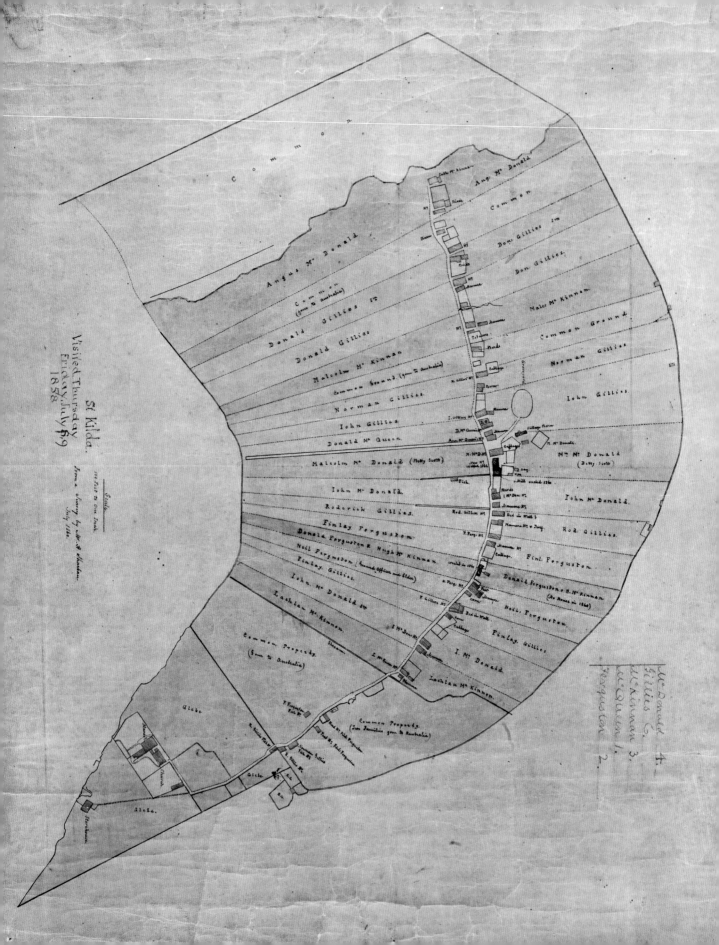

St Kilda.

Visited Thursday
Friday, July 8 & 9
1858.

From a Survey by Mr A Sharbau
July 1860

Scale
100 Feet to One Inch

C O M M O N

Angus McDonald

Common
(gone to Australia)

Donald Gillies 1st

Donald Gillies

Malcolm McKinnon

Common Ground (gone to Australia)

Norman Gillies

John Gillies

Donald McQueen.

Malcolm McDonald (Molly Scott)

John McDonald.

Roderick Gillies.

Finlay Ferguson.

Donald Ferguson & Hugh McKinnon.

Neil Ferguson (Ground, Officer now Elder)

Finlay Gillies.

John McDonald 2nd

Lachlan McKinnon.

Common Property
(gone to Australia)

Glebe

Glebe

Glebe

Storehouse

Beth McKinnon

Ang McDonald

Common

Don Gillies Jun.

Don Gillies.

Malm McKinnon

Common Ground

Norman Gillies

John Gillies

Village Room

M. McDonald

M. McDonald
(Betty Scott)

John McDonald.

Rod Gillies.

Finl Ferguson.

Donald Ferguson & H. McKinnon
(No House in 1860)

Neil Ferguson

Finlay Gillies.

J. McDonald.

Lachlan McKinnon.

Common Property
(Two Families gone to Australia)

McDonald 4.
Gillies 6.
McKinnon 3.
McQueen 1.
Ferguson 2.

Chapter Two
Antiquaries and Archaeologists

While the work of RCAHMS in the Outer Hebrides, Skye and the Small Isles between 1914 and 1926 resulted in the first detailed regional study of the area's archaeology, earlier accounts from the late 17th century had interwoven information about the antiquities with general topographic matter, ethnography, folklore and natural history.[1] Martin Martin's *A Voyage to St Kilda* (1698) and *A Description of the Western Isles of Scotland* (1703) not only offer the historian and the archaeologist a uniquely detailed insight into life at that time, but also demonstrate how antiquities were then understood not only on St Kilda, but throughout the Western Isles. The geographer Charles Withers noted that Martin's accounts were of especial importance for three reasons: as a native of Skye and a Gaelic speaker, he was of the places and people he writes about; they pre-date the full development of the romantic vision of Highland Scotland; and he was a 'practising scientist with national connections', writing largely at the behest of members of the Royal Society.[2] The descriptions Martin provides of the cleitean and bothies on St Kilda, as well as of specific structures such as the Amazon's House and Taigh Stallair are invaluable

This plan by Henry Sharbau and Captain Frederick Thomas portrays how the crofting landscape in 1860 was apportioned between the various families.

Society of Antiquaries of Scotland Collection, National Museum of Scotland, 1860, MS158

and can be compared with the descriptions he gives of the 'several ancient forts' on Harris and of fowling practices generally in the Hebrides.[3] Martin's account of St Kilda was followed by those of the Reverend Alexander Buchan (1727), an incumbent on the island, and the Reverend Kenneth Macaulay of Harris (1764), both of whom touch on antiquities that are broadly understood to be ancient, Danish or Druidical.[4] And only a few years later, the first record of a chance find is reported, when 'fisher-men ... dug up ... two antique urns, containing a quantity of Danish silver coin'.[5]

Further discoveries of archaeological interest were prompted by phases of the same agricultural improvement that brought sweeping changes to rural life across much of Scotland after 1700. Thus, while the removal of an archaeological site in the 17th century or earlier is rarely recorded in the Outer Hebrides, this changed during the 18th and 19th century. The notes taken by the Reverend Neil Mackenzie relating to the discovery of cists and an underground structure during the creation of fields and enclosures around his manse on Hirta between 1832 and 1844 are a case in point; although they were only published much later by his son.[6]

While the majority of the early accounts of St Kilda's antiquities are parochial, the island was also visited by Thomas Muir, the well-known scholar and author of *Ecclesiological notes on some of the islands of Scotland*, who excavated at the Amazon's

The finds retrieved from the souterrain by the Kearton brothers and the factor's son in 1896 are displayed as a semi-ordered jumble. They included a Norse spearhead, as well as a collection of undated stone tools and implements.
Cherry Kearton, 1896, DP113396

House in 1858.[7] Two years later, Hirta was visited by Captain Frederick Thomas, a member of the Royal Navy's hydrographic survey, who undertook the first 'substantive archaeological work' in the Outer Hebrides.[8] As well as providing Muir with additional information for his published note on the Amazon's House, Thomas conducted a series of important surveys on buildings in Village Bay and Gleann Mòr which are now preserved in the archives of the Society of Antiquaries of Scotland; and there is also little doubt that the fine illustration of the township prepared by his assistant Henry Sharbau in July 1860 was created at his behest.[9] For Thomas, St Kilda's buildings were a critical element of his thesis explaining architectural development in the Outer Hebrides, featuring in two out of three of his key publications. His empirical work is of great interest, but his contention that blackhouses and shielings reflected 'the past in the present' contributed to a sense that the architectural traditions of the islands were somehow ancient or backward.[10] Another notable figure in Hebridean history, Alexander Carmichael, visited Hirta in 1865 and again in 1878, gathering the songs and traditions of the islanders, some of which were later to appear in his compendium *Carmina Gadelica* (1900), but there is little evidence that he was concerned with the archaeology of St Kilda.[11]

Although Thomas was interested in 'earth-houses', he was unaware of the souterrain on Hirta known to the inhabitants as Taigh an t-Sithiche. This had been accidentally discovered by 'a man who was digging the ground above it' in 1844, but its exploration was left to John Sands, who had a lengthy stay on the island in 1875 and returned in 1876, when he 'determined to get it opened and examined'.[12] Subsequently, Sands read the first detailed study of St Kilda's antiquities to the Society of Antiquaries of Scotland in April 1877, including within it a notice of structures on Hirta, Dun, Soay and Boreray, as well as some observations on certain customs that 'may throw light on the habits of ancient and primitive populations'.[13] His general interest in islands resulted in forays to Tiree and Foula, and at least one other paper on antiquities.[14]

The souterrain attracted further attention in 1896 when it was re-excavated by the estate factor's son, John Mackenzie, at the behest of Richard and Cherry Kearton.[15] John Mackenzie's interest in antiquities was also relied upon by John Mathieson and he is known to have helped in the exploration of Dùn Fiadhiart on Skye in 1914.[16] Richard Kearton's book, along with another contemporary volume by Norman Heathcote, provided a number of general notes and photographs of antiquities, together with a general descriptive commentary on the islands.[17] A further description of St Kilda's antiquities was read to the Society in 1905 by Reverend James Bannatyne Mackenzie, the son of Reverend Neil Mackenzie, who recounted the 'antiquities and old customs' of the archipelago from notes that had been made by his father some 60 years earlier. This combined the discovery of prehistoric features with observations on 19th century buildings and agricultural practice.[18] Mackenzie, who had contributed a number of articles to the *Proceedings of the Society of Antiquaries of Scotland* on subjects such as cup-markings, stone axes, and stone circles, was also a keen photographer.[19]

In 1928, John Mathieson published a fresh overview of St Kilda's antiquities. Mathieson, a Gaelic speaker from Durness in northern Scotland, had retired as a Division Superintendent of the Ordnance Survey in 1909, in order to take up the role of chief surveyor in a study of Svalbard.[20] As a corresponding member of the Society he had published a note on an 'earth-house' near Durness a few years earlier, and had advised RCAHMS on the use of Gaelic in 1910.[21] However, his main focus on St Kilda was the creation of the first accurate map of the islands, which had been omitted from the Ordnance Survey's coverage of Harris and North Uist some 50 years earlier. He and his assistant, the geologist Alexander Murray Cockburn, prepared this over a four month period in the summer of 1927 and it was published the following year as a fold-out in the *Scottish Geographical Magazine* along with a descriptive memoir. In line with Ordnance Survey practice, the map included the position of known antiquities, including the locations of the three chapels on Hirta. It was subsequently adopted and republished by the Ordnance Survey.[22]

The evacuation of the islands in 1930 created opportunities for all sorts of individuals like Robert Atkinson, who photographed many of the buildings between 1938 and 1953,[23] while numerous visits were made by naturalists, who were also interested in history and archaeology.[24] Thereafter, major developments in the study of the islands' archaeology had to wait until the late 1950s, when St Kilda was being considered with the Outer Hebrides as the site of a Joint Services Guided Missile Range,[25] at the same time as the ownership of the islands was transferred to the NTS, who conferred the day-to-day management to the Nature Conservancy in 1957.[26] The Ministry of Works' response to the proposed range was almost immediate, with their Inspector Roy Ritchie undertaking a detailed reconnaissance of the archaeology on Hirta threatened by the plan in 1956. He was especially impressed by the abandoned township, where 'the history of village planning can be seen on the ground and dated from the accounts of those who have written about the island … . Probably no other community has been so well documented and no other community will offer such an opportunity for studying the development of village planning'.[27] This was an important observation, as it was perhaps the first recognition that St Kilda might prove suitable for rural settlement studies, some six years before Horace Fairhuirst's excavations at Rosal in Sutherland established this as a sub-discipline.[28]

The detailed story of the Ministry of Works' programme has yet to be told, but it was developed with the School of Scottish Studies who would arrange for Ian Whittaker to record and study the cleitean and agricultural structures on St Kilda; Donald MacGregor to plan the township and the surrounding countryside; Patrick Nuttgens to study the architecture of the houses; while Wilhelm Nicolaisen would analyse the islands' placenames.[29] Unfortunately, apart from a collection of photographs in the safekeeping of the School, only Macgregor's study was published.[30]

The Reverend Neil Mackenzie helped the St Kildans establish a crofting landscape during the 1830s, before moving to Kilchrenan on the shores of Lochawe in his later years. His son, an active antiquarian and photographer, captured this view of the family outside the manse there in 1871. It seems likely that the man pictured on the left is the minister.
Reverend James Bannatyne Mackenzie, 1871. DP157052.

At much the same time, the staff of the Nature Conservancy also turned their attention to the islands' archaeology. Regional Officer John Morton Boyd and Warden Kenneth Williamson, operating independently of the Ministry of Works and the wider archaeological community, focussed their efforts on two particular problems: the whereabouts of the medieval village and an explanation for the archaeological remains in Gleann Mòr.[31] Their conception with regard to the latter is best expressed in the following quotation: 'Could it be (we often wondered) that this, the remotest glen in all Scotland, on the very brink of Europe, once cradled a forgotten culture?'[32]

Mary Harman began her study of St Kilda's archaeology and culture in 1977. With the assistance of Stuart Murray, she visited the most inaccessible structures such as this bothy perched on the steep slopes of Stac an Àrmainn. Her data forms the foundation of St Kilda's sites and monuments record.

Mary Harman, 1977, SC1305308

Boyd and Williamson's perception of the archaeology of St Kilda was essentially naive. They understood it to be uniquely distinctive and largely independent of its wider context on account of its remoteness – a notion that studies of the St Kilda mouse and the wren had already shown to be true.[33] However, the tacit contention that the human occupation of the islands might somehow have followed this same Darwinian arc was new. So it was that while the archaeological establishment was excavating Iron Age and Norse sites in the Uists under the auspices of the rescue programme agreed with the Ministry of Works, Williamson and Boyd were formulating a theory about a 'Gleann Mor Folk' on St Kilda,[34] which not only divorced the islands from the remainder of the Hebrides, but was quite at odds with

the models then being developed in archaeology.[35] Nevertheless, their ideas were influential because they were published widely at a time when the profile of the Nature Conservancy in relation to the islands was especially high.[36]

Some excavation did take place. An NTS work party led by Professor Andrew O'Dell of the Department of Geography at Aberdeen University spent at least a day in 1958 'digging out the floors of the buildings' in Gleann Mòr,[37] while James Mackay, an educational officer with the Royal Artillery, excavated Calum Mòr's House in Village Bay with the aid of another party.[38] However, by 1963 Roy Ritchie's recommendations with regard to the most significant archaeological sites on Hirta had been accepted and these were now offered protection as Scheduled Ancient Monuments under Act of Parliament. This defined elements within the landscape as of special significance and brought into play a process of official consent that was to provide an important counterbalance to some of the more invasive and ill-thought-out actions that had been previously initiated.[39] In 1966, Francis Celoria, leading a summer school from the University of Keele, surveyed many of the cleitean on Hirta and undertook a small excavation of a turf feature at An Lag Bhon Tuath, subsequently interpreted as a raised cultivation bed;[40] and that same year, the Ordnance Survey's Archaeology Division began to revise and update their card index of sites and finds for future editions of their maps.[41] The initial research was conducted by Beverly Stallwood,[42] but fieldwork the following year was undertaken by Jimmy Davidson.[43] Unusually, Davidson produced a separate report in which he identified what he thought might be prehistoric structures and provided a detailed commentary on the development of the township and its cleitean.[44]

Piecemeal surveys were undertaken by Rutherford in 1970[45] and Tom Hetherington in 1972 and 1973.[46] More extensive work was carried by Barry Cottam of the Department of Geography in the University of Dundee and the NTS in 1973 and 1974[47] on Dun, in Gleann Mòr and at An Lag Bhon Tuath on Hirta, where a 'boat-shaped' setting that had been identified as a possible Viking grave yielded a radiocarbon date that seemed to place it firmly in the 2nd millennium BC.[48] In 1977, Mary Harman began her research of the cleitean,[49] in the course of which more than

1,350 were identified, measured and described. Most were also photographed and her study forms the foundation of the NTS' sites and monuments record and the later RCAHMS mapping programme.

The RCAHMS survey of Village Bay from 1983 to 1986 proved to be a catalyst in the initiation of a new programme of work permitted by the Scottish Development Department (SDD) and sponsored by the NTS from 1984. This could be justified on four counts: it would contribute to a better understanding of Scotland's archaeology generally; it would assist the interpretation and presentation of St Kilda; it would diversify the deployment of the summer work parties; and it would facilitate the conservation and repair of a few of those structures that seemed to be deteriorating.[50] A small excavation within the interior of two buildings, Blackhouse U and House 16, by Timothy Quine of the University of Strathclyde had been carried out in 1983,[51] but now the NTS sought the advice of John Dunbar, the Secretary of RCAHMS, who invited one of the Commissioners, Professor Rosemary Cramp of the Department of Archaeology at the University of Durham, to discuss the possibility of further work with the SDD and the NTS in early 1984.[52] Overseen by a committee of eight, the resulting programme was undertaken by Durham University between 1986 and 1990 and published by Norman Emery in 1996.[53] Excavations concentrated upon House 6, in advance of its reconstruction, House 8 (together with the building that it replaced) and 'Blackhouse' W, which confirmed that the latter had been built originally as a kiln barn.[54]

One of the committee, Chris Morris, moved north from Durham to the University of Glasgow, instigating a second phase of investigation between 1991 and 1997 under the directorship of Alex Morrison. This included mapping, geophysical surveys and excavations in the vicinity of Mullach Sgar and An Lag Bhon Tuath; and also a programme of palaeobotanical sampling undertaken by Jacqui Huntly of the University of Durham.[55] During this period, Mary Harman continued to record structures throughout the islands, which resulted in a PhD thesis presented to the School of Scottish Studies at The University of Edinburgh in 1994. This was subsequently published in shortened form as *An Isle Called Hirte* (1997). Thereafter, between 1995 and 1998, Andrew Fleming of the

The enclosures on the floor of An Lag Bhon Tuath nestle between Conachair and Oiseval. They were the site of an extensive programme of survey, excavation and environmental sampling undertaken by the University of Glasgow in the 1990s. Steve Wallace RCAHMS, 2008. DP044901

University of Wales and Mark Edmonds of the University of Sheffield embarked upon a detailed search for evidence of prehistoric activity on the islands, ultimately culminating in the publication of Fleming's *St Kilda and the Wider World* (2005).[56] As a landscape archaeologist, Fleming recognised the complexities of multi-period landscapes and in his book he also challenged the perception of St Kilda as both distinctive and isolated. These are the themes that will be developed further in the course of this book. Research on the soils across Hirta by Andrew Meharg of the Department of Plant and Soil Science at the University of Aberdeen, led to the discovery of surprisingly high levels of toxins in the enclosed fields of the crofts – a finding that was explained by the islanders' former practice of recycling seabird carcasses containing contaminants when making a fertiliser from an admixture of peat and turf ash.[57] Geophysical survey and trial excavations were undertaken in these fields and elsewhere in Village Bay by GUARD between 1998 and 2006. The results of all the work that has been undertaken by the Archaeology Department of Glasgow University and GUARD since 1991 have been recently published in *Winds of Change: The Living Landscapes of Hirta, St Kilda* (2011) authored by Jill Harden and Olivia Lelong.[58]

Chapter Three
First Visitors – 10,000 BC to AD 400

Mesolithic, 10,000 to 4000 BC

Discarded food waste and evidence for stone tool manufacture indicate that people were living along the Atlantic seaboard from about 9,000 years ago. Persistently occupied sites such as An Corran and Camas Daraich on Skye, and Kinloch on Rum, not only reveal something of the Mesolithic economy, but more importantly indicate that these communities moved freely in and around Scotland's coastline.[1] Coastal-hopping and short sea journeys were clearly part of everyday life and the clear view to St Kilda from the Outer Hebrides, coupled with clement weather conditions, would only have encouraged attempts to reach these islands. It has been argued that the decline in woodland on South Uist in the late 7th millennium BC was induced by fires caused by people[2] and this indication of a human presence in the Outer Hebrides has now been strengthened by the first secure evidence for Mesolithic activity at Northton on Harris, dating from about 7000 BC, as well as strong indications of activity elsewhere.[3] Peat formation and the rise in sea level may now hinder the detection of hunter-gatherer camps.

Making the journey across open water from the Outer Hebrides, St Kilda's first visitors would have been confronted by the sheer cliffs fringing the eastern edge of Hirta as they sought a safe place to land.
Steve Wallace RCAHMS, 2008, DP046608

The key factor that holds true throughout St Kilda's history is that the most attractive areas for settlement and land-use have been consistently exploited and re-exploited; under these circumstances the survival of evidence from earlier periods becomes increasingly at risk through time. While there is no evidence for ocean-going craft in Britain until the Bronze Age, it is possible that earlier, occasional and short-lived attempts at settlement did occur; and perhaps artefact scatters and the remains of ephemeral structures, together with their associated middens, lie buried beneath the low-lying land now occupied by the later field systems in Village Bay on Hirta. The numerous small-scale excavations that have taken place across this area have focussed upon other questions, but nevertheless the fact that no Mesolithic finds have been noted is perhaps telling. Other possible occupation sites like the flooded caves beneath the present cliffs have never been systematically investigated.

Neolithic, 4000 to 2500 BC

If the occupation of the Outer Hebrides in the Mesolithic is attested only by fragmentary remains and little more than circumstantial evidence, the Neolithic is more clearly represented by a range of great megalithic chambered tombs that have been studied since the early 20th century.[4] These include sites such as Barpa Langais[5] and Clettraval (Cleitreabhal a Deas)[6] on North Uist, both of which provide views to St Kilda on clear days and are located on high ground

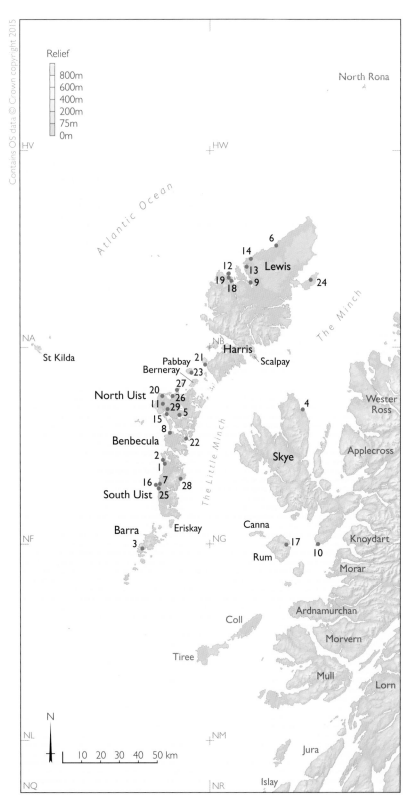

Relief

800m
600m
400m
200m
75m
0m

Contains OS data © Crown copyright 2015

North Rona

Atlantic Ocean

HV

HW

6
14
12
13   Lewis
19 18   9
24

The Minch

NA

St Kilda

NB

Harris

Pabbay   21
Berneray   23
27
North Uist   20   26
11   29   5
15
8
Benbecula
22
2
1
16   7
South Uist   25   28

Barra
3

The Little Minch

Scalpay

4

Wester Ross

Skye

Applecross

Knoydart

Morar

Eriskay

Canna

NG

Rum   17   10

Coll

Ardnamurchan

Morvern

Mull

Lorn

NF

NL

N

10   20   30   40   50 km

NM

NQ

NR

Jura

Islay

Tiree

The Western Isles –
sites referred to in this chapter

1   A' Cheardach Bheag
2   A' Cheardach Mhòr
3   Allt Chrisal
4   An Corran
5   Barpa Langais
6   Barvas
7   Bornais
8   Bruthach a' Tuath
9   Callanish
10   Camas Daraich
11   Clettraval
12   Cnip
13   Dalmore
14   Dun Carloway
15   Dùn na Càrnaich
16   Dun Vulan
17   Kinloch
18   Loch Baravat
19   Loch na Berie
20   Loch Olabhat
21   Northton
22   Rosinish
23   Seana Chaisteal
24   Shulishader
25   Sligeanach
26   Sollas
27   The Udal
28   Uisinis
29   Unival

RCAHMS, 2015, GV005721

away from the coast; others such as Dùn na Càrnaich,[7] also on North Uist, occupy lower lying locations and yet more are to be found on the smaller islands nearby.[8] A handful of cup marked rocks are also found in this coastal zone,[9] as are some of the earliest stone circles like Callanish (Calanais) on Lewis, where traces of cultivation have been observed that predate its construction.[10] Indeed, there is now an increasing body of evidence for contemporary settlement along the coastal margins of the Hebrides, as well as on islets in lochans, beneath peat bogs and in the machair.[11] The best studied of these is that at Loch Olabhat on North Uist, but others at The Udal, also on North Uist, and at Northton on Harris suggest many more await discovery.[12]

The material culture associated with the Neolithic in the Outer Hebrides includes pottery, a wide range of stone and bone tools, as well as more unusual objects such as carved stone balls. Some of these artefacts were produced locally, but others reveal a well-developed network of exchange for items made from Rum bloodstone, Arran pitchstone and Antrim porcellanite.[13] A remarkable example is a porcellanite axe which was recovered intact within its wooden haft during peat cutting at Shulishader (Sulasiadar) on Lewis in 1982.[14]

Although no unequivocal sign of Neolithic occupation was noted on St Kilda by RCAHMS, there is some evidence to suggest human activity. A pollen sequence from Gleann Mòr on Hirta, taken in the summer of 1980, demonstrated a steady rise of ribwort plantain around 3800 BC.[15] At that time, ribwort plantain was interpreted as a natural component of maritime plant communities, rather than as an indicator of pastoral or arable activity; but Andrew Fleming of the University of Wales has argued that this may have been an over cautious analysis,[16] as more recently, a discontinuous sequence obtained from the peat bog between Mullach Mòr and Conachair, indicated the presence of 'cereal-type pollen' around 3100 BC.[17]

To these sparse environmental indicators can be added the discovery of two sherds of Neolithic pottery recovered from the sea-cliff fronting Village Bay in 1996.[18] The use of diagonal incised decoration on both is in keeping with the character of Hebridean Neolithic pottery,[19] although it would be more satisfactory if sherds of this kind were better dated. Further aspects of material culture are provided by

The eroding Atlantic coastline at Northton on Harris has provided evidence for Mesolithic, Neolithic and Bronze Age activity, while only a short distance further round the coast stand the remains of an Iron Age broch and a medieval chapel. In the foreground, the crofts of the present day township extend to either side of the modern road.
Robert Adam RCAHMS, 2005, DP010491

The burial monuments of Scotland's Neolithic find expression in the chambered cairn at Unival on North Uist, from where St Kilda is often visible on the horizon.
Erskine Beveridge, 1904, SC335940

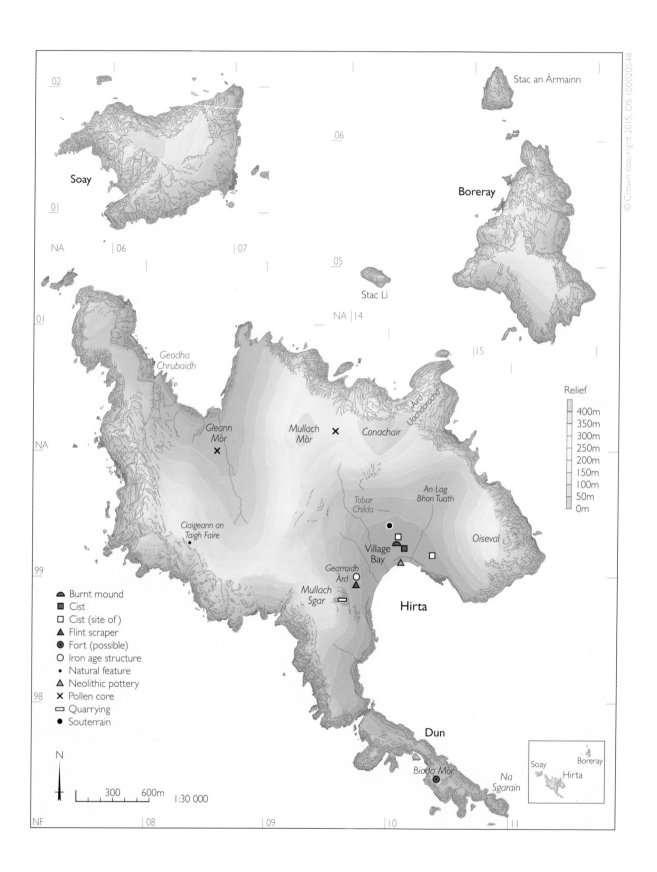

© Crown copyright 2015. OS 100020548

Stac an Àrmainn

Soay

Boreray

Stac Li

NA | 14

| 15

Geodha
Chrubaidh

Àird
Uachdarachd

Gleann
Mòr

Mullach
Mòr ✕

Conachair

An Lag
Bhon Tuath

Tobar
Childa

Oiseval

Claigeann an
Taigh Faire •

Village
Bay

Gearraidh
Àrd ○

Hirta

Mullach
Sgar

Relief

400m
350m
300m
250m
200m
150m
100m
50m
0m

⬤ Burnt mound
◼ Cist
☐ Cist (site of)
▲ Flint scraper
◉ Fort (possible)
• Natural feature
△ Neolithic pottery
✕ Pollen core
▭ Quarrying
● Souterrain

N

300   600m

1:30 000

Dun

Bioda Mòr

Na
Sgarain

Soay   Boreray
        Hirta

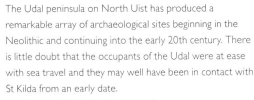

5cm   1:1.25

The Udal peninsula on North Uist has produced a
remarkable array of archaeological sites beginning in the
Neolithic and continuing into the early 20th century. There
is little doubt that the occupants of the Udal were at ease
with sea travel and they may well have been in contact with
St Kilda from an early date.

Dave Cowley RCAHMS, 2011, DP111325

Evidence for early prehistory on St Kilda is difficult to identify
securely. In 1996, archaeologists Andrew Fleming and Mark
Edmonds made the exciting discovery of two rim sherds of
Neolithic pottery eroding from a section of the sea-cliff in
Village Bay. Both are decorated with incised diagonal lines and
are comparable to other Neolithic wares in the Hebrides.

Mike Copper, University of Bradford, 2015, GV005692

a couple of pieces of worked and unworked flint
recorded on Hirta, including a small scraper found
fortuitously during the excavation of a quarry pit at the
foot of the scree slopes on Mullach Sgar.[20] There are
no natural deposits of flint on the island and it is likely
that these artefacts were introduced at an early date.[21]

By contrast, there are a large number of locally
made stone tools of many different types, some of
which may be Neolithic.[22] These were first observed
in a midden near the Iron Age souterrain and
subsequently in the 'ruins of old houses'.[23] Andrew
Fleming conducted a careful search of the walls and

opposite

St Kilda – sites referred to in this chapter

RCAHMS, 2015, GV005726

buildings of the township in 1994, which disclosed
flaked stone bars, pounders or grinders and objects
similar to the Skaill knives found on Orkney. In
addition, Fleming and his colleague Mark Edmonds,
recorded numerous examples of roughouts, hammers,
mauls and working debris in the area around Clais na
Bearnaich during fieldwork and excavation between
1995 and 1998.[24] Later excavations conducted by
GUARD on the slopes below Mullach Sgar from 1998
until 2003 unearthed many more, some of which came
from secure Iron Age contexts.[25]

Flaked stone bars, interpreted as hoe blades, are
present in prolific numbers and are made from greyish
green dolerite.[26] Many bear traces of heavy wear or
appear to have broken during use.[27] They are generally
wider than those that have been found in Neolithic

and later contexts in Shetland and Orkney[28] and some have tangs which imply that they may have been hafted.[29] Skaill knives, often associated with butchery, are an especially distinctive element of the Later Neolithic on Orkney, being known from the settlements at Skara Brae, Links of Noltland, Rinyo, Pool and Tofts Ness.[30] Like flaked stone bars, their production appears to have outlasted many other tool types[31] and it is curious that assemblages like those on Hirta and in the Northern Isles have not been identified in the Outer Hebrides.[32]

As has been indicated, roughouts and waste material from the quarrying of these tools have been discovered in the screes below Clais na Bearnaich, Mullach Sgar, where traces of workings are visible in both the cleft and along an undercut horizontal ledge that runs to either side of it. However, Fleming and Edmonds also observed that the upper slopes of Gearraidh Àrd were heavily disturbed by what they took to be 'quarries, some of them large and deep, with numerous heaps and runs of waste material'.[33] They were not able to confirm this through the test pits that they excavated and in the opinion of RCAHMS these hollows are more likely to be the product of natural geomorphological processes. However, it is recognised that only further excavation will clarify the matter.

Fleming and Edmonds' research led them to advance the hypothesis that 'a viable community evidently occupied Hirta well before the Iron Age',[34] and suggested that it was perfectly possible that the origin of many of the stone tools lay in a Neolithic or Bronze Age horizon.[35] At present, it must be

acknowledged that there is no scientific dating to support this and the distribution of the tools in stone dykes, walls and soils across Village Bay is in itself only evidence for the recycling of stone in the making of a pre-crofting landscape.

Bronze Age, 2500 to 800 BC

Although it is possible that St Kilda was included in some way in the networks that developed throughout the Atlantic seaways during the Neolithic and Bronze Age, the evidence for this is scanty to say the least. However, the islands could not have supported anything resembling permanent occupation unless this condition was met. Elsewhere in the Outer Hebrides, new ideas and new technologies associated with metal-working can be seen to take hold, although how far these disrupted or altered the traditional pattern of life is very difficult to gauge. Bronze is noteworthy by its scarcity, but one introduction was the Beaker, a distinctive tulip-shaped pottery vessel that spread widely throughout Western Europe from about 2800 BC. The majority of Beaker pottery from the Outer Hebrides comes from domestic contexts; elsewhere in Scotland it is commonly found in funereal contexts with a recurring association of grave-goods from about 2500 BC.

It is possible that the known settlements with Beaker pottery in the Outer Hebrides represent an expansion into the west of Scotland but some, like Northton on Harris[36] and The Udal on North Uist,[37] had been established in the machair before the introduction of Beakers. The same is true of Allt Chrisal on Barra,[38] which is situated in a rocky coastal environment that may once have overlooked a gentler landscape now lost to marine incursion. Northton, Allt Chrisal, together with Barvas (Barabhais)[39] and Dalmore (Dàil Mòr)[40] on the north-west coast of Lewis, have revealed oval-shaped, semi-sunken, stone-revetted buildings associated with hearths, internal pits and midden material. Apart from pottery and stone pounders or grinders, typical assemblages include chipped stone tools and others made from bone and antler. There is evidence for cultivation at Rosinish (Roisinis) on Benbecula[41] and Sligeanach[42] on South Uist, and also at Cnip on Lewis;[43] Rosinish has produced carbonised grain including naked and hulled barley, as well as emmer wheat. The excavators argued that the economic basis of Northton may have been focussed on pastoral farming, as there is little

Jimmy Davidson of the Ordnance Survey identified small groups of what he thought might be prehistoric houses in 1967. This example, above Geodha Chrùbaidh on Hirta, is probably an enclosure of more recent date.

Steve Wallace RCAHMS, 2008, DP051805

evidence of food processing, while grain impressions are absent from the pottery. However, the bones of sheep and cattle were present in equal proportions, while red deer, cetaceans and birds were also exploited. In addition, a wide range of shellfish contributed to the diet of its inhabitants.[44]

No trace of comparable Bronze Age roundhouse settlements or field systems is known on St Kilda, but the signature of ribwort plantain continues in the pollen record of Gleann Mòr and Conachair.[45] Traditionally, the earliest roundhouses in Scotland are assigned to the Bronze Age, when they occur in association with enclosures, field boundaries and clearance cairns. They are found widely throughout much of Scotland, although rarely in the Outer Hebrides due to subsequent peat growth or later clearance where they occupied the more fertile ground. The oval-shaped hut-platform identified by Roy Ritchie of the Ministry of Works in 1957 at Claigeann an Taigh Faire has been reinterpreted by RCAHMS as a natural terrace surrounded by exposures of outcrop.[46] Furthermore, considerable doubt attaches to the antiquity of the clusters of small 'hut circles' that are spread east-south-east and west-south-west of Tobar Childa, Village Bay;[47] and the same can be said for those situated on the natural shelf above Geo Chrùbaidh north-west of Gleann Mòr and on

the promontory Àird Uachdarachd.[48] In all three cases, RCAHMS has identified these as the remains of relatively modern pens, small enclosures or simply natural features.

Burnt mounds present another kind of structure found widely throughout much of Scotland, although again rarely in the Outer Hebrides, where less than a dozen have been recognised. They occur throughout prehistory, but frequently date to the Bronze Age, especially to the latter part of the period. The evidence for burnt mounds on St Kilda is equivocal, but small numbers of heat-shattered beach pebbles have been observed in the make-up of the central consumption dyke on the line of one of the 19th century croft boundaries in the township. These burnt stones are especially numerous where the consumption dyke overrides a low spread, oval mound.[49] More have been noted in a stone heap near the souterrain and elsewhere, but it may be questioned whether they derived originally from a burnt mound or simply from the disturbance of domestic middens.

If the evidence for settlement is opaque, there are antiquarian and more recent accounts of monuments which, if substantiated, would throw additional light on St Kilda in the Bronze Age. Stone circles are traditionally assigned to this period and, writing in 1764, Kenneth Macaulay[50] was quite sure there was one on Boreray: 'What I call a Druidical place of worship, is a large circle of huge stones fixed perpendicularly in the ground, at equal distances from one another, with one more remarkably regular in the center, which is flat in the top, and one would think sacred in a more eminent degree.'[51] He was evidently conscious that his readership might be sceptical and so he tried hard to convince them, creating a romantic if improbable vision that appears to draw upon the ideas of such influential antiquaries as John Aubrey, John Toland and William Stukeley.[52] Margaret Curtis has suggested that Euphemia Macrimmon, the islands' oldest inhabitant in the early 1860s, was referring to this circle when she spoke about the chapel on Boreray, but this is clearly not the case.[53] Neither John Sands, John Mathieson nor RCAHMS observed any traces of such a monument on their visits to the island and Sand's report in 1878 that 'the St Kildans seem never to have heard of it' can be accepted as authoritative.[54]

In 1967, Jimmy Davidson of the Ordnance Survey noted a roughly circular stone setting of twelve irregularly spaced small boulders set into a low bank on the mid slopes of Gleann Mòr on Hirta. This measures about 15m in diameter.[55] Over four decades later, Ron and Margaret Curtis visited and planned the site referring to it as a 'prehistoric stone circle'.[56] Since then, it has been re-evaluated in the field by RCAHMS and, while its date remains unresolved, it has been reclassified as an enclosure, as this seems to best describe its character.

During this period funerary rites began to change. Chambered tombs were closed and abandoned giving way to single grave inhumations or cremations, deposited in cists under cairns or mounds. Although these are numerous in the Outer Hebrides, only a few have been adequately dated: a crouched inhumation in a cist from one of the three cairns at The Udal on North Uist yielded a date in the middle of the 2nd millennium BC[57] and similar dates have also been obtained for both a cremation and an inhumation at Cnip on Lewis.[58]

No such discoveries have been made on St Kilda in recent times, but antiquarian accounts provide tantalising evidence that similar burial sites may once have survived in Village Bay as late as the 1830s. These features came to light during clearance work initiated by Neil Mackenzie, who was then the resident minister, sometimes within the boundary of his own glebe. Mackenzie relates how, in the course of agricultural improvements, numerous green mounds were removed. The mounds were known colloquially as the *cnocan sithichean*, the abodes of the fairies,[59] a common association attached to cairns and natural hillocks throughout Scotland. On being opened, Mackenzie's mounds were found to be 'composed of stones mixed with a little earth to a depth of two or three feet. At some distance below this layer were stone coffins formed in two different ways. At times they were formed of four flat stones set on edge and covered by a fifth. At other times both the sides and roof were formed of several stones set in the same way.' [60] In recognising two distinct architectural styles, Mackenzie believed them to be of different dates. His account continues by noting that while only a few contained bones, nearly all contained sherds of pottery – although it is unclear whether this comment referred to both kinds of grave, or simply to those of the latter type. Whatever the case, these contents have long since disappeared.

Mackenzie also refers to another subterranean feature that may have been a cist, but his description

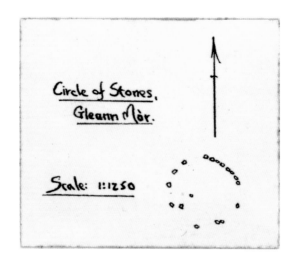

References to the existence of a 'stone circle' on St Kilda reach back to the 18th century and one possible contender was discovered in 1967. This small plan, one of many hundreds produced for Ordnance Survey large scale maps in Scotland, shows an intermittent ring of boulders which probably define no more than the remains of an enclosure.
Jimmy Davidson, Ordnance Survey, 1967, DP214154

of a 'curiously built space' secreted beneath a stone capped with ashes is too obscure for certainty.[61] This, too, was discovered while he cleared the ground for agriculture 'in a small park near the centre of the glebe',[62] situated at the foot of Oiseval. Nevertheless, in keeping with the account, the Ordnance Survey map of 1928 depicts this in what seems to be roughly the correct location, along with the annotation 'Underground Chamber found 1835'.[63] By contrast, the discoveries of the cists are plotted collectively on croft land immediately below House 9, with the annotation 'Stone Coffins found 1835.'[64] However, as this map was produced nearly a century after the discoveries it records, such closely defined locations should be treated with caution.

In practice, much hinges on Mackenzie's original descriptions. Those 'stone coffins' with capstones, sides and ends formed by single edge-set stones strongly recall Early Bronze Age cists. Their presence can be read as a clear indicator of permanent settlement, but it remains open to question whether this should be understood to be continuous. Less confidence can be ascribed to those constructed of 'several stones set in the same way', although their contents of bones and pottery are also in keeping with prehistoric

2.5m 1:100

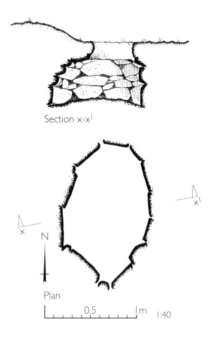

Section x-x¹

Plan

0.5   1m   1:40

A number of 'boat-shaped settings' first identified in the 1950s can be found in An Lag Bhon Tuath (top and above). Originally understood as Bronze Age or Norse funerary monuments, they have been reinterpreted more recently as stances for peat and turf which the St Kildans used for fuel. A more convincing candidate for a Bronze Age burial is this small corbelled chamber (right). Found in the lower croft land of Village Bay, it may once have been covered by a small mound.

Steve Wallace RCAHMS, 2008, DP044995

RCAHMS, 1985, GV005689 and GV005688

inhumations. It is possible that they were small drystone corbelled chambers of which the remnants of one is still to be seen on the croft boundary below Houses 7 and 8.[65] This corbelled chamber is similar to those that have been excavated at Northton on Harris,[66] at Rosinish on Benbecula[67] and at Cnip on Lewis;[68] and if the comparison is accepted it reinforces the likelihood that Hirta, at least, was occupied for a time during the Bronze Age.

A number of U-shaped stone settings at An Lag Bhon Tuath were identified before 1964 by Aitken and Moira, architects with the Ministry of Public Buildings and Works, who 'made plans of several boat-shaped mounds' some of which were based upon sketch-plans made by a Mrs Crouse.[69] While these features were initially believed to be funerary monuments of Norse origin and were recorded as such by Davidson in 1967,[70] they were subsequently attributed to the Bronze Age following the excavation of one of fourteen examples identified by Barry Cottam of Dundee University in 1973. This yielded a sample of peat which returned a date of about 1850 BC;[71] but this and their interpretation as burial monuments was later challenged by Mary Harman and it is now generally accepted that the date refers to the peat itself.[72] This structure and its counterparts, including another excavated by Robin Turner of the NTS in 1995, have since been reinterpreted and re-attributed to a very much later period.[73]

The Iron Age, 800 BC to AD 400

As with the Bronze Age, the beginning of the Iron Age in the Outer Hebrides is not demonstrated by a clear archaeological horizon; and while artefacts of iron must have gradually replaced the less efficient tools made from other materials, there is no reason to suppose that this was accompanied by disruption to the structure of society. However, climatic deterioration in the early part of the 1st millennium BC seems to have led to an increase in waterlogging with a concomitant growth of peat and this is believed to have led to social stress as some ground became less productive. Roundhouse farmsteads on marginal land were gradually abandoned, and settlement became more restricted instead to the kinder, better drained lands of the coast. This is where the novel and distinctive architecture that belongs specifically to the second half of this period is generally to be found, including brochs, wheelhouses and simpler types of

domestic structure. Forts, duns and crannogs are also commonly ascribed to the period, but some of these may have been built or occupied at earlier or later dates.

Brochs are found throughout most of Scotland, but by far the majority are located in the Northern and Western Isles. They are the most distinctive Iron Age structure in the Outer Hebrides where more than 60 are known. A small number have been excavated over the last 30 years, including those at Loch Baravat (Bharabhat)[74] and Loch na Berie (Beirgh)[75] on Lewis and at Dun Vulan (Mhùlan) on South Uist.[76] However, they are apparently absent from some of the smaller islands on the Atlantic seaboard such as Scalpay (Scalpaigh), Berneray (Beàrnaraigh), Eriskay (Èirisgeigh) and St Kilda.

The idea that brochs can be associated with relatively well-defined territories has become widely accepted and it has been estimated that South Uist may have had eleven or twelve such zones reaching back from the coast.[77] This number could perhaps be increased for North Uist, but it should probably be reduced for Harris on account of its more rugged landscape. It is uncertain whether these territories should be understood as 'estates', but it is an interesting coincidence that the site of Seana Chaisteal, a broch on Pabbay, became one of the centres of the MacLeod domain at least as early as the 14th century[78] and that this may have already included St Kilda as a detached portion of their holdings. There seems no reason why this idea of territoriality in the Iron Age should not have embraced the offshore islands and it is possible that those which lack evidence for brochs were also in some sense subsidiary portions of a larger whole.

Wheelhouses were usually built as semi-subterranean structures with a series of spoke-like compartments arranged around a central hearth, but also linked by a circular aisle to their rear. They have a similar, but less dense, distribution in the Outer Hebrides and appear to have been introduced towards the end of the 1st millennium BC. A number of examples were excavated in advance of the establishment of the Hebridean Rocket Range in the 1950s, including Sollas on North Uist,[79] A' Cheardach Mhòr[80] and A' Cheardach Bheag[81] on South Uist and Bruthach a' Tuath on Benbecula.[82] Others have been investigated in more recent years at Cnip on Lewis,[83] The Udal on North Uist[84] and

Bornais on South Uist.[85] Like the brochs, they often appear to be isolated structures, but the complex landscape of prehistoric sites at Uisinis on South Uist, which was recorded by RCAHMS in 2013, includes two wheelhouses amongst a series of roundhouses and enclosures.[86] Both wheelhouses and roundhouses were directly associated with souterrains – underground, stone-lined and lintelled passages running away from surface buildings that in some cases were probably used as storehouses for agricultural produce.

A souterrain known as the House of the Fairies (Taigh an t-Sithiche) has been recognised on Hirta since the mid 19th century, but it was initially interpreted as a dwelling in its own right. John Sands, writing in 1877, noted that 'this house was found by accident about 32 years previously by a man who was digging the ground above it', probably John Gillies,[87] who was then the tenant of the croft. It was subject to a 'hasty survey' before being covered up, but Sands relocated the 'door in the roof' in 1876 and commenced his own exploration.[88] He reported that it was 25ft (7.6m) in length and that there appeared to be a side-passage on the north. However, his description clearly indicates that the south-east end was not visible at this time. Twenty years later the souterrain was explored for a second time by Richard and Cherry Kearton, who noted that 'the entire credit of properly investigating and restoring this interesting home of primitive man belongs to our friend, Mr. John Mackenzie, jun., who takes a great deal of interest in the history of the place'.[89] Mackenzie was probably the factor's son and although the family lived on Skye, he was eventually to take over from his father in 1910.[90] The illustration of the entrance and the fact that Richard Kearton recorded the length of the souterrain as '30 or 40ft' (9–12m), suggest that Mackenzie excavated further south-east along the passage, perhaps creating the opening visible today.[91] In 1927, three years after Captain Grant recorded the souterrain for RCAHMS, John Mathieson and

opposite
The broch at Dun Carloway on Lewis is one of the best surviving examples of Iron Age architecture in the Outer Hebrides. It nestles within a landscape of later cultivation remains, buildings and enclosures, some of which were constructed from the stone robbed from its walls.
Dave Cowley RCAHMS, 2011, DP110854
RCAHMS collection, c1910, SC1242412

The plan of a typical Iron Age wheelhouse was revealed by excavation at Sollas on North Uist in 1957. Claims for the existence of such structures on St Kilda are as yet unsubstantiated.
Historic Scotland Collection, 1957, SC518388

Alexander Cockburn 'in the course of two afternoons digging' found that it extended a further 9ft (2.7m) to the south and illustrated this with a photograph and plan.[92] The open end appears little changed when their photograph is compared with others taken in 1957 and 1986, so whatever renovations Roy Ritchie effected in 1974 must have been relatively limited.[93] RCAHMS mapped, planned and photographed the souterrain between 1985 and 1986 as part of the survey of Village Bay.[94] More recently, excavations by GUARD on behalf of the NTS in 2004 sought to assess the extent of these earlier investigations and the degree of consolidation work that might have been undertaken.[95] This led not only to the discovery of undisturbed archaeological deposits and evidence for a side-chamber to the north, but also to the recognition of footings that may represent the building with which the souterrain was associated at ground level. Indeed, it is possible that an unusual cleit a few metres to the north may incorporate further fragments of this almost indiscernible structure.[96]

All but a small handful of the stone artefacts collected during these excavations come from the topsoil or disturbed deposits.[97] Tools made from

The Iron Age souterrain has been explored on several occasions. Its passage has been cleared out, but its original entrance extended a little further south-east.

Steve Wallace RCAHMS, 2008, DP043051 and DP043048

cobbles, such as pounder or grinders and smoothers, which were probably used in the preparation of food, made up roughly a sixth of the assemblage and are familiar from Iron Age contexts. Skaill knives made up a further quarter and although prevalent on Neolithic and Bronze Age sites on Orkney and Shetland, they are also found on Orkney in early Iron Age contexts.[98] Just over a third comprised flaked stone bars, together with roughouts and waste material, suggesting that they were manufactured nearby. More than 700 sherds of pottery also derive from these investigations, but most are of recent date.[99] However, some are 'Iron Age or late Iron Age' and fit into the wider ceramic traditions of Atlantic Scotland.[100] They can be compared with specific sherds from the wheelhouse at Cnip on Lewis, or more broadly with the assemblages from Sollas on North Uist and Dun Vulan on South Uist.[101]

If little or nothing can be said about the building associated with the souterrain, its shadowy presence at least clearly indicates that Hirta was occupied during the Iron Age and that Village Bay once again was the most attractive location for settlement. There seems little doubt that there must have been a farm here, although only the poorly dated flaked stone bars confirm that tillage contributed to its economy. Nevertheless, excavations by GUARD in the screes below Mullach Sgar between 1998 and 2003 revealed a small, semi-subterranean, corbelled, oval building dating from the 2nd century BC,[102] which appears to have been constructed at the same time as various walls and revetments across the screes. Although it was not interpreted as a dwelling and no formal hearth was noted, stone tools and burnt deposits recovered from its roughly paved floor, in addition to sherds from the top of the wall, recalled a domestic function.[103] A wall was subsequently inserted reducing the internal space before it fell from use and several thick deposits of midden-like material were deposited in its interior. The stone tools recovered from the floor included nine flaked stone bars, a hammer stone, a pounder or grinder, a handful of flakes and a facetted cobble, while the pottery was likened to that known from Dun Vulan and Sollas.[104]

Glasgow University's Archaeology Department had previously explored at least three other semi-subterranean structures of indeterminate date situated in the unvegetated screes, while another had been dug out by Sands in 1876.[105] Two were elongated, sunken structures with very slightly corbelled walls, just like those of Sands' example. However, the third was quite

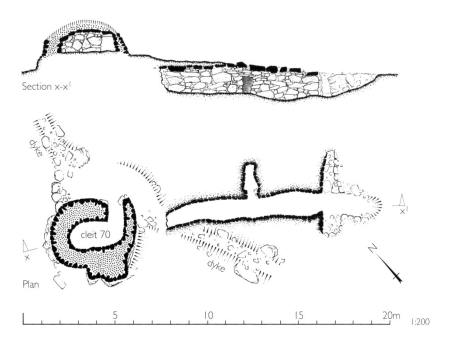

Section x-x¹

dyke

cleit 70

Plan

dyke

N

5   10   15   20m   1:200

This section and plan of the souterrain indicate that its full extent has not yet been established. Recent excavations have also suggested that fragments of an associated building may still survive. RCAHMS, 1985, GV005690

different, being circular in plan with an entrance and corbelling that survived almost to roof height. Artefacts from the infill of the former included a flaked stone bar, a pounder or grinder, the lower stone of a saddle quern and four possible smoothers, while the infill of the latter yielded two flaked stone bars, two tanged implements, two roughouts and four cobbles. All of these structures had been dug into the scree, so that they may have been largely hidden and some have thought that they could have acted as places of refuge.[106]

Another building that has long been attributed to this period is Taigh Stallair (the Steward's House) on Boreray.[107] This was first recorded by Martin Martin in June 1697, who related that it was much larger than the Amazon's House in Gleann Mòr, but otherwise 'of the same model in all respects'.[108] He thought it had been built by a hermit, who 'had he travelled the universe he could scarcely have found a more solitary place for a monastick life'.[109] Macaulay, who

plainly believed it had been occupied by the druid who officiated at his nearby stone circle, provided a much fuller description in 1764. He related how it was almost entirely buried, but had an interior that was circular on plan with a corbelled roof rising to a height of 18ft (5.5m). Spatially, it seems to have been symmetrically arranged about a central hearth with seating around the walls interspersed with four bed nooks, each entered through 'separate openings resembling, in some degree, so many pillars'.[110] However, it is Euphemia Macrimmon's recollections in 1862 that have inadvertently invited the notion that the structure might be attributable to the Iron Age. She not only confirmed that the interior of this semi-subterranean building was circular and contained bed nooks, but noted that these nooks could be reached by a passage within the wall without entering the central chamber.[111] Macrimmon also explained that the structure had been used as a bothy until about 20 years before 'when the roof fell in'.[112] As Captain Frederick Thomas perceived, this description was resonant of Uamh Ìosal at Uisinis on South Uist[113] and for him, both belonged to the same class of monument.[114] Andrew Fleming was to agree with Thomas that the descriptions of Taigh Stallair would not be out of

above

In 1876, the writer John Sands dug out this structure in the screes below Clais na Bearnaich. Tradition holds that it was a 'hidey hole' used by the St Kildans to escape the attention of unwelcome visitors.

Steve Wallace RCAHMS, 2008, DP045519

keeping with that of 'an aisled wheelhouse dating from the Iron Age', while admitting that the presence of such a building in this inhospitable location was perhaps a challenging concept.[115] Nevertheless, he argued forcefully that fowling might well have been as important to the Iron Age community on St Kilda as it was in later centuries. By the time John Sands visited Boreray in June 1876, Taigh Stallair was said to have been robbed of its stone for cleitean.[116] However, Mathieson was still able to identify and map its location in 1927,[117] although some thirty years later, Kenneth Williamson, who was one of a team that visited the site in 1959, observed that 'Tigh Stallar was no more'.[118]

The site was re-examined by RCAHMS and Jill Harden in 2010, when it was identified as an artificial oval mound containing the remains of a substantial stone structure at the location recorded by Mathieson. The shape of the building could not be determined, but they noted the presence of a substantial external kerb and a cell. A very small area was de-turfed at the north corner of the cleit that had been built over the mound, revealing a void in the corbelled roof of another cell. Through this they were able to glimpse the full extent of the cell, as well as a choked entrance leading south. They considered that this and the other cell may have opened off a third cell that lay hidden from view and concurred with Martin that the best local analogy for the structure lay with the Amazon's House. This comparison suggests that Taigh Stallair is of medieval date.

Although many parts of the Western Isles have strong natural defences, in certain instances the inhabitants sought to improve these lofty eminences by

left

This unusual and enigmatic oval building, excavated by GUARD, has been dug into the scree at Mullach Sgar. Heather charcoal from the infill of peat and domestic waste yielded dates ranging from the 2nd century BC to the 1st century AD.

GUARD, 2002, 1182/2/2

opposite

The remains of a substantial stone building at Taigh Stallair on Boreray are now overlain by a later cleit. Commentators have drawn analogies between it and Iron Age structures since the mid 19th century, but these remain unsubstantiated.

RCAHMS, 2010, GV005691

Jill Harden, 2010, DP114404

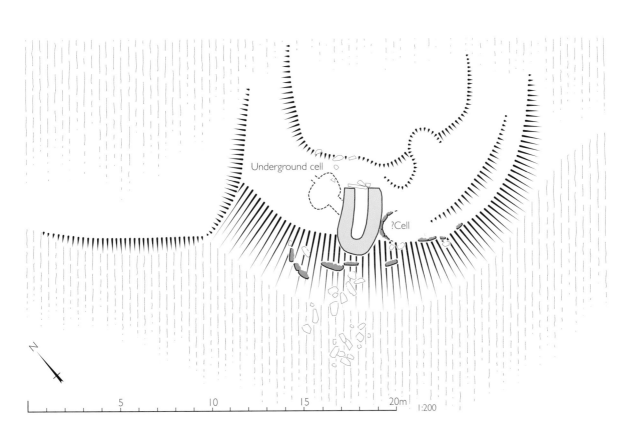

Underground cell

?Cell

N

5   10   15   20m
                                          1:200

The impressive and well-preserved wall that cuts off the south end of Dun at Na Sgarain has long been equated with the 'little old ruinous fort' described by Martin Martin in 1697. However, it seems more plausible that it was built to keep the islanders' sheep away from the rough boulder-strewn headland beyond.
George Geddes RCAHMS, 2013, DP150376

building defensive works, thereby defining enclosures. Forts are traditionally assigned to the later prehistoric period. There is no evidence for such on Hirta, Boreray or Soay, but there are two stretches of rubble wall extending from either side of a rocky knoll at Na Sgarain on Dun that have been traditionally associated with Martin's description of a 'little old ruinous fort' that 'may be reckoned amongst the strongest ... in the world [which] nature has provided ... with store of ammunition for acting on the defensive; that is, a heap of stones in the top of the hill'.[119] It is also mentioned by Macaulay, although he added little more beyond

the fact that the fort was named Dùn Fir-Bholg by the natives.[120] Neither provided a clear indication of its location.

Captain Frederick Thomas, in noting that Euphemia Macrimmon's testimony indicated that Macaulay's Gaelic name had been replaced by the more prosaic 'Castle of Dun', regretted not having visited the site to ascertain its character.[121] However, he drew his reader's attention to a note by James Wilson who, while referring to the wall, was sceptical as to whether it could really have been a fortification.[122] By contrast, Sands believed that it was defensive and that it had been 'evidently intended to keep an enemy who had landed on the island from getting to the extremity', noting the presence of 'parapets inside, on which the defenders could have stood'.[123] Mathieson was unconvinced, observing that it looked quite modern and instead suggested that it was built 'simply for the purpose of temporarily separating the sheep on the island'.[124]

A candidate for an enclosure of early date on Dun survives on the summit of Bioda Mòr, where traces of a substantial drystone wall can be observed crossing the north-east side of the summit between two sheer cliffs.
George Geddes RCAHMS, 2013, DP150334

There is nothing about the wall that suggests a prehistoric date and it does not fortify the promontory. It simply cuts off an area of very rough ground containing two rock shelters, a cave and a possible hut, all of which are probably of relatively recent date.[125] The likelihood is that it was a dyke built to keep the sheep away from the precipitous headland.

However, there is another length of walling on Dun that is altogether more mysterious.

Photographs taken by Robert Atkinson in 1953 and Mary Harman in 1977 show a grass-grown wall of massive boulders below Bioda Mòr, the highest point on the island.[126] This was investigated by RCAHMS and Jill Harden in 2013, who confirmed its siting across the north-east side of the summit, between two sheer cliff faces, where the approach was least precipitous. Although its purpose and date are unknown, its location, dimensions and condition are indicative of an early date.

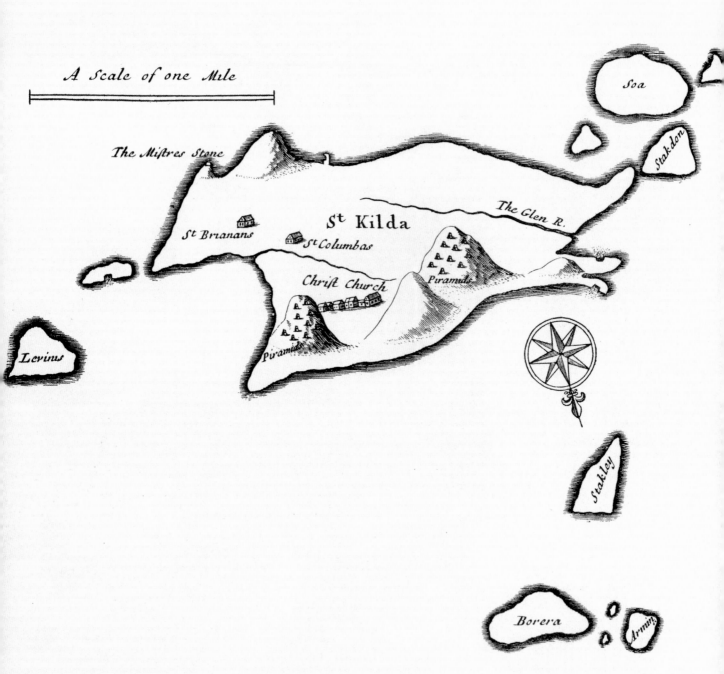

Chapter Four
Clerics, Clans and Cultivators – AD 400 to 1600

Early Medieval

The 1st millennium AD was a period of significant change in the Outer Hebrides. Many of the brochs, wheelhouses and duns that had gradually fallen into disuse were quarried for the construction of less substantial buildings. New cultural and political groupings appeared, while the Celtic Christian church was established bringing novel rites and practices.

The majority of settlements in the middle of the 1st millennium AD are situated on the machair, where continuity from the previous millennium is demonstrated by numerous examples of re-occupation, marked by the construction of smaller buildings within brochs like Dun Vulan on South Uist and Loch na Berie on Lewis.[1] Elsewhere, entirely new structures appear at sites such as The Udal on North Uist and at both Cnip and Bostadh on Lewis, introducing novel buildings of a regular size and shape.[2] While these settlements cannot be assigned to a specific cultural group, some have yielded finds such as composite bone combs, which are normally ascribed to the Picts.[3]

Examples of the burial rite practised during this period are found at the long cist cemetery at Galson (Gabhsann) on Lewis dated to the first half of the 1st millennium AD and a grave of similar type excavated at Kilpheder (Cille Pheadair) on South Uist, which disclosed the remains of a woman within a cist overlain by a square cairn of the kind attributed to the Picts and dated to AD 700.[4] This is similar to a less well-preserved square cairn discovered at Àird Ma-Ruidhe on Berneray.[5] There is also a small corpus of Pictish symbol stones, which includes a slab discovered at Strome Shunnamal (Sròm Shùnamul) on Benbecula and a standing stone on the island of Pabbay off Barra.[6] The Pabbay stone incorporates recognisable Pictish motifs, although part of its interest lies in the addition of a more deeply incised Latin cross which was possibly added at a later date.[7] Stones and rocks bearing early crosses are found on eighteen sites in the Outer Hebrides, from Berneray in the south to North Rona.[8] While there is a distinct hiatus in the distribution on Lewis and Harris, examples have been recorded on Taransay (Tarasaigh) and in the Shiant Isles (Na h-Eileannan Seunta), while there is a notable concentration on North Uist.[9]

Ian Fisher of RCAHMS has described the spread of Christianity from the late 6th century and how this led to the establishment of monasteries along the western seaboard of Scotland, including the foundation of Iona by St Columba (Calum Cille)

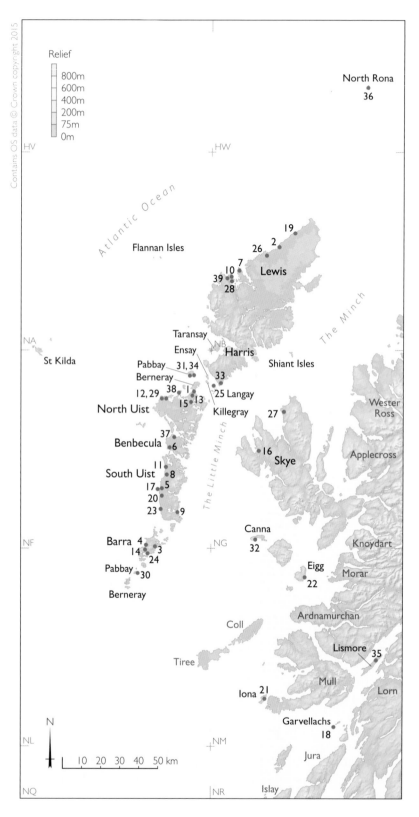

Relief

800m
600m
400m
200m
75m
0m

North Rona
36

Atlantic Ocean

Flannan Isles

19

26 2

7
10
39
28

Lewis

The Minch

Taransay

Ensay

NB

Harris

Shiant Isles

Pabbay 31, 34
Berneray

33

12, 29 38 1
15 13

25 Langay

Killegray

27

North Uist

37

Benbecula 6

Wester
Ross

Applecross

11

South Uist 8

16 Skye

17 5

20

The Little Minch

23 9

St Kilda

Barra 4

14 3
24

Pabbay 30

Berneray

Canna
32

Eigg
22

Knoydart

Morar

Ardnamurchan

Coll

Lismore 35

Tiree

Mull

Lorn

Iona 21

N

Garvellachs
18

10 20 30 40 50 km

Jura

Islay

The Western Isles –
sites referred to in this chapter

1	Àird Ma-Ruidhe
2	Barabhas
3	Ben Gunnary
4	Borgh
5	Bornais
6	Borve Castle
7	Bostadh
8	Caisteal Bheagram
9	Calvay
10	Cnip
11	Drimore
12	Druim nan Dearcag
13	Dùn an Sticer
14	Dùn Mhic Leoid
15	Dùn Torcuil
16	Dunvegan
17	Dun Vulan
18	Eileach an Naoimh
19	Galson
20	Gearraidh Bhailteas
21	Iona
22	Kildonan
23	Kilpheder
24	Kisimul
25	Langaigh
26	Loch an Duna
27	Loch Chaluim Chille
28	Loch na Berie
29	Loch Olabhat
30	Pabbay, Barra
31	Seana Chaisteil
32	Sgor nam Ban-Naomha
33	St Clement's
34	St Mary's Church and St Moluag's Chapel, Pabbay, Harris
35	St Moluag's, Lismore
36	North Rona
37	Strome Shunnamal
38	The Udal
39	Valtos

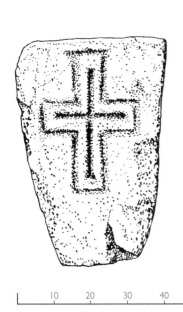
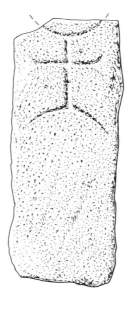

10   20   30   40   50cm
1:10

St Kilda has long been thought of as a place where Christian monks seeking solitude may have settled. Three cross-incised stones have been discovered on the island, each re-used in later structures. Two can be stylistically dated to between the 8th and 10th centuries AD, but the third (centre) has no direct parallel in Scotland.

top RCAHMS, 2015, GV005693
left John Keggie RCAHMS, 1986, SC1463894
middle Alan Leith RCAHMS 2009, DP165014
right John Keggie RCAHMS, 1986, SC1463859

and his Irish followers in AD 563.[10] Lismore (Lios Mòr) is of a similar date and is associated with St Moluag, whose death is recorded there in AD 592.[11] A smaller monastic site is believed to have been established at Kildonan (Cill Donain) on Eigg by St Donnan, while literary evidence also indicates that there was another on 'Hinba' associated with St Columba, as yet an unidentified location.[12] Other undocumented sites of monastic character among the islands include Eileach an Naoimh on the Garvellachs,[13] Loch Chaluim Chille on Skye[14] and Sgor nam Ban-Naomha on Canna[15] – this last quite possibly an eremitic site. However, perhaps the most interesting of the possible eremitic sites is North Rona,[16] which has a small collection of simple stone crosses, an oval enclosure and a chapel or oratory. Unfortunately its date is by no means fully resolved.[17]

St Kilda has long been considered a candidate for the location of an eremitic site on account of dedications to St Brianan (St Brendan) and St Columba, and its remote situation.[18] While no upstanding structural evidence of this date has been recorded by RCAHMS, there are three cross-incised stones of which two have been dated to between the 8th and 10th centuries AD by their typological similarity to other Early Christian examples.[19] The third, found by Strat Halliday of RCAHMS, is also likely to be early, but it has no direct analogy in Scotland.[20] They were all discovered within 150m of the oval burial ground which is situated a little to the north of the Street running through the township. There is also a record of a 'stone with an inscription on it [which] had been carried off by a former factor' before 1876,[21] while yet another stone 'upon which

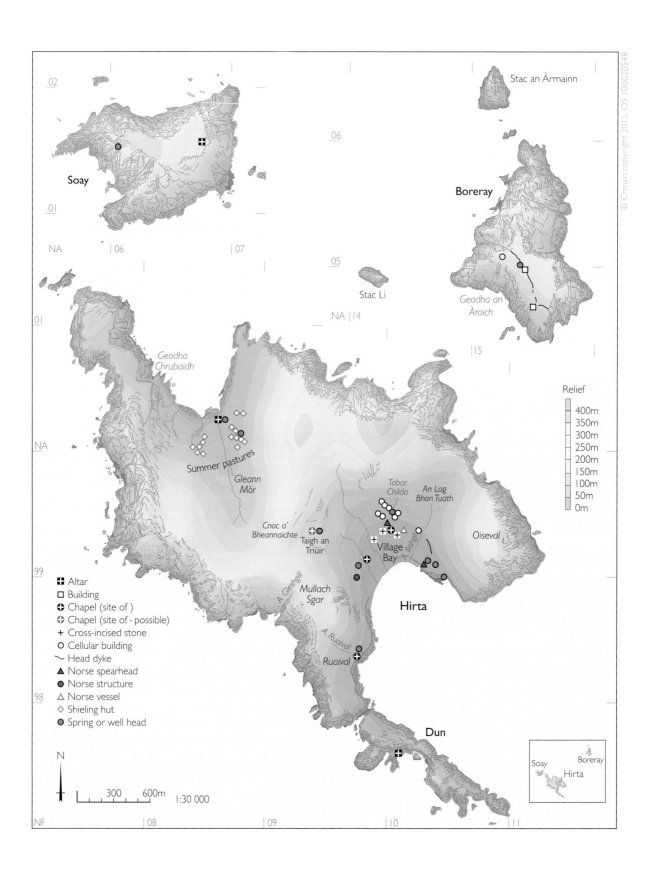

Stac an Àrmainn

Soay

Boreray

Geodha an Àraich

Stac Li

Geodha
Chrubaidh

Summer pastures

Gleann
Mòr

Tobar
Childa

An Lag
Bhon Tuath

Oiseval

Cnoc a'
Bheannaichte

Taigh an
Triùir

Village
Bay

Hirta

Mullach
Sgar

Ruaival

Dun

Relief

400m
350m
300m
250m
200m
150m
100m
50m
0m

Altar
Building
Chapel (site of)
Chapel (site of - possible)
Cross-incised stone
Cellular building
Head dyke
Norse spearhead
Norse structure
Norse vessel
Shieling hut
Spring or well head

N

300   600m   1:30 000

Soay   Boreray
       Hirta

© Crown copyright 2015, OS 100020548

there is writing' is recorded from Boreray,[22] but these
could be much later in date. References to as many as
six chapels in the 17th century[23] and the well-preserved
'monkish cells' noted in the 18th century must of
course also be treated with some caution.[24]

Norse Settlement

The Anglo-Saxon Chronicle provides a vivid record of
the first Norse arrival in Britain in AD 787,[25] followed
by the sacking of Lindisfarne in AD 793.[26] The next
year there was widespread raiding and St Columba's
monastery on Iona was pillaged in AD 795, AD 802
and AD 806.[27] The Atlantic seaways passing south
through the Minch or west along the coast of the
Outer Hebrides towards Iona, the Isle of Man and
Ireland provided relatively sheltered routes and it
seems likely that provisions were sought along the
west coast of Scotland. How violent and frequent the
initial incursions were remains unclear, but in time
this period of raiding gave way to colonisation and
the establishment of farming settlements.[28] Once
occupied, the Outer Hebrides remained part of the
Norse world until their succession to the Scottish
Crown in 1266.[29]

For many years, historians and archaeologists
have wrestled with the fact that the most widespread
evidence for Norse activity in Britain is represented by
placenames, but these do at least provide an indication
of the extent and density of settlement throughout
the Hebrides. In Lewis, for example, John Barber has
estimated that 99 of 126 current township names
are wholly of Norse origin, while a further nine also
retain Norse elements.[30] Common Norse names
include those that describe types of settlement and
others that are topographically descriptive. A journey
north of Leverburgh on Harris takes one past Loch
Steisebhat (from *vatn*, lake), between the mountains of
Greabhal and Ceapabhal (from *fjall*, mountain), to the
townships of Sgarasta and Horgabost (from -*stadh* or
-*bost*, denoting different types of farm).

All the Norse settlements that have been excavated
in the Outer Hebrides are located on the machair
that fringes the Atlantic coast. Nonetheless, the areas
around the deeper harbours of the east coast, such
as Stornoway, were also occupied.[31] Erosion of the

opposite
St Kilda – sites referred to in this chapter
RCAHMS, 2015. GV005727

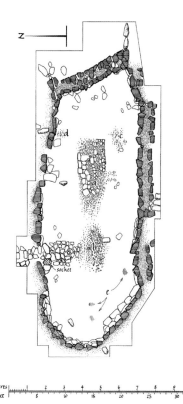

Settlements of Norse date are difficult to locate even
in areas where they are well attested by other forms of
evidence. This house at Drimore, which was excavated
by Alastair MacLaren of RCAHMS, was one of the great
discoveries made in the course of the rescue programme
undertaken before the construction of the Hebrides Missile
Range in the 1950s.
RCAHMS, 1971, SC1468575

machair at Barabhas on Lewis disclosed a large midden
containing Norse pottery, and subsequent excavations
uncovered the remains of at least two sub-rectangular
buildings, associated with pottery of the 10th and 11th
centuries AD.[32] Similar circumstances at Bostadh on
Lewis revealed a Norse building marking the final
phase of an occupation that reached back into the
late 1st millennium BC,[33] while the sub-rectangular
buildings at The Udal represent the introduction of a
new and innovative building tradition, although it is
unclear how far this simply reflects Norse influence,

A pair of Viking brooches, probably associated with a woman's grave, was found on St Kilda sometime before 1846. In that year, the famous Danish archaeologist Jens Worsaae studied them at the Andersonian Museum in Glasgow, publishing this illustration of one in 1872. Both are now lost.

Jens Worsaae, 1872, SC1478812

rather than colonisation.[34] There is less dispute about the Norse building at Drimore (Druim Mòr) on South Uist, which was excavated by Alasdair MacLaren of RCAHMS in 1956, as part of the rescue excavations undertaken prior to the introduction of the Rocket Range.[35] This yielded finds of late 9th or early 10th century date, which included a decorated single-sided bone comb, spindle whorls and vessels made of steatite, together with pins and other objects of bone and ivory. More recently, excavations at Bornais on South Uist uncovered several sub-rectangular stone buildings, including a house.[36] This produced a substantial assemblage of artefacts comprising stone tools, objects of lead, copper alloy and iron, together with quantities of worked bone and antler, much of which was discarded material from comb making. As the only specialist 'rural comb-making site so far found in Britain', this emphasises the importance of the settlement, which may have been the administrative centre of South Uist.[37]

The inhabitants of the earliest Norse settlements were pagan and, like their non-Christian predecessors, their graves are not often located. Antiquarian discoveries are known from Borgh on Barra,[38] Langaigh Island in the Sound of Harris,[39] an unspecified location on South Uist[40] and at Valtos on Lewis.[41] In addition, sand erosion at Cnip on Lewis has revealed a small cemetery which has been assigned to the 9th and 10th centuries AD.[42] Such inhumations are sometimes accompanied by grave goods that seem gender-specific – weapons for the men and pairs of brooches or other artefacts for the women; but these stereotypical interpretations, especially in the case of weapons, always require care in the absence of osteological corroboration.

There is one specific documentary reference to St Kilda in this period and it relates how an Icelandic cleric and his entourage took shelter on 'the islands that are called Hirtir' in 1202.[43] Otherwise evidence of Norse activity is provided largely by placenames and a few old finds. Alexander Taylor has affirmed that Hirte is of Norse origin (although its meaning is far from clear), as are Soay (sheep island) and Boreray (fort island).[44] He has also shown how St Kilda, although ultimately of Norse origin, has a fascinating and complex origin that belies a saintly individual and instead finds an explanation in cartographical error and confusion reinforced by transposition.[45] Topographic features with Norse names include some of the highest hills on Hirta, such as Ruaival (red hill) and Oiseval (eastern hill); as well as some of the more local features like burns, such as Abhainn Gleshgill (shining stream in the gulley) and Abhainn Ilishgil (deep stream of the spring).[46] Furthermore, a number of the field names that were hopelessly Latinised by Martin and Macaulay may have a Norse origin too.[47]

Although the archaeological evidence for the Norse presence on St Kilda is slight, it is nonetheless compelling. There seems little doubt that the minister Neil Mackenzie recorded the discovery of an undisturbed burial mound containing a male inhumation during the improvements of the 1830s in Village Bay. He relates that: 'In clearing the glebe I removed a mound in a little field, and found in it a long and narrow whetstone, an iron sword, a spear-head, and various other pieces of iron, mostly of irregular shape, and the use of which was not obvious.'[48] A second iron spearhead generally attributed to this period was discovered by the

Keartons during their explorations of the souterrain.[49] The so-called 'boat-shaped' structures in An Lag Bhon Tuath that were once thought to mark Norse burials are discussed elsewhere, but what was probably a Viking woman's grave is represented by the two brooches that were examined by the great Danish archaeologist Jens Worsaae on a visit to Scotland in 1846.[50] Unfortunately, both the location of this grave and the circumstances of its discovery are unknown. There is also a newspaper reference to a hoard of 'Danish' coins that were dug up by two fishermen in 1767, but this cannot now be substantiated.[51] The more recent discovery of several small pieces of carved steatite during the excavation of the area around House 8 in Village Bay should probably also be attributed to this period.[52] Although vessels of this material were traded from Shetland as early as the Neolithic, steatite was the subject of a very extensive and well-organised Norse market.

Buildings of Norse type have proved elusive on St Kilda, despite the evidence of placenames, burials and chance finds – although one candidate, 'Blackhouse' W, which has been put forward from time to time,[53] is now discounted.[54] Only the slight remains of a very small, crescent-shaped structure situated on the grass-grown screes of Mullach Sgar have produced dates of the 10th to 13th centuries and these originated from midden material that was dumped within it.[55] This presumably reflects some kind of domestic or agricultural activity, but clearly the main settlement lay elsewhere. The likelihood is that this was centred on Village Bay, where all surface trace has been lost through the robbing and recycling of stone in later times. Nevertheless, Andrew Fleming has put forward the suggestion that the fragmentary head dyke to the north of that constructed in the 1830s could be a Norse 'ring-garth', although there is nothing to substantiate this at present.[56]

AD 1266 to 1600

The end of Norse control in the west, and therefore St Kilda, came in 1266 following the Treaty of Perth, when King Magnus VI of Norway ceded the Hebrides and the Isle of Man to Alexander III, the King of Scotland. The Hebrides fell to the Lordship of the Isles and there followed the construction of a series of impressive medieval strongholds, the most notable of which were Dunvegan (Dùn Bheagan) on Skye, Kisimul (Chìosamul) on Barra and Calvay (Calbhaigh)

Dunvegan Castle on Skye, the seat of the MacLeods, is one of the great medieval strongholds of the Western Isles. For most of its history, trade, travel and warfare were undertaken by sea. This inland view, which appears in Thomas Pennant's A Tour in Scotland and Voyage to the Hebrides, 1772 is rather unusual in offering a road traveller's perspective.
Moses Griffiths, 1774, DP023548

on South Uist.[57] A number of smaller tower houses were also built in this period, including Caisteal Bheagram on South Uist, Dùn Mhic Leoid on Barra and Borve Castle (Caisteal Bhuirgh) on Benbecula.[58] In many cases, these buildings reoccupied the sites of earlier strongholds, a process that is most readily seen in the frequency with which brochs, duns and crannogs were transformed into medieval houses. The best known of these conversions are those of the brochs of Dùn an Sticer and Dùn Torcuil[59] on North Uist, but Seana Chaisteal on Pabbay is another.[60]

The Hebridean elite also invested in ecclesiastical foundations and their patronage is reflected in St

Clement's at Rodel on Harris, where the tomb of Alasdair Crotach, 8th Chief of the MacLeods, represents the high point of West Highland sculpture in the early 1500s.[61] The church dedicated to St Mary on Pabbay is probably of early 16th century date.[62] This stands immediately adjacent to what is almost certainly an earlier chapel dedicated to St Moluag – one of a small group of such buildings that are located on offshore islands in the parish of Harris, including Ensay, Killegray and Taransay.[63] None is securely dated, but excavation has determined that the earliest of the graves investigated in part of the burial enclosure on Ensay probably date from the 16th century, while the chapel is likely to be earlier still.[64]

The dwellings occupied by the main population in this period remained elusive until recently. A summary of a detailed archaeological survey of Barra and the islands to its south noted that these might possibly be identified in a number of 'sub-rectangular buildings about 7–8m long externally and a little over half as wide'.[65] Firmer evidence was discovered at Bornais on South Uist, where a house of similar length and a kiln barn were excavated, both of which were assigned a date in the 13th to 15th centuries.[66] A much smaller sub-rectangular structure was excavated at Eilean Olabhat on North Uist, which was divided into two compartments with one containing a hearth.[67] The ceramics suggested that this dated to the 14th and 16th centuries.[68] A slightly later settlement was situated nearby at Druim nan Dearcag comprising two houses, two barns and an enclosure. One of the houses was excavated and this was found to be generally similar to that at Eilean Olabhat, although it had been heavily modified.[69] Another settlement at Gearraidh Bhailteas on South Uist was also shown to contain evidence for occupation between the 14th and 17th centuries.[70] Typically, buildings of this period had

In medieval times, St Kilda was controlled by a Hebridean elite who invested in ecclesiastical sites such as St Clement's Church at Rodel on Harris (top). The church contains the 16th century tomb of its founder Alasdair Crotach, 8th Chief of the MacLeods, the finest example of medieval sculpture in the Outer Hebrides (middle). That same century, the church of St Mary's was constructed on Pabbay, an island in the Sound of Harris with a long association with St Kilda (bottom).

thick walls, not unlike those of the later blackhouses, and they would have had roofs of timber covered with turf and thatch.

The township, consisting of a number of buildings in a cluster, was the principal settlement of Hebridean communities from the medieval period. Each was associated with a large hinterland intended for the procurement of resources, including building materials and fuel, as well as ground that was given over to cultivation and the grazing of stock. Although it is possible to point to a number of settlements that have their origin in this period, medieval field systems in the Outer Hebrides are little known and have yet to be closely studied. The practice of transhumance, whereby some members of the community would relocate in the summer months to live beside their grazings known as 'shielings' is well attested in the Hebrides, but very few of the many huts that formed this seasonal accommodation have been excavated. However, the earliest phase of an oval example with stone foundations at Ben Gunnary (Beinn Ghunnaraidh) on Barra has been attributed to the Norse period on the basis of finds, although it continued to be rebuilt and occupied into medieval times.[71] Shieling practice continued well into the 19th century in the Outer Hebrides and many of the best preserved huts survive on Lewis and Harris. When encountered by antiquaries in the 19th century, these buildings were thought to reflect ancient building traditions and this has led to confusion as to their date. Many are unquestionably of simple construction, but some at least were built after 1750, including well preserved examples recorded by RCAHMS at Sròn Smearasmal and Both a' Chlair Bheag on Harris and at Ascleit and Àirigh a' Sguir on Lewis.[72]

There is no castle or tower on St Kilda, presumably because the archipelago formed a small detached portion of the MacLeod lands, the caput of which was eventually established at Dunvegan. Nor is there clear physical evidence for an early medieval chapel, although there must surely have been one at that time, and in the following centuries that witnessed the establishment of a parochial system after 1200.[73] One account suggests there were seven chapels on St Kilda (not necessarily on Hirta), another account suggests six, with dedications to Christ, St Brendan (St Brianan), St Clement, St Columba, St John and St Peter.[74] While these references are difficult to verify, at least three of the dedications survived into the 1690s

when Martin described Christ's Chapel, St Brianan's and St Columba's in some detail. Christ's Chapel was 'covered and thatched after the same manner with their houses'.[75] It was associated with a burial ground about 'an hundred paces' [80m] in circumference which was surrounded by a wall.[76] This was used for services as the building itself was too small to house its congregation. The other two chapels were apparently similar, each being spaced at intervals of about a quarter of a mile (700m).[77] Subsequently, Macaulay noted that Christ's Chapel measured 24ft (7m) by 14ft (4m), but had fallen into disuse save for burials, while St Columba's on the west side of the settlement lacked an altar, a cross and an accompanying cell. St Brianan's also seems to have been abandoned, for although it still had 'an altar within and some monkish cells without', the fact that these were reportedly 'almost entire' clearly was intended to contrast it with the ruinous condition of its counterparts.[78] The sites of the three chapels were plotted by Mathieson in 1927, but he records how he found them 'difficult to locate'[79] and that he had had to rely upon the testimony of the factor, John Mackenzie, and the ground officer, Neil Ferguson.[80] From this it would be safe to assume that there may be some margin of error in their plotted positions.

The site of Christ's Chapel was noted on Mathieson's map of 1928 about 30m from the burial ground, but that position was amended by Jimmy Davidson of the Ordnance Survey in 1967 on account of the evidence provided by Sands, who stated in 1878 that a ruined chapel stood 'in the little churchyard' but 'was demolished some years ago'.[81] Wilson, on a visit in 1841, noted that the burial ground 'surrounds what may be called the debris rather than the ruins of the ancient chapel', perhaps the area in the western half of the burial ground that is devoid of grave markers.[82] Although there is no evidence that the burial ground was moved during the Christian era, the present enclosing wall and the roughly level surface of the interior are of 19th century date and so perhaps provide an indication of the date for many of the rude markers within.[83] St Brianan's chapel, which was 'indistinct though perceptible' in 1841,[84] was located by Mathieson, with Neil Ferguson's help, within a well-preserved enclosure just north-east of Abhainn Ruaival, where geophysical surveys undertaken in 1991 and 1992 identified a series of anomalies, none of which were excavated.[85] Instead, two features

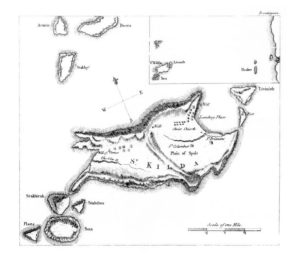

situated about 150m to the north-north-east were examined and although these were initially interpreted as the remains of Macaulay's 'monkish cells', this was subsequently discounted.[86] The site of the third chapel, St Columba's, was located by Mathieson on a raised knoll between two burn gullies and now lies just within the head dyke, where it is overlain by two cleitean, two clearance cairns and a series of terraces resulting from peat cutting.[87] An alternative location, within the remains of an enclosure some 60m away, was explored by geophysical survey in 2007, when a 'well defined rectilinear response' was identified, although this has not been explored further.[88]

In addition to these chapels, those dedicated to St John, St Peter and St Clement have yet to be discovered. One may have stood at Taigh an Triùir (the House of the Trinity), an unusual cleit which stands on a knoll that may have inspired the placename Cnoc a' Bheannaichte (blessed knoll). Macaulay did not describe the building, but instead drew his reader's attention to a 'sacred stone' and the 'plain of spells, exorcisms, or prayers' that lay nearby.[89] Another chapel may have been located on the island of Boreray, where an altar was also recorded.[90] When the minister's niece Anne Kennedy wrote to Captain Thomas in 1862, she included a description of 'a temple on Boreray built with hewn stones', which an elderly St Kildan, Euphemia Macrimmon, remembered seeing. Kennedy went on to say that 'there is one stone yet in the ground where the temple stood, upon which there is writing; the inhabitants of St Kilda built cleitean or cells with the stones of the temple'.[91] Although Mathieson failed to find either the altar or the inscribed stone in 1927, there is no particular reason to doubt that a small chapel of pilgrimage, analogous with the medieval building on the Flannan Isles, once stood on Boreray.[92] Another may have been situated on Soay, where what has been taken to be an 'enclosure' around the altar may in fact be the remains of a building.

The chapels and wells depicted on Kenneth Macaulay's map of 1764 have often been regarded as ancient rather than relatively recent, while James Wilson's etching of the interior of a ruinous chapel owes more to flights of fancy than reality. More recently, archaeological investigations at the site of St Brianan's Church (bottom) failed to locate it.

Kenneth Macaulay, 1764, DP214155

James Wilson, 1842, DP212775

Dave Cowley RCAHMS, 2012, DP134129

A natural spring, protected by an impressive well head, is situated at the foot of Gleann Mòr, the best part of an hour's walk from Village Bay. In the 17th and 18th centuries Tobar nam Buaidh (the well of virtues) attracted pilgrims from Harris who sought a cure for various aches and pains. They are said to have placed offerings on an adjacent altar.

Steve Wallace RCAHMS. 2008, DP051807

St Kilda is rich in natural springs or 'wells' and these must have served the islands' inhabitants since the earliest times. The Ordnance Survey map of 1928 records eight named springs on Hirta, not all of which can be easily associated with those described by early visitors. However, five were noted by Martin, who related that three had a 'cover of stone'.[93] As far as he was aware, only Tobar nam Buaidh (the well of virtues) was associated with healing. This was clearly of some renown at the time, as it attracted 'the inhabitants of Harries [who] find it effectual against windy-cholicks, gravel, [and] head-aches'.[94] This stands at the foot of Gleann Mòr and has the largest and most striking of the well heads. Macaulay records in some detail the placement of 'offerings' on an adjacent altar by

'pilgrims', raising the interesting possibility that Hirta was indeed a place of pilgrimage in the medieval period.[95] A second, unnamed spring with a simple well head also survives in Gleann Mòr, much closer to the Amazon's House, but no historical records for this are known.[96]

The remaining four named by Martin are situated in Village Bay and served the township. There is a substantial well head named Tobar Gille Chille (the well of the servant of the church) to the north-east of the present church, but this perhaps post dates the construction of this edifice in the late 1820s, as there is no mention of it any earlier.[97] The well head at Tobar Childa (the cold well), situated just north of the head dyke near Calum Mòr's House, is less substantial although reputed to be 'in universal use by the community in the 18th century'.[98] A 'second holy well', 'Toberi Clerich' (the clergyman's well), is mentioned by Macaulay, who reported that it was situated 'below the village, and gushes out like a torrent from the face of a rock'.[99] This was said to be inter-tidal and it is almost certainly that recorded as Tobar a' Chlèirich in 1927, which was plotted on the rocky foreshore to

The survival of an altar on Soay, set within the ruined walls of an earlier building or enclosure, suggests the possibility of a pilgrimage route around the archipelago that included Hirta, Dun, and probably Boreray five miles distant.

Stuart Murray, 2010, DPl64867

the south-east of the gun emplacement.[100] There is no reason to confuse this well with Tobar a' Mhinisteir (the minister's well), which stands about 30m north-north-west of the church and supplies the military base. It, too, was covered with a well head comparable with that of Tobar Gille Chille.[101]

Two other wells recorded by Martin are more difficult to identify, but one named 'Conirdan', which was also provided with a well head, may be equated with Tobar Chonastan, situated south-west of the Abhainn Riasg,[102] while another, Tobar na Gille (the servant's well), was situated near St Brianan's chapel, but this now lacks any kind of covering.[103] Another well was recorded in 1928 at Taigh an Triùir, and Mathieson also recorded Tobar Ruadh on Soay, but omitted a spring on Boreray, where the lining of a ruined well head survives near the site of the recent bothies.[104]

Macaulay is the first to record the presence of four freestanding altars on St Kilda, three of which were 'at considerable distances from the holy places'.[105] One, in particular, was situated 'on top of a hill to the south-west, [being] dedicated according to tradition to the God who presides over the seasons'.[106] He also reported that another lay close to Tobar nam Buaidh, which 'during the reign of Popery' the St Kildans revered on account of the water's miraculous ability to cure 'a great variety of distempers, deafness particularly, and every nervous disease' – a list of conditions that differs quite markedly from those that had been outlined by Martin some 50 years earlier.[107] Every supplicant was required to make at least some simple offering even if these consisted only of 'shells and pebbles, rags of linen or stuffs worn out, pins, needles, or rusty nails … and sometimes, though rarely enough, copper coins of the smallest value'.[108] The records of altars on Boreray and Dun are more circumspect, although the traditional site of the latter was noted by Mathieson in 1927.[109]

Only the altar on Soay remains largely intact in part due to its remote location and in part to the efforts of recent visitors, who may well have contributed stones

This area in Village Bay has long been considered the likely site of the 'medieval village', based largely upon the number of cleitean that appear to incorporate earlier cellular structures. However, the dating of these earlier features remains an open question.
Steve Wallace RCAHMS, 2008, DP044840

to its fabric. The altar, a solid rubble-built structure measuring 1.5m square and 1m high, is situated within a small, grass covered 'enclosure' (perhaps a ruined building) towards the east end of the island, at the edge of a break of slope and about 100m below the island's summit.[110] While its date is open to question, it may bear comparison with the undated 'hut' known as 'the altar' recorded by RCAHMS at the eremitic site of Sgor nam Ban-Naomha on Canna and possibly with another on North Rona.[111] Martin also records what may be an altar on the Flannan Islands[112] and such 'leachta' as they are known are relatively common in Ireland where they are praying stations and also occasionally mark out a route for pilgrims.[113] Some of these date back to the Early Christian period, but there is no reason to suppose that the altars on St Kilda were so ancient.

Traces of the field systems and settlements that preceded the crofting township established in the 1830s have proved difficult to identify. There seems little doubt that cultivation will have centred on Village Bay, but apart perhaps from the fragmentary head dyke that survives on the east within the circuit of its later counterparts, there are no surface traces that can be attributed with confidence to this period. Following fieldwork in 1957, with Macaulay's description of the settlement in 1764 to hand, Kenneth Williamson of the Nature Conservancy felt able to describe the 'medieval village' in some detail in an unpublished report in which he noted a group of buildings that were 'too pretentious to be mere store-chambers, and are broader and have greater head-room than the general run of structures'.[114] These included 'Calum Mòr's House'[115] situated south-east of the well head named Tobar Childa. He also noted that their plans embraced a cellular element which he believed to be an early feature, although he had no conception of how intricate the evolution of this settlement might have been. His analysis was published in *Scottish Field* in March 1958 and reiterated in three further

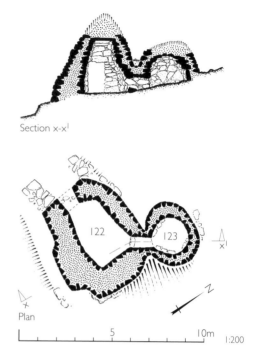

Section x-x¹

122   123

Plan

5   10m

1:200

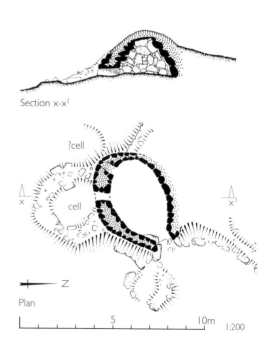

Section x-x¹

?cell

cell

Plan

5   10m

1:200

publications before 1963.[116] Subsequent authors have tended to support his thesis, accepting that Tobar Childa lay at the settlement's centre.[117]

In 1966, during the record revision of the Ordnance Survey, Beverley Roy Stallwood synthesised and evaluated earlier accounts of the medieval village which he then ascribed to the broad period from 1400 to 1830. However, his colleague, Jimmy Davidson, sounded a note of caution in relation to the likely complexity of the field archaeology.[118] Nevertheless, they agreed that the village probably extended from Tobar Childa south-eastwards, but that there was only evidence for three or four of the 'medieval or "beehive" type dwellings' similar to Calum Mòr's House having been converted into cleitean at a later date. During the survey of 1983–6, RCAHMS planned the area that had been highlighted and created a series of measured drawings of eight buildings, all but one of which provided evidence for contiguous cells, so distinguishing them from the average cleit.[119]

In his careful study of 2003, Andrew Fleming argued convincingly that the settlement that preceded that of the 1830s, which had been sketched by Thomas Dyke Acland and George Atkinson before its demolition,[120] was not to be traced in these substantial buildings, which he called 'super-cleits'.[121] Instead, it lay in the rather more ephemeral traces of rectangular buildings situated east and south-east of the burial ground.[122] However, the structural history of the township prior to 1830 will undoubtedly have been complicated, as the multifaceted remains of the settlements abandoned on the island Pabbay in the 1840s attest.[123]

The group of 'beehive' dwellings first identified by Williamson and described in detail by RCAHMS in the 1980s remains to be securely dated, although all the available evidence at present suggests they should originate *before* the 17th century. 'Calum Mòr's House', which was described in 1875 as 'an old cellar',[124] was the subject of a series of notes and photographs over the following 85 years and was identified by Williamson as 'the most ancient' of his 'medieval' buildings.[125] The building appears now as a grass-grown mound apparently overridden to the north by a small cultivation plot. The interior measures 4.6m by 2.6m and is entered through a small opening. Two smaller apertures lead off to what may have been sleeping cells on the south and west. A larger building, which was re-roofed as late as 1896, stands outside the head dyke to the north.[126] Known simply by its numerical signifier as 'Cleit 122 and 123', this building is unique in that the attached cell still remains roofed, although it is only accessible via a small opening from the main compartment. Its walls, particularly on the south and west, show signs of modification.

These corbelled and cellular buildings bear comparison in terms of their size with small medieval structures excavated elsewhere, while parallels for the corbelled side-chambers are found on Lewis, where they are generally contained in the thickness of a wall.[127] Indeed, domestic structures throughout the medieval period are characterised by thick walls constructed of turf or turf and stone. As such, it is possible that these 'beehive' buildings have been modified to such an extent that neither their plan, nor their outer walls, nor their roofs, authentically represent their original appearance – in practice, a change of function from dwelling to cleit has led to them being entirely transformed. Such changes are reflected in the plans of the buildings, which often show signs of having been reduced in size and of having had walls that were originally thicker. The likelihood is that all these buildings were originally roofed with timber and thatch, but that these were subsequently renewed in stone. Walls were reduced in thickness to allow air to circulate and the entrances were remade, while the surviving cells, which have sometimes been reduced to mere footings, simply became redundant.

By contrast, the cellular buildings in Gleann Mòr appear relatively unaltered. The suggestion that these

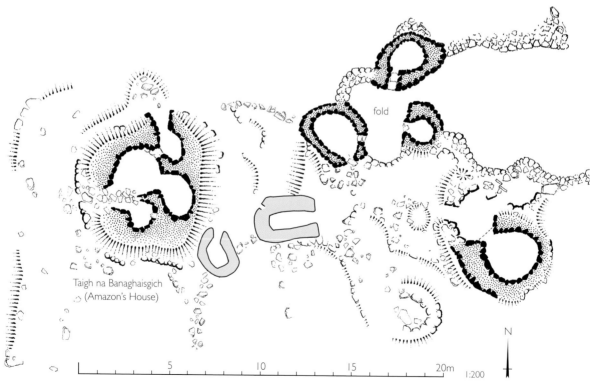

Taigh na Banaghaisgich
(Amazon's House)

fold

5   10   15   20m   1:200

N

opposite
One of the best known structures on St Kilda is Taigh na Banaghaisgich (the House of the Female Warrior). This complex of structures includes more recent gathering folds and cleitean, as well as the shieling huts which were visited by Martin Martin in 1697. He introduced the notion of the exotic Amazon and it is now commonly known as the 'Amazon's House'.
Steve Wallace RCAHMS, 2008, DP045011
RCAHMS, 1985, GV005694

above and right
Cellular buildings are distributed across the rich pastures of Gleann Mòr. While at times they have been assigned to the prehistoric period, they are more probably shielings of medieval date. Many, such as Structure G shown here, have a later gathering fold set into their ruins, while the majority are overlain by at least one cleit.
Steve Wallace RCAHMS, 2008, DP045030
RCAHMS, c1985, GV005695

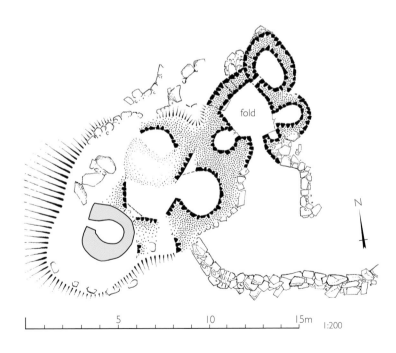

fold

N

5   10   15m   1:200

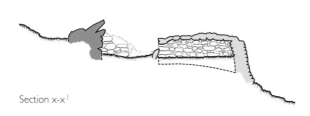

Section x-x¹

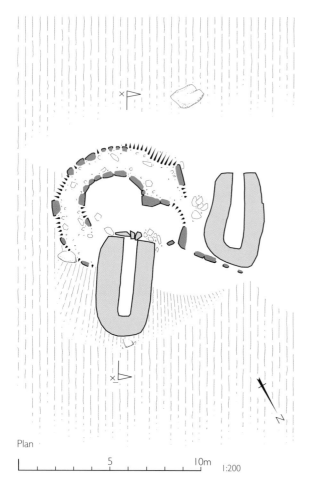

Plan

| 5 | 10m |
| 1:200 |

This small corbelled shieling hut, Structure N, which is set into the slope and comprises two ruined cells, has been robbed for stone to build two cleitean.

RCAHMS. 2009, GV005696

may represent the settlement of an ancient community persisted until very recently. Indeed, RCAHMS described them in 1988 as 'more obviously embodying wheelhouse building traditions' and as appearing to belong to the 'the same species as the surviving cellular buildings in the village'.[128] This view has now been superceded and there is little doubt that they are shieling huts.[129]

Transhumance was universal in the Outer Hebrides at this time and on St Kilda it is well attested both by the placename Àirigh Mòr (the big shieling) and the implicit description of the practice in the late 17th century, when some islanders stayed in Gleann Mòr 'all summer'.[130] The best known of the huts was named to Martin as Taigh na Banaghaisgich (the House of the Female Warrior), a being that he configured as an Amazon for his readership.[131] Describing the building and its traditional association in some detail, he recorded what was probably a reference to the Mulletach or Scáthach characters of Gaelic mythology,[132] while also comparing its architecture with Taigh Stallair on Boreray.[133] Since then it has been described on many occasions, most recently by RCAHMS.[134]

Although once likened by RCAHMS architect Charles Calder to Neolithic buildings on Shetland,[135] the similarity does not extend beyond an approximation of the floor plan. Further comparisons have been made with Pictish buildings like those within the broch at Dun Vulan or at Bostadh, South Uist;[136] Iron Age wheelhouses;[137] Loch an Duna broch on Lewis;[138] 'Pict's houses of the Orkneys';[138] and with the 'beehive' shielings on Lewis and Harris.[140] Field visits and surveys by RCAHMS at these sites suggest that the closest comparison is with the corbelled shieling huts of Lewis and Harris, despite the fact that they are of a much later date than Captain Thomas implied. He considered them to be evidence for 'the expiring modes and habits of the Celtic race as they have been practised for two thousand years'.[141]

However, in many ways the statement offered by RCAHMS in 1988 still holds true: 'all that can be confidently asserted on the basis of the survey and historical evidence is that the "Amazon's House" is of about 1600 AD or earlier'.[142] Gleann Mòr is dotted with similar buildings, which no doubt reflects a lengthy history of shieling, an intensive use of the glen for grazing and, possibly, its careful management by a certain number of families. While many have been

The rich grassland of Gleann Mòr is dotted with cleitean and shielings constructed over the last 500 years. The largest group of structures (above, left) was known in the 20th century as Àirigh Mòr (the big shieling), reflecting the glen's use as pasture for cows and sheep.

John Keggie RCAHMS, 1986, SC1467611

robbed for later structures, whether gathering folds or cleitean, shieling huts of this period and in this state of preservation are rare survivals in the Outer Hebrides, particularly when associated with such specific historical documentation.

As has been indicated, Martin drew attention to the resemblance between Taigh Stallair on Boreray and the Amazon's House.[143] The former is one of a group of three similar mounds on Boreray,[144] but the only one to betray structural evidence in the form of walling. It has long been considered an ancient survival and indeed by some as the home of a druid or priest,[145] but it has been reinterpreted here as evidence for the late medieval – early modern occupation of Boreray. These mounds appear to be related to an extensive multi-phase field system situated on the steep south-west

facing slope of the island, where a head dyke crossing from north-west to south-east separates the upper slopes used for grazing from the lower ground, where a series of heavily eroded banks divide the terrain into a number of sub-rectangular enclosures.[146] This arrangement has no close analogies in the prehistoric period and essentially recalls the late medieval system of infield and outfield. It probably relates to a relatively lengthy period when an attempt was made to permanently occupy and cultivate the island; and in every instance where it can be observed, the cleitean and bothies are later than the field boundaries and the mounds. The islanders who created this system must have lived somewhere and the only candidates known at present are Taigh Stallair and its counterparts.

There is also a series of terraces on the extremely steep slopes above the rocky cleft of the Geo an Àraich on Boreray which defy a ready explanation. They were first noticed by Mary Harman and Morton Boyd in May 1979, when the latter suggested they may be related to the exploitation of puffins, or perhaps otherwise were built by the St Kildans who were stranded during the smallpox epidemic of 1727–8[147]

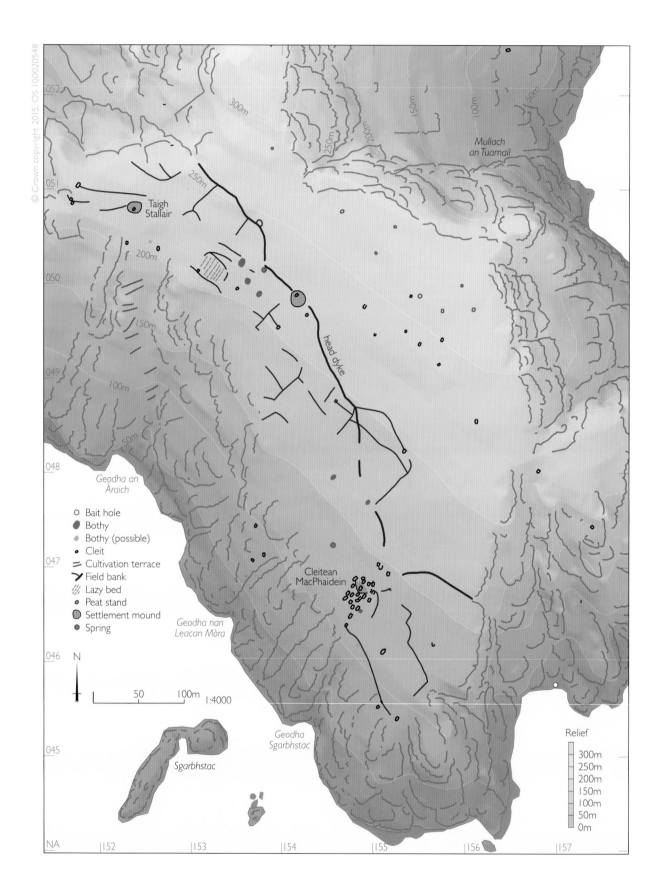

© Crown copyright 2015, OS 100020548

300m

052

051 Taigh
Stallair

250m

050 200m

150m

049 100m

head dyke

Mullach
an Tuamail

150m
100m
50m

250m
200m

048

Geodha an
Àraich

○ Bait hole
● Bothy
◆ Bothy (possible)
• Cleit
═ Cultivation terrace
➤ Field bank
▥ Lazy bed
○ Peat stand
◯ Settlement mound
● Spring

047

Cleitean
MacPhaidein

046

N

Geodha nan
Leacan Mòra

50   100m   1:4000

045

Sgarbhstac

Geodha
Sgarbhstac

Relief

300m
250m
200m
150m
100m
50m
0m

NA |152 |153 |154 |155 |156 |157

The survey of Boreray in 2010 recorded an extensive field system on the grassy south western slope which may be late medieval in origin, contemporary with a series of settlement mounds that predate the numerous cleitean and bothies. The single patch of lazy bedding suggests an attempt at cultivation in the mid 18th century.

opposite RCAHMS, 2010. GV005732

above Stuart Murray, 2010. DP164561

– although in practice they are reputed to have been marooned on Stac an Àrmainn. The terraces possibly represent garden plots, as they are located in a comparatively well-sheltered hollow and again, presumably date to a period when permanent occupation was attempted. Equally poorly dated are the bait holes situated on the rocks just above the sea at the south end of the island. They indicate that the inhabitants of Boreray augmented their diet with fish caught by rod and line – the only archaeological evidence for this activity known at present in the archipelago.[148]

During this period, then, the archaeology of St Kilda intimates that the islands were occupied by a permanent population practising arable and pastoral agriculture. Unfortunately, the part that may have been played by fishing and fowling in their economy is almost completely unknown, but the fact that the St Kildans were part of a wider community linked by the Hebridean seaways is also reflected in the suggestion that for some they seem to have been a place of pilgrimage. This more extensive community also shared the same history, whether falling under the influence of Christianity, or being brought under the successive suzerainties of distant Norwegian kings, semi-independent Lords of the Isles, or the Chieftancy of the MacLeods. Indeed, the islanders' dependency on their wider network only strengthened with time. And whereas this reliance is only dimly perceptible in the sparse documentation extant before the 17th century, the ties they had with their neighbours to the east become clearer as the administrative and ecclesiastical records begin to accumulate in the subsequent years.

Chapter Five
From Chiefs to Landlords – 1600 to 1780

St Kilda became part of the territory of 'McCloyd of Haray', the second principal branch of the Clan MacLeod at some point before 1549.[1] Both the MacLeods of Harris and those of Lewis claimed descent from Leod, a son of Olaf the Black, King of Mann from 1226 until 1237.[2] While the power of the MacLeods of Lewis waned in the 17th century, the MacLeods of Harris emerged from the superiority of the Lordship of the Isles to control an extensive territory. The Outer Hebridean interests of the clan were initially centred at Seana Chaisteal on the island of Pabbay, where the 4th chief died in the 14th century,[3] but in later years the caput of the estate was at Dunvegan on Skye.[4]

The MacLeods controlled St Kilda until 1779, when they were forced to sell much of their estate to fend off bankruptcy. However, sentimental associations ensured that the clan chief bought back the archipelago in 1871 and it was not sold again until 1931 shortly after the evacuation. In addition to St Kilda, the MacLeods territory in the early 18th century comprised most of the offshore islands in the Sound of Harris, the main island of Harris itself, Glenelg in Lochalsh, and

opposite
Dunvegan Castle on Skye, the ancestral seat of the MacLeods, occupies the summit of a rocky boss on the eastern shore of Dunvegan Loch. The castle was usually accessed from the sea until the mid 18th century when a network of roads was established. c1890, SC948763

a number of farms in northern Skye that included Dunvegan, Waternish, Duirinish (Duirinis), Minginish (Minginis) and Bracadale (Bracadal) – a total of almost 400,000 acres (160,000ha).[5] Although the preceding chapter looked largely to the Outer Hebrides for St Kilda's historical context, here the focus is narrowed to the MacLeod estate itself which, with the important exception of the fowling economy, provides the most appropriate framework for considering the archaeological heritage of the archipelago in the 17th and 18th centuries.

Historians such as Robert Dodgshon and Michael Newton have described the complex nature of the society and economy that the chiefs controlled.[6] The MacLeod sat at the top of a hierarchical social system organised around kin-based communities with strategic control of land and resources. This was a system that had long emphasised and distinguished status through the practices of feuding and feasting.[7] Skirmishes over territory were commonplace. In the Battle of Bloody Bay, which took place off the north coast of Mull in the late 15th century, the MacLeods supported John of Islay, 4th Lord of the Isles, in a dispute with his son;[8] while in the Blàr Milleadh Gàraidh (the battle of the destruction of the dyke), which took place on the Waternish peninsula in the late 16th century, the MacLeods vanquished a force of Uist MacDonalds who had burned the congregation in Trumpan Church in revenge for a similar massacre on Eigg a year or so earlier.[9] As for feasting, this

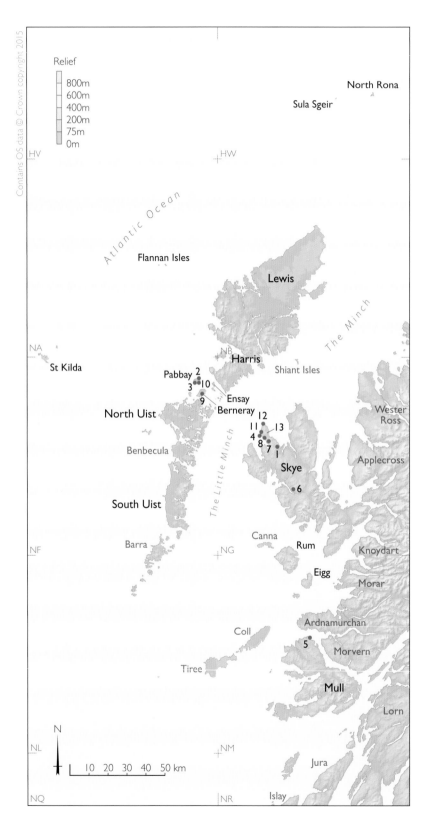

Relief

800m
600m
400m
200m
75m
0m

Contains OS data © Crown copyright: 2015

North Rona

Sula Sgeir

Atlantic Ocean

Flannan Isles

Lewis

The Minch

St Kilda

Harris

Shiant Isles

Pabbay 2
3 ●●10
9
Ensay
Berneray

North Uist

The Little Minch

Wester Ross

12
11 ● ● 13
4 ●
8 ● 7 1

Skye

Applecross

Benbecula

● 6

South Uist

Canna

Rum

Knoydart

Barra

Eigg

Morar

Coll

Ardnamurchan
5 ●

Morvern

Tiree

Mull

Lorn

N

10 20 30 40 50 km

Jura

Islay

The Western Isles –
sites referred to in this chapter

1	Allt na Smuide
2	Baile-fo-thuath
3	Baile Lingaidh
4	Blàr Milleadh Gàraidh (Battle Site)
5	Bloody Bay (Battle Site)
6	Dunvegan
7	Fàsach
8	Halistra
9	Risgary
10	Seana Chaisteal
11	Trumpan
12	Unish
13	Waternish

RCAHMS, 2015, GV005723

Dunvegan lay at the heart of an extensive domain controlled by the MacLeod's factor and tacksmen. While many of the tenants' buildings were in a vernacular style, the estate buildings and farmhouses were altogether grander.

William Daniell, 1819, DP009314

Unish House stands at the centre of an extensive contemporary landscape within the Waternish peninsula on Skye. Perhaps dating from the early 17th century, it was renovated as the house for the local tacksman in the 18th century.

Geoff Quick RCAHMS, 1990, SC717508

was an overt expression of wealth that relied upon the surplus produced by the estate which included St Kilda.[10]

The management of the estate was mediated on the one hand through a system of land grants to younger sons or the most senior cadet branches of the family, and on the other through land rentals to the cadet branches, with their senior members being employed as tacksmen.[11] The principal holdings on Harris were held by cadet families who were often associated with particular places. Thus, while the chief was known as MacLeod *of MacLeod*, his factor at one time included Norman MacLeod *of Berneray* (b 1614) and one of his tacksman was Neil MacLeod *of Pabbay* (b 1596);[12] and these men would sometimes be referred to simply by their holding. The factors of MacLeod took control over his business in large districts, while the tacksmen formed the interlocutors for smaller areas within the estate, in the management and the organisation of the economy of the tenants and the landless cottars. The tacksmen rented one or more townships, generally for their lifetimes, with an additional numbers of years for an inheriting son.[13] This is the model that was followed for St Kilda, which was included in a tack (or rental) with Pabbay.

The nature of the MacLeod economy has been explored by Robert Dodghson through the rentals for the century following the 1680s.[14] Rentals at this time comprised a combination of payment in cash and in kind, as well as a range of obligatory services – the balance and detail varying widely across the territory and through time. They record that the islands of the Sound of Harris were 'far more productive' in arable than Harris itself, with Pabbay and Ensay providing nearly 60% of the Harris grain rent.[15] The grain rents of these islands and Berneray exceeded any other part of the MacLeod estate during this period,[16] but it is difficult to establish the contribution of St Kilda at this time.

Dunvegan Castle was the seat of the estate, where the 13th century fortification was supplemented by major extensions in the 17th and 18th centuries.[17] The estate buildings grouped near the castle are generally of later date,[18] although one 18th century building survives in the form of a crow-stepped range which acted as the factor's house and estate office.[19] Communications between the estate and its outlying reaches including St Kilda were by sea rather than by land and there was 'no landward entrance at Dunvegan until 1748'.[20] The small size of the vessels in use before the 18th century required little more than a naust for a place to berth. Although tracks had long been in existence, a road network was only developed from about 1800.[21]

The estate of Dunvegan roughly corresponds with the modern parishes of Duirinish and Bracadale on

The many structures on the island of Pabbay confirm that it was one of the more productive components of the MacLeod estate. Pabbay and St Kilda belonged to the same rental, or tack, for much of their history.

Getmapping, 2011, PGA

Skye, Harris (including St Kilda) and Glenelg. It was subdivided topographically into a series of large areas (Skye, Harris, Glenelg) managed by a factor or factors who, in turn, oversaw the tacksmen.[22] The MacLeod's factors on Harris during this period usually resided at Risgary on Berneray, where the much altered remnants of their house survive.[23] Some of the tacksman's houses were of a comparable stature to those of factors, such as the substantial 17th and 18th century building at Unish on Skye, which was surveyed by RCAHMS in 1990.[24] By contrast, a tacksman's house can sometimes only be recognised during field survey on account of its floor plan being larger than that of a tenant's house.[25]

The MacLeod townships of this period generally contained from 35 to well over 100 people,[26] the latter being comparable with the size of the St Kildan community.[27] The size of each was broadly related to

the areas of arable and pasture, but was also reflected in both the complexity and number of buildings. Over 500 townships have been recorded in the Outer Hebrides, while the parishes of Duirinish and Harris both boast over 90.[28] Nevertheless, not all of these were occupied between 1600 and 1800; and Canon Roderick Charles MacLeod's list of over 130 townships with entries in the rentals of the MacLeod estate in the early 18th century provides a much better guide.[29] The estate at that time covered a large area and there are numerous examples of joint-tenanted mixed farms with evidence for arable cultivation, grazing and shieling. RCAHMS has had the opportunity to survey two landscapes within the MacLeod's holdings and these provide a useful comparison with St Kilda. The first on the island of Pabbay in the Sound of Harris was once considered the bread-basket of the estate; and it is the island with which St Kilda was most strongly connected in this period. The second is the much larger peninsula of Waternish, forming part of the parish of Duirinish on Skye, which illustrates the general character of the landscapes under MacLeod control at this time. Fowling, however, which was

Trumpan, overlooking the Ardmore peninsula, lay relatively close to Dunvegan. It was the location for a medieval church and the site of a clan battle in the 16th century. Although separated by many miles of open sea, St Kilda and Trumpan were MacLeod possessions during the medieval period.

Dave Cowley RCAHMS, 2011, DP111350

such a distinctive component of the St Kildan economy, was not practised extensively elsewhere on the estate, although it was common amongst the coastal communities of Scotland, as well as in other parts of the Outer Hebrides and the Northern Isles.

The 17th and 18th century archaeological landscape of Pabbay is both rich and diverse, although it has received scant attention in the archaeological literature.[30] Over 80 sub-rectangular buildings have been recorded on the island and at least two candidates for a tacksman's house have been noted.[31] Perhaps of most interest is the nucleated township that comprises the northern part of Baile Lingaidh,[32] which includes fourteen buildings of varying dates and function, and

the farmstead consisting of six buildings at Baile-fo-thuath, where the largest may have been a tacksman's house.[33]

Despite the damaging effects of a sand blow which occurred in 1697 and covered a large area of the lower ground,[34] extensive evidence of cultivation can still be observed in the ploughlands on the lower slopes, the lazy bedding (feannagan) at higher altitudes and the individual garden plots close by the buildings. Usefully, the nature of cultivation on this and other islands in the late 18th century is described at some length in the *Statistical Account of Harris*.[35] Root crops were important and there were arrangements for their storage in pits at a number of locations,[36] while at least two corn drying kilns can be attributed to this period.[37] Much of the arable ground is enclosed within a series of head dykes which separate the more fertile lands in the south-east of the island from the rockier terrain in the north-west, although numerous enclosures containing lazy bedding survive beyond them which must have been included in the 600 acres (243ha) of arable surveyed by Bald in 1805.[38] Four groups of shieling huts have

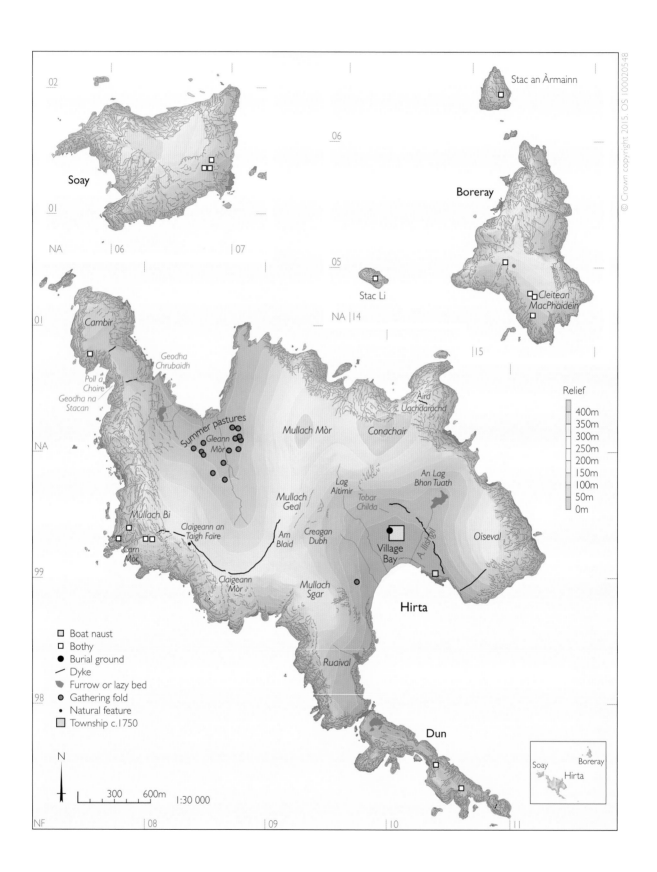

Soay

Stac an Àrmainn

Boreray

Stac Li

Cleitean
MacPhaidein

Cambir

Geodha
Chrubaidh

Poll a
Choire

Geodha na
Stacan

Summer pastures

Gleann
Mòr

Mullach Mòr

Conachair

Aird
Uachdarachd

Relief

400m
350m
300m
250m
200m
150m
100m
50m
0m

Lag
Aitimir

An Lag
Bhon Tuath

Tobar
Childa

Mullach
Geal

Mullach Bi

Claigeann an
Taigh Faire

Carn
Mòr

Am
Blaid

Creagan
Dubh

Village
Bay

Oiseval

Claigeann
Mòr

Mullach
Sgar

Hirta

Ruaival

◻ Boat naust
◻ Bothy
● Burial ground
╱ Dyke
▨ Furrow or lazy bed
◉ Gathering fold
• Natural feature
▧ Township c.1750

Dun

N

300   600m   1:30 000

Soay   Boreray
        Hirta

One of the two drystone bothies on Eilean Mòr, the largest of the Flannan Isles. Now undermined by the burrowing of puffins, this once provided shelter for the men who came to the island to catch seabirds.

George Geddes RCAHMS, 2014, DP190358

been identified on the higher ground, each a string of circular drystone structures that were presumably attached to one of the farm holdings.[39]

The density of the pre-Clearance remains on the MacLeod estate on the Waternish peninsula might be partly explained by a rise in population in the later 18th century; but the vestiges of earlier phases were distinguished at Halistra and Fàsach.[40] Some 775 buildings were recorded in the course of the RCAHMS survey and 202 of these were depicted as roofed on the 1st or 2nd editions of the Ordnance Survey 6-inch map.[41] The majority of the structures were located in coastal townships, but 202 shieling mounds and 144 shieling huts were recorded on land above 75m OD. Most of the shielings were fairly evenly distributed throughout the peninsula beyond the core areas of permanent settlement, although some were found within the boundaries of the head dykes, while others had been levelled by cultivation. Many are now simply mounded sites showing little architectural form, but others are stone-walled, sub-rectangular huts, or multi-celled structures like that at Allt na Smuide.[42] The farmsteads situated within the head dykes usually consist of one long building and at least

opposite

St Kilda – sites referred to in this chapter.

RCAHMS, 2015, GV005728

one other attached to an enclosure, with additional small huts and pens. Several freestanding corn drying kilns, a handful of kiln-barns and two grain mills were also noted, one of which had been constructed by the estate in the 1730s.[43] Plots of both plough and spade cultivation are a recurrent feature of the landscape and are sometimes found within enclosures. Clusters of sub-circular fields measuring roughly 1ha are relatively common and appear to have been integrated with the cultivated ground, although it is unclear whether their boundaries had been constructed to include or exclude grazing animals.

Although St Kilda was the only part of the MacLeod estate that practised fowling extensively, the harvesting of seabirds and their eggs was undertaken throughout much of coastal Scotland in the 17th and 18th centuries. However, the intensive exploitation of these resources was restricted to the most significant seabird colonies, whether in the Northern and Western Isles, or on certain isolated islands such as the Bass Rock.[44] Seabird bones occur regularly in archaeological assemblages, but there has yet to be a study attempting to relate them to the colonies that were exploited. Moreover, little research has been undertaken on the field archaeology of fowling, although recent work by RCAHMS and Jill Harden has begun to address this issue.[45] Bothies still accommodate the seabird hunters on the small island of Sula Sgeir, which lies close to North Rona about 70km north of the Butt of Lewis (Rubha Robhanais), thus maintaining an annual tradition stretching back to the 16th century or earlier.[46] These are of drystone construction and mostly oval or sub-rectangular on plan.[47] Other examples have been recorded on the Flannan Isles, where two attributed to the Clan MacPhail have a complex plan incorporating a central area and side cells. These were originally protected by a covering of turf, but are now ruinous and only partly roofed, while today the ground around them is riddled with puffin burrows. Martin, writing in the late 17th century, noted that the islanders of Lewis visited the Flannan Isles to 'make a great purchase of fowls, eggs, down, feathers, and quills' and how they sought blessings on their endeavours at the small chapel provided for the purpose.[48] No storage structures have been found in association with the bothies on Sula Sgeir and the Flannan Isles, presumably because all the catch was removed when the hunters returned to their homes.[49] However, huts known as skeos were used for drying meat and fish on Shetland;[50]

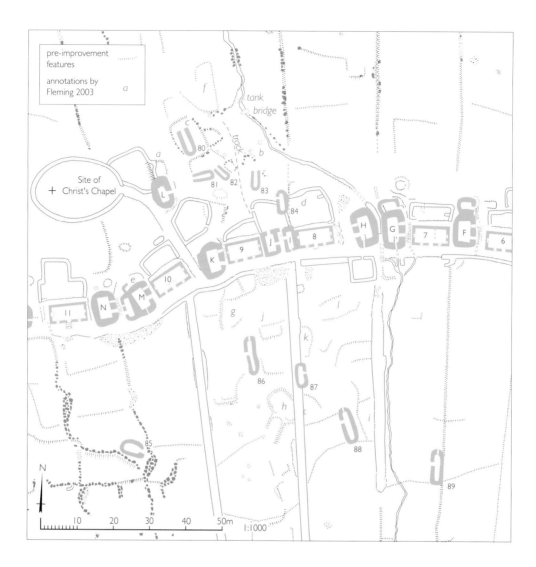

This detailed plan of the centre of the 18th century settlement in Village Bay highlights the features identified by Andrew Fleming in 1999. So great were the improvements made to the houses and the fields in the 1830s that only slight and sometimes ambiguous vestiges of the earlier settlement can now be traced.
RCAHMS, 2014, GV005697

and a few structures of the same basic form as St Kilda's cleitean were recorded by RCAHMS in 2014 on Swona in Orkney, where they were used to dry dogfish.[51]

As will become clear, St Kilda is surprisingly rich in remains dating to the 17th and 18th century and, with the exception of those connected with fowling, these conform to the same general arrangements as

found elsewhere on the MacLeod estate. The township described by Martin in 1697 cannot be distinguished from any other in the Outer Hebrides: 'The walls of their houses are rudely built of stone, the short couples joining at the ends of the roof, upon whose sides small ribs of wood are laid, these being cover'd with straw; the whole secured by ropes made of twisted heath, the extremity of which on each side is poised with stone to preserve the thatch from being blown away by the wind.'[52]

As has been indicated in the previous chapter, the location of this pre-crofting township is uncertain, but it has usually been assumed that its buildings would have clustered close together somewhere in Village Bay. Much effort has been made to discover its

precise location since the 1950s and it became generally accepted that it lay around the well head called Tobar Childa, where there are numerous stone features and nearby structures with side cells that have been rebuilt as cleitean. In 1983 RCAHMS surveyed the complex surface remains within the current head dyke and, almost 20 years later, this provided the foundation for an analysis by Andrew Fleming which resulted in a major reinterpretation of the evidence. His thesis, based upon his own careful field observations and George Atkinson's sketch of the settlement taken in 1831, determined that the post-1720s township, if not that before, had lain well to the south of Tobar Childa and on both sides of the current Street.[53] Another drawing by Thomas Dyke Acland dating to 1812 provided Fleming with confirmation, although the character of the horizon casts some doubt on the nature of this sketch and whether it is truly representational.[54]

When the RCAHMS survey was digitised in 2007–9, a special effort was made to confirm Fleming's proposition on the ground. On the north side of the Street Fleming had noted two features (a, e), associated with standing buildings, in addition to three others underlying cleitean (c, b and d) and a 'faint feature' north-east of Cleit 80 (f). Each of these appeared to be the remnants of earlier buildings oriented from north to south as shown in Atkinson's drawing.[55] A reanalysis of this landscape using both Fleming's plan and that of RCAHMS taken in 1983–4 was undertaken in 2014. One feature (d) appears to be the remnants of a croft boundary constructed in the 1830s, while another (f) is too ephemeral to be interpreted as a building. The two features (a, e) associated with standing buildings could be of mid 19th century date. Those that remain (b, c) and the faint traces underlying Cleitean 81 and 82 are more convincing; and Fleming also identified a water tank, an old track represented by a hollow way

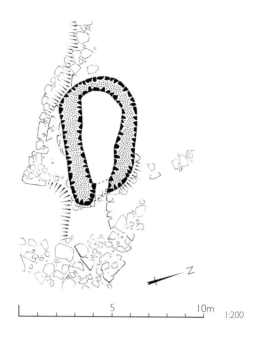

This building is famously associated with Lady Grange and her incarceration on St Kilda in the 1730s. It has been entirely remodelled as a typical, if rather large, cleit. There is little doubt, however, that its footings contain the remnants of an earlier and much larger structure.

above John Keggie RCAHMS, 1986, SC416660

right RCAHMS, c1985, GV005698

and a clapper bridge. To the south of the Street, he noted at least two further buildings (g, h) among other fragmentary remains which he assigned to the same date. One (h) is unquestionably a rectangular building with another attached to its south, but the other (g) is more difficult to characterise.[56]

A small trench was opened within the interior of one of the putitive buildings (h) following geophysical survey by GUARD in 2005. This revealed a 'curvilinear concentration of boulders', presumably the remains of wall, which delimited a soil flecked with heat-affected sediments and charcoal or burnt peat. What may have been part of a drain was discovered in the south-west corner of the trench, but the only finds (which included a spindle whorl) were recovered from the topsoil and so could not provide a clear indication of the date of the building.[57]

The remains of this township are relatively ephemeral, but one building (Cleit 85) has been identified as the site of the house occupied by Rachel Erskine, Lady Grange, during her incarceration on the island between 1734 and 1742.[58] While the current structure can be securely classed as a cleit, it is certainly possible that particular elements of its make-up represent the footings of a larger 18th century building, especially when considered in conjunction with the neighbouring foundations situated to its east.

Between August 1727 and May 1728, St Kilda was struck by an epidemic of smallpox, a fate it shared with other islands such as Foula.[59] Although there is some disagreement as to the numbers that survived, a letter from Daniel Macaulay, read to the Scottish Society for the Propagation of Christian Knowledge on 25 July 1728, noted that 'nine men, ten women, fifteen boys and eight girls' remained alive. Eleven had escaped the epidemic by virtue of becoming stranded on 'the Rock called Stackriarmin' during the winter.[60] It is no surprise that St Kilda is absent from the MacLeod's rentals in the following year of 1728–9, as the products of the archipelago would have been greatly reduced through want of labour.[61] There is no unambiguous evidence that the remaining St Kildans left the island and their evacuation would have caused the tacksman significant inconvenience. Furthermore, despite the argument of Bill Lawson, who maintained that it is improbable that the houses of the deceased would have been re-occupied due to fear of the disease,[62] RCAHMS is now of the opinion that it seems unlikely that many buildings in the township would really have been abandoned. During the winter of 1727–8, the great majority would have been in use to shelter the islanders' valuable cattle, with a smaller number still occupied by the depleted number of islanders. Crops were presumably sown in the following spring and when the tacksman finally arrived in the summer of 1728, there must have been discussions between him and the remaining tenants with regard to the maintenance of the other buildings, the harvest and the care of the deceased islanders' livestock. Moreover, preparations would also have been set swiftly in hand to accommodate all the new tenants who were to be added to the community over the following years.

While the location of the pre-crofting township has been clarified recently, the lack of excavation means that only documentary sources can provide an insight into the character of the buildings and the internal organisation of the islanders' houses. Macaulay noted the unusual flatness of their roofs, perhaps contrasting them in his mind with the steeper thatched pitches found elsewhere in the Hebrides, although it could be that these had simply slumped due to lack of maintenance.[63] He also describes how the beds were in the thickness of the walls – a tradition that was widespread in Scotland and Ireland;[64] while the existence of a partition separating the byre from the living quarters adverts to a complex transition that occurred in the Western Isles in the 18th and 19th centuries.[65] However, Macaulay's particular focus was the way the St Kildans periodically prepared the floors of their houses in order to provide seasonal manure. They first spread peat ash and then added a mixture of earth and peat dust, before watering and treading this into a mulch that was thereafter dried off with the fire. This process was repeated regularly until they were ready to remove the accumulating floors from the houses to spread on the arable ground before sowing barley in their fields.

In addition to the fragmentary remains of the township, the medieval church and burial ground continued in use. The relationship of the Church of Scotland with St Kilda reached a more permanent footing from 1705, when a succession of ministers and missionaries took up residence on Hirta. The Reverend Alexander Buchan built 'houses and accommodations' for himself and his family before 1712. These also housed a small library and a school room, but their location is uncertain and they have not been identified.[66] However, having a minister on the island did not ensure the upkeep of the church and it is said to have fallen into disrepair later in the century.[67] Other buildings used by the islanders included a corn drying kiln mentioned by Martin, which is also currently unlocated. It probably stood a little apart from the settlement on account of the fire risk.[68] In addition, he also described the 'Gallies Dock' – a place where a boat could be secured and this may possibly be identified with a naust-like feature that appears on Henry Sharbau's map immediately west of the storehouse.[69]

If much of this still remains shadowy and elusive, extensive remains of pre-crofting enclosure and cultivation are preserved in both Village Bay and Gleann Mòr. In the late 17th century Martin described how the islanders cultivated barley and a little oats with the cas-chrom (crooked spade), the common tillage implement of the Northern and Western Isles, but that they also used a wooden harrow with tines of seaweed. The land was divided into ten principal lots, which were further sub-divided amongst the tenants by the ground officer once every three years.[70] Writing in the middle of the 18th century, Macaulay observed that:

All the ground hitherto cultivated in St Kilda lies round the village. The soil is thin, full of gravel, and of consequence very sharp. Originally it was covered and lined with a vast number of stones, which have been all cleared away by the inhabitants in some former period. All the arable land is divided out into a great many unequal plots, and every one of these is in a manner enclosed and kept invariably within the same bounds, by the help of the stones just now mentioned: These serve for boundaries, and are not to be removed or any how violated … [The] several plots, though very numerous, have every one of them, the smallest as well as the largest, a distinction … from all the rest, the whole body of the people may in a stormy day assemble together in one place, and without any difficulty divide all their ground at a fire-side.[71]

The most conspicuous elements of the field system in Village Bay are the well-preserved drystone head dyke and its contemporary enclosures and cleitean. While some of these features are demonstrably early in date, others are remodelled versions of 17th and 18th century predecessors.
John Keggie RCAHMS, 1986, SC1463901

The principal components of the most recent Village Bay field system are the drystone head dyke and the linear crofts set out in the 1830s, as well as groups of smaller walled fields. These smaller walled fields have a complex history and while some demonstrably continued in use after the introduction of the crofts, often in a modified form, others are versions of predecessors that date from the 17th and 18th centuries, if not earlier.[72] These early vestiges are part of a pattern that also includes low banks and scarps that are clearly pre-crofting in origin as they underlie the head dyke and croft boundaries. The

opposite
Plan of the Tobar Childa field system.
RCAHMS 2015, GV005719

interiors of some of these stone-walled enclosures have been supplemented with manure and other forms of fertiliser to increase the soil depth, much in the way described by Macaulay.

Fleming and Edmonds excavated a cutting across one of the better preserved of the boulder walls defining part of the pre-crofting field system and uncovered a substantial, multi-phase revetment.[73] Apart from 18th and 19th century artefacts found under the turf to its north (which indicated that the ground had been cultivated during that period), many hoe blades were also retrieved from the boulder wall itself and the deeper soil behind it. The excavators took the presence of the hoe blades as an indication of a prehistoric date. However, as the materials for the wall and also the soil it retained were almost certainly introduced from elsewhere, these blades evidently belong to secondary contexts and so the ostensible date they seem to provide may be unreliable. Within the same analysis, Fleming and Edmonds also drew attention to the relationship between elements of the field system and a handful of cellular buildings (Cleitean 123, 137, 142).[74] While these cellular

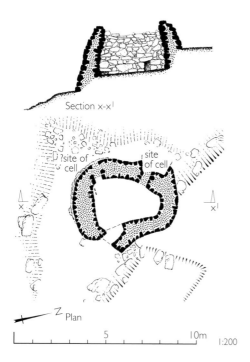

Section x-x¹

?site of
cell

site
of cell

Z
Plan

5   10m
                1:200

Cleit 32 was in use until the evacuation, but it betrays evidence for substantial remodelling. Its relationship to the old head dyke is confused by later rebuilding, which included the reconstruction of its wall faces and entrance.
RCAHMS, c1985, GV005703

The courses of two earlier head dykes are visible as grass-grown stony banks running from left to right. Badly robbed features like these are notoriously difficult to date, but the upper one may be of 18th century date.
John Keggie RCAHMS, 1986, SC1467635

buildings have been described here as being of medieval origin, they have been heavily modified. The boulder banks appear to underlie, abut, or respect the cellular buildings, but these relationships are far from clear chronologically.

In addition, Fleming and Edmonds observed that two 'old tracks' which had been denoted by RCAHMS in the 1980s were in fact the remnants of similar boulder walls and that the northern example was probably a head dyke delimiting this field system.[75] It can be traced in sections from the south-east of Village Bay all the way up to the scree slopes below Conachair. Some areas enclosed by this dyke, particularly uphill from Cleitean 32 and 149, have never been cultivated and are still strewn with scree. It is likely that this northern head dyke continued west, and then south to enclose the arable land. In his account of 1764, Macaulay noted that the arable ground of Hirta extended to about 80 acres (32ha)and it may not be a coincidence that this equates with the size of the area that is enclosed within this pre-crofting head dyke.[76]

The lower 'old track' is also a head dyke that is best preserved in a section between Cleit 10 and Cleit 32. It is a much more substantial feature than its northern pre-crofting counterpart, but presumably survives merely as a fragment of its original length. The only relative dating evidence for this at present is the supposition that the upper head dyke represents an expansion of this earlier system, together with its association with structures along its length. Cleit 32, which is now set into its south-west facing scarp, retains evidence for an earlier cellular structure, but the relationship between this predecessor and the dyke is unknown.

Although most of the cultivated ground was contained within the northern head dyke, there are also isolated plots elsewhere on Hirta, Dun and Boreray, at least one of which can be ascribed with confidence to the mid 18th century. On an exposed, rocky, east-facing slope on the route between Gleann Mòr and the Cambir, there is an area of lazy bedding of about 0.6ha. This type of cultivation is almost ubiquitous in north-western Scotland, but few examples can be closely dated. Although there is a small plot of unenclosed beds 170m to the north-west, most of this is constrained within a ruinous rubble wall overlain by two cleitean. Some of the ridges are markedly curvilinear on plan.[77] It seems likely that this field system corresponds with the plots 'on the north-west of the island' which Macaulay relates were cultivated a few years before 1758 at the behest of the tacksman, a MacLeod of Pabbay.[78] The St Kildans were reluctant participants in this experiment from the outset, as they resented the loss of good grazing; but the grain sown here produced such weak plants that the trial was swiftly abandoned.[79] Indeed, the islanders' lack of enthusiasm might explain why this was situated in a part of Gleann Mòr that was not especially well located for sunlight or endowed with the deepest soils. The MacLeods of Pabbay resided on an island that is covered with the remains of lazy bedding; and while some are undoubtedly much later in date, it is unlikely to be a coincidence that the tacksman attempted to translate a method of cultivation to St Kilda with which he was so familiar.

Similar plots have also been recorded in two other areas of Hirta, both of which were subject to detailed investigation by Glasgow University Archaeology Department in 1991–4. The first (Mullach Sgar South), about 1.2ha in extent, survives on the south-east slopes of Ruaival amidst a complex of agricultural features, immediately north-east of Abhainn Ruaival.[80] An initial analysis, later refined by RCAHMS, suggested that these features could be broken down into phases, each of which post-dated the abandonment of St Brianan's chapel. The earliest appears to be represented by a field system made up of curvilinear, grass-grown stony banks, some of which constrain lazy beds, although at least three patches lie further upslope to the south-west. Within the stony banks are also areas of sub-rectangular raised beds. This field system is partly overlain by larger, more substantial enclosures delimited by drystone walls which were probably constructed in the 19th century.

In addition to the lazy bedding and the raised beds, there are also a number of distinctive, broad, linear ridges in this area, especially on the south. The published plan indicates that one ridge is overlain by a bank associated with the earlier curvilinear field system, but otherwise there is no reason to suppose that these differ in date from the lazy beds.[81] Similar

ridges and lobed features are also found in An Lag Bhon Tuath, where they are overlain by stone-walled enclosures dating to the 19th century. This area has been subject to turf cutting which has disturbed these indications of cultivation. Nevertheless, the excavations by Glasgow University Archaeology Department confirmed the earlier judgement of RCAHMS that some of these features also resulted from the natural effects of solifluction.[82] As at Mullach Sgar South, stone tools were notable by their absence – quite possibly an indication that the cas-chroms or spades that were used to create these ridges were tipped with iron.

There are also isolated small plots of lazy bedding on Dun and Boreray. The plot on Dun is unenclosed and about 1ha in extent. The lack of enclosing banks probably indicates that it was only exploited at a time when there were no animals grazing on the island; and so is likely to pre-date the 19th century when sheep are known to have been taken there for this purpose.[83] Fleming suggested that this setting overlaid a field bank that might date to the Norse period, but in practice this appears to be no more than a feature of the natural geology.[84] The plot on Boreray was first noted by Williamson and Boyd, but it was not closely examined until it was mapped by RCAHMS in 2010.[85] It is situated south-east of Taigh Stallair on a relatively steep slope, occupying an area of about 0.15ha within the larger field system.

While the use of shieling huts in Gleann Mòr was discussed in the section describing the period AD 1266–1600, it is very likely that at least some of these buildings continued in use into the 18th century.[86] The community certainly continued to use Gleann Mòr for the summer pasture of their sheep and cattle, and they continued to use, repair and adapt the old shieling huts.[87] Some of them are found in association with enclosures and small drystone cells, which attracted the attention of Frederick Thomas. He planned and described two of them, referring to them as 'gathering folds' (Buaile Crothaidh).[88] Although these have been examined on several occasions, no-one has questioned his interpretation.[89]

Where the gathering folds are found in association with the shieling huts, they are clearly secondary. A total of fourteen have been recorded and half of these have been constructed with stone robbed from earlier buildings which they overlie. Each has a similar layout comprising two walls that funnelled the sheep into the

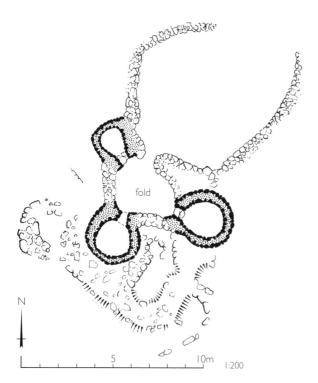

fold

N

5   10m
1:200

During his study of St Kilda in the summer of 1860, Captain Frederick Thomas recorded the use of the gathering folds in Gleann Mòr. After the sheep and lambs were caught within the fold, the lambs would be separated off in to the adjacent cells, allowing the islanders to take a proportion of the ewe's milk. This practice continued into the 1920s.

left RCAHMS, 1985. GV005699

above Steve Wallace RCAHMS, 2008. DP045078

fold, which according to Thomas, was closed with a 'straw mat'.[90] A number of small drystone cells opened directly off the fold, and these were used to shelter the lambs. This also allowed the islanders to take a proportion of milk for themselves: 'the huts or cotanan were for the lambs and kids, from whence they were in sight and smell of their dams, but were prevented from sucking'.[91] The iron head of a shepherd's crook was recovered from the tumble of a similar fold excavated on the eastern flank of Mullach Sgar.[92] One islander, Donald Gillies, who left in 1924, recalled the use of the folds overnight during his childhood;[93] and the overnight penning of ewes and lambs in such structures may have been common during the post-medieval period in the Western Isles more generally, as examples have been recently recorded by RCAHMS on Harris, South Uist and Rum (Rùm).[94]

A turf and stone dyke at the head of Gleann Mòr is probably related to the management of stock during this period. It was presumably intended to limit the movement of cattle that had been turned out to the summer grazings. It is 1.4km long and where best preserved it presents a vertical inner stone face. Mary Harman has compared this dyke to a short stretch that was evidently constructed to prevent animals from

wandering on to the Àird Uachdarachd promontory, on the steep north-east side of Conachair.[95] There is little to date the Gleann Mòr boundary dyke, but it must have continued in use into the 19th century, as the islanders used to travel there twice a day to milk the cattle which were left to fend for themselves overnight.[96] A ruinous drystone wall running up the south-west slope of Oiseval may have performed a similar role; and both may be compared to the wall on Dun that cuts off its south-eastern end and the walls that separate the Cambir from the rest of Hirta to the south. Here, two successive lengths interupt the narrowest approach to the headland, while others stretching to the east, north-east and south-west are clearly related to the management of stock.[97] Another wall crosses the neck between Geodha na Stachan and Geodha Chrubaidh, while fragments of what is probably the same feature are situated to the north and south. These, too, were built to prevent the cattle from falling down the steep slopes. Shorter stretches of dyke in more inaccessible locations probably relate to the management of sheep grazing, the most striking example being that cutting off a gully down on the steep slopes south-west of Claigeann Mòr.[98]

The north glen of Hirta has long been regarded as a place where ancient structures might survive. The valley was used intensively from at least the medieval period when it provided the main summer grazing, but there are no structures within its confines that can be firmly dated to an earlier period.

Dave Cowley RCAHMS, 2012, DP134168

Enclosures and stretches of dyke also extend across the lower reaches of Gleann Mòr. Some of the dykes appear very slight, being little more than low bands of stones. It has been suggested that turves could have been used to raise their height and make them more of an obstacle,[99] but there is little evidence of either turf stripping in their immediate vicinity or of an eroded turf component in their make-up.

The systematic mapping of the dykes and enclosure boundaries by RCAHMS in 1985 and 2008 has offered a number of clues regarding relative chronologies, shown on the following page. At least some of the features relate to the use of the gathering folds and the management of stock. To the west of the Abhainn a' Ghlinne Mhòr the majority of the dykes have been constructed around the folds and

although there is a high degree of complexity in the vicinity of structures K–P and the phasing has yet to be fully understood, there is no reason to suppose that these enclosures relate to any activity other than those associated with the shielings or later folding. The lengths of dyke east of structures O and P would have helped direct sheep into these folds;[100] and it is likely that the largest and most complex (K) is associated with a group of enclosures. Another dyke encloses about a hectare of ground near the shore, within which there are several buildings, a number of cleitean, a smaller enclosure and three other shorter stretches of dyke. Apart from the enclosed plots of lazy bedding to the west, there is no evidence for cultivation in Gleann Mòr and this steep rocky ground must also have been used for pasture. Indeed, features relating to the introduction and maintenance of cultivation terraces of the kind found in Village Bay are notable by their absence.

The east side of Gleann Mòr has a higher concentration of dykes, enclosures and gathering folds, as well as a greater density of the earlier shieling huts. However, this area has long been thought of

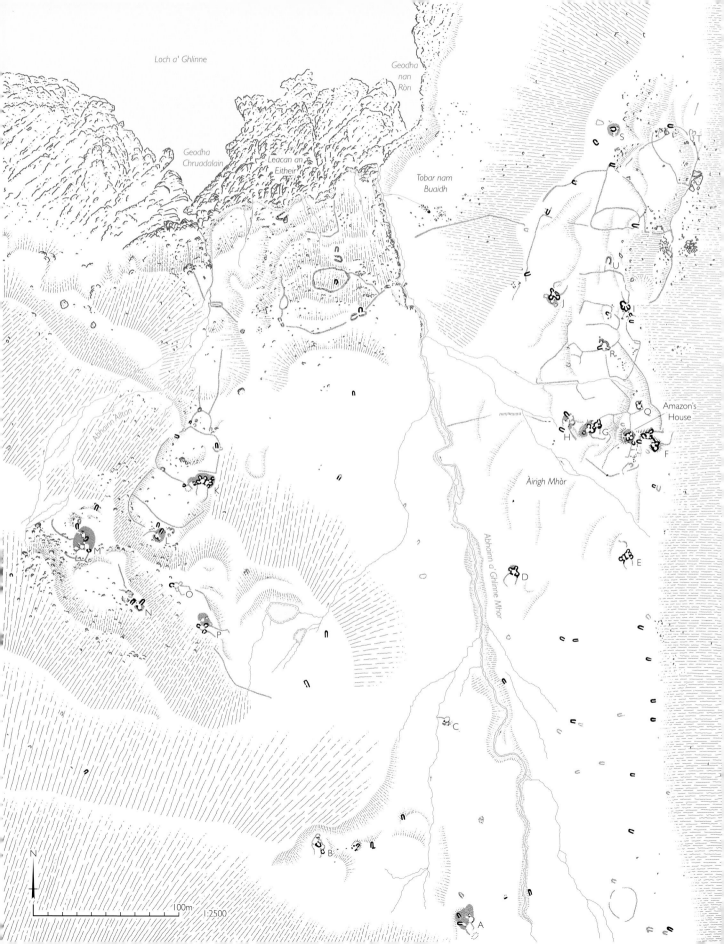

Loch a' Ghlinne

Geodha
nan
Ròn

Geodha
Chruadalain

Leacan an
Eitheir

Tobar nam
Buaidh

S

T

U

J

U

I

R

Q

Amazon's
House

H

G

F

Àirigh Mhòr

Abhainn Alltan

K

E

L

D

M

C

O

N

P

Abhainn a' Ghlinne Mhòr

B

N

A

100m   1:2500

One group of enigmatic structures on Hirta comprises a handful of sub-rectangular buildings in the lower reaches of Gleann Mòr. Their date and function are unknown, but they may have been used for specialist storage.

above Steve Wallace RCAHMS, 2008, DP045081

right RCAHMS, 2009, GV005700

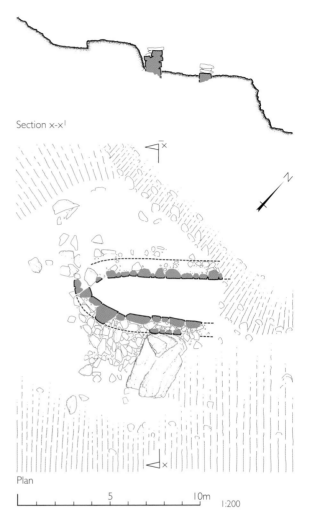

Section x-x[1]

Plan

as the site of prehistoric settlement and there is thus a perception that the enclosures and dykes might represent an associated field system. A recent analysis by Andrew Fleming and Mark Edmonds has favoured this hypothesis, as they drew an analogy between these and the small, curvilinear fields north of Tobar Childa, which they also believed to be prehistoric.[101] In addition, they also argued that the shielings in Gleann Mòr (represented by the Amazon's House) were later in date than the enclosures and dykes, although they admitted that there was nowhere that this could be demonstrated clearly. The absence of stone tools in the fabric of any of the elements making up the Gleann Mòr landscape was explained as resulting from the want of more recent episodes of cultivation during which they might have been uncovered.

In practice, any period attribution can only be resolved through excavation, which might demonstrate the chronological relationships unequivocally or provide samples for scientific dating. However, until

opposite

The steep sides of Gleann Mòr confine a holy well, shieling huts, gathering folds, enclosures and dykes. It was intensively used and closely managed; and it has been suggested that the number of folds and shielings (A to U) roughly equates with the number of families on the island.

RCAHMS, 2015, GV005704

this is undertaken, it seems more plausible that the shieling grounds used in the medieval period simply evolved into a more ordered landscape that encompassed a complex system of grazing and stock management. Where there is a relationship the gathering folds post-date the shielings, the enclosures seem to be associated with the gathering folds and the cleitean are all later still. In other words, the same sequence seems to hold here as to the west of the burn. Furthermore, the absence of stone tools noted by Fleming and Edmonds might be seen as an indication that the remains in Gleann Mòr were never associated with an early phase of arable agriculture.[102]

More problematic are a group of four or five sub-rectangular buildings situated within the 1ha enclosure up to 150m from the rocky foreshore,[103]

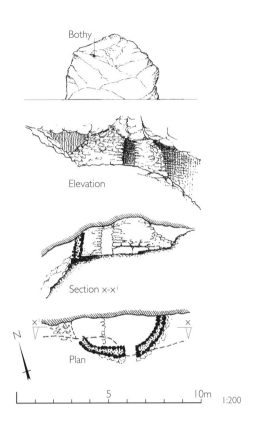

Bothy

Elevation

Section x-x¹

Plan

N

5   10m   1:200

above and right

The exploitation of seabirds varied across the archipelago
depending upon the species and the time of year. On Stac Lì,
there is only one simple drystone bothy (above, top right). On
Stac an Àrmainn (bottom right), the bothy is a much larger
structure set amongst numerous cleitean and it was used for
more extensive periods.

opposite

The precipitous slopes of Stac an Àrmainn, seen here with Boreray
and Stac Lì to its right (top), play host to more than 80 structures.
The boulder field of Carn Mòr on Hirta (bottom) has almost 200
cleitean and rock shelters, which are often no more than a stretch
of walling creating a niche beneath massive boulders.

together with another located about 100m north of
the Amazon's House.[104] Each is set across the slope and
the best-preserved example occupies a terrace above
the rocks scoured by the sea.[105] This is round-ended
on the south-west, but open to the north-east and
good stretches of wall face survive on both sides. At
least two of these buildings have fallen roof lintels.
The others have been extensively robbed, in two cases
to form cleitean, one of which overlies the earlier
structure, which in its turn appears to overlie an
enclosure wall.[106] Their function is unclear; but there
is no evidence of phasing and they are not especially
complex structures. It is possible that they were used
for storage related to some activity that had its focus in
the lower reaches of Gleann Mòr.

The final component of the islands' economy was
fowling. While it can be demonstrated that cultivation
took place on three of the main islands and grazing
on four, fowling also extended to the two principal

sea stacks off Boreray – Stac an Àrmainn and Stac Lì. The structures associated with fowling are limited to three types: ephemeral nooks with walls of just a few stones that were used during the hunting of seabirds; bothies used by the hunters for accommodation; and cleitean used for the storage of the produce of hunting and gathering. In most cases, the association of these structures with fowling relies entirely on their location, as they have no distinctive architectural traits.

More than 70 small storage nooks were recorded by Mary Harman in the 4ha boulder field known as Carn Mòr, situated below Mullach Bi on Hirta.[107] This is only accessible by descending the steep grassy slopes from Claigeann an Taigh Faire, or by a lengthy and awkward traverse via the Cambir.[108] They range in character from short lengths of wall that enclose a small space under an overhanging rock or boulder, (typically classified as a 'rock shelter'), to stacks of as few as three stones. While the former may have been used for storage or even as a sleeping platform, the latter were probably used for temporary storage during hunting expeditions.[109]

Bothies provided the islanders with accommodation during these hunting trips.[110] While some are of relatively recent origin, documentary and archaeological evidence suggests that others date to the 17th or 18th century, if not earlier. Martin noted that bothies were provided on both Stac Lì and Stac an Àrmainn in 1697.[111] The first of these stands on a ledge only accessible after a strenuous climb. It is really a rock shelter, with a single wall fronting a small area beneath the overhanging rock. There is little reason to doubt that this structure is the same as that to which Martin alluded, although it has clearly been carefully maintained over the years. There is also a single bothy on Stac an Àrmainn, which is situated on the steep grassy slopes on the south-east side of the stack. It is a freestanding, sub-rectangular structure occupying a stone-revetted platform, with an entrance in the centre of the south-east wall. The roof was originally corbelled but has now collapsed.

At least two similar bothies have been recorded on Soay. They must have stood for many years before the 19th century, when they were used by women staying on the island while harvesting birds and plucking the carcasses.[112] John Sands described how a third structure, the rock shelter attached to Taigh Dugan, was used to house six women, but its roof had collapsed by 1896.[113] The remains of two further

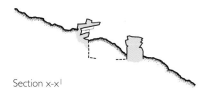

Section x-x¹

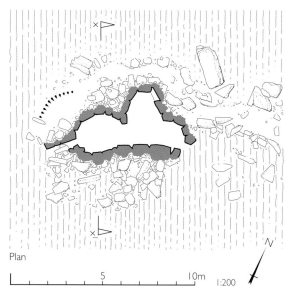

Plan

5   10m   1:200

Bothies were not confined to the outer islands and stacks, although a lack of historical references suggests that those on Hirta may have gone out of use at an early date. This example perched above Geodha Chrubaidh at the north-west tip of the island is well sited for access to the cliffs around the Cambir and Mullach Bi.

top Alex Hale RCAHMS, 2008, DP214063

above RCAHMS, 2009, GV005702

bothies were recorded by Mary Harman on Dun. These buildings are more poorly preserved than those previously described and they are not mentioned in historical documents.[114] Other examples, perhaps better described as rock shelters, together with a cave, may also have been used as temporary accommodation on the island; one even contains a hearth.[115] Their regular use may be linked with the revetted path that permitted passage across the steep slopes.[116]

There are also a series of ruined bothies on the vertiginous slopes of Boreray. Four probably date to the 17th and 18th centuries and can be distinguished from the well-preserved 19th century examples, as they have been robbed to provide material for later cleitean. One stands about 75m north of Cleitean MacPhaidein, at the junction of three lengths of field bank,[117] while another is situated a further 40m west-north-west.[118] The third stands a little below the concentration of cleitean,[119] while the fourth is situated south-south-west of Taigh Stallair.[120] All were probably originally encased in turf.

A number of bothies are also known on Hirta, where they are not only distinguished by their locations in the north-west and west of the island, but also by their unusual cellular form. The best-preserved example is situated on the steep south-facing slopes on the west side of the Cambir overlooking Poll a' Choire, where it can be readily accessed by traversing a route to the south-east.[121] This can be compared with another which is located on the east side of the Cambir, while the others stand at the northern extremity of the Carn Mòr boulder field and in the lee of the long spine of outcropping rock running down the steep slope to the west.[122]

However, it is the cleitean of St Kilda that are the most numerous and distinctive feature of the islands. RCAHMS has mapped 1337 on Hirta, 60 on Boreray, 33 on Soay and 80 on Stac an Àrmainn, using information collected by Mary Harman in the 1970s, as well as its own data gathered between 2007 and 2010.[123] Cleitean are narrow, sub-rectangular drystone buildings, roofed with transverse lintels and covered with an earth and turf cap. They are usually aligned up and down a slope and are provided with a single entrance. While it is likely that the tradition of building cleitean developed with the need to store a large quantity of eggs and fowl, the earliest references occur in the 17th and 18th centuries when they were also in use as peat stores. Martin noted the existence of 'about forty' cleitean on Boreray, and 'several' on Stac an Àrmainn in 1697. Although he is likely to have conflated these with corbelled buildings used for other purposes, he estimated that there were 'above five hundred' in the archipelago.[124] This total would account for about a third of those known, so there is little doubt that some of those that are present today were in existence before 1697. Macaulay's description provides an interesting note on their ownership in the 18th century, as he reports that every islander had his share of them 'in proportion to the extent of land he possesses, or the rent he pays'.[125]

Peat and turf were vital commodities on the islands, as they could be used as building materials or fuel, but the evidence for the exploitation of these resources in the form of cuttings, stands and tracks can be easily overlooked. Martin and Macaulay referred to the deep soils on the top of the hills, which afforded the islanders 'good turf',[126] yet the small number of cuttings that have been identified on St Kilda can in no way represent the full extent of these activities. In practice, large areas of the land surface on Hirta have been depleted through the wholesale removal of the turf and peat over many centuries. This is particularly true at Am Blaid (the col between the two glens) and south-west of An Lag Bhon Tuath above the modern head dyke in Village Bay, where cleitean can be seen perched upon remnants of the earlier land surface;[127] but it is also evident across the grassy slopes of Mullach Geal, Mullach Sgar and Oiseval. Direct evidence of exploitation in the form of 'hags' or cuttings is restricted to the area around the enclosures at An Lag Bhon Tuath and also to a large area south-east of Lag Aitimir extending south-eastwards into the modern croft land.[128] Much of this may be relatively recent in date, as it has led to the destruction of the pre-crofting field system.[129] Mary Harman also observed similar features on Soay,[130] but none has been located within Gleann Mòr or on Boreray, although there is little doubt that exploitation occurred there too, as at least seven peat stands were recorded there in July 2010.

Peat stands consisting of low artificial mounds often delimited by a rough kerb of stones are rare on Hirta. Only seven examples have been located and these are all situated in the shelter of An Lag Bhon Tuath.[131] As has already been indicated, these have been misinterpreted in the past by several authorities, although Jimmy Davidson, who recorded them in 1967, recognised that they might be 'the remains of old cleitean'.[132] One example was surveyed by RCAHMS in 1985,[133] while others were mapped on Boreray beyond the head dyke in

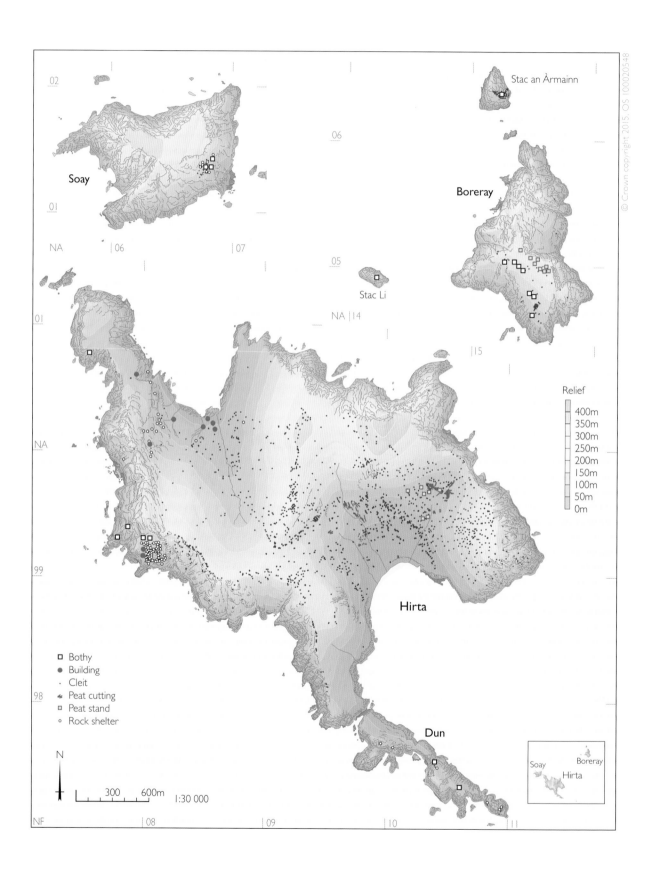

02

06

Stac an Àrmainn

Soay

Boreray

01

NA | 06 | 07

05

Stac Li

01

NA | 14

15

NA

Relief

400m
350m
300m
250m
200m
150m
100m
50m
0m

Hirta

98

□ Bothy
● Building
· Cleit
⚞ Peat cutting
◻ Peat stand
○ Rock shelter

Dun

N

300   600m   1:30 000

Soay   Boreray

Hirta

NF | 08 | 09 | 10 | 11

© Crown copyright 2015. OS 100020548

Evidence for turf and peat cutting is often difficult to identify, especially in areas where the entire land surface has been stripped away. This cleit stands proud on a little knoll on the route up to the Gap from An Lag Bhon Tuath. The ground around it has been removed for fuel, building material or to enrich the soil elsewhere, leaving the cleit perched on a residual tump.

Steve Wallace RCAHMS, 2008, DP044883

opposite

St Kilda – the distribution of structures relating to fowling and to the exploitation of peat and turf.

RCAHMS, 2015, GV005731

2010.[134] A typical example is little more than a stony tump with a small platform on the downhill side.[135] However, cleitean were also used for the storage of peat and turf from at least the 18th century[136] and there is little doubt that the high density of these structures and widespread distribution across the slopes of Oiseval, Mullach Sgar, Mullach Mòr and at Creagan Dubh, south-east of Mullach Geal, reflects the stripping of peat and turf in their neighbourhood and its subsequent storage.[137]

While the archaeology of St Kilda in the years between 1600 and 1780 reflects the influence of the MacLeod estate and the nature of a clan economy, the following period was to witness a number of significant changes. The reorganisation of the MacLeod estate was precipitated by financial collapse, as occurred throughout the Outer Hebrides and the implications of this are explored in the next chapter.

THE TOWN & BAY, ST. KILDA, FROM THE WEST. 6190. G.W.W.

Chapter Six

The Making of the
Crofting Community – 1780 to 1930

The archaeology of St Kilda during the 150 years before the evacuation reflects wider patterns of change that are recognisable throughout much of rural Scotland. Archaeological landscapes on the mainland are dominated by features that were created or abandoned during a phase of agricultural Improvement which lasted more than 100 years and resulted in the wholesale replacement of the country's agricultural buildings, the re-organisation of much of the land and the development and specialisation of smaller industries.

In the Outer Hebrides this revolution was coincident with a change in the character of land ownership, as clan chiefs that had familial ties with their tacksmen and tenants re-focused the management of their estates to produce a surplus for sale within an ever-widening market. Few were successful and in the end the whole island chain was sold to new owners, often absentee landlords with significant investments elsewhere, during the period from 1779 to 1844.[1] The exploitation of kelp, the intensification of agriculture and the expansion of sheep farming were to have dramatic effects on the landscape and its people, leading in turn to disruption,

emigration and the fossilisation of large areas of farmland and settlement and to the creation of new types of farmholding and buildings.

The MacLeods, who owned St Kilda, were the first of the large clan families that possessed land in the Outer Hebrides to experience significant financial difficulty and they acted to forestall calamity by raising rents significantly in 1769. Correspondence held in the MacLeod archive includes a letter from 1773 referring generally to 'chiefs who have screwed up their rents to obtain the means of luxury' and there is no doubt that such increases were to have a serious outcome, leading MacLeod's factor to express concern at the emigration of tacksmen from other estates.[2] Later that year the factor's worry was confirmed when Alexander MacLeod of Pabbay, St Kilda's tacksman, emigrated to North Carolina with several of his sub-tenants.[3] The increase in rent and the emigration of such an important figure on this account were harbingers of major changes afoot.

In 1779 the whole estate of Harris was sold by MacLeod of Dunvegan to a son of one of the cadet families and, despite his wish to retain St Kilda for 'sentimental reasons', it was included in the final sale.[4] The new owner was Captain Alexander MacLeod, the second son of Donald MacLeod of Unish, the 'Old Trojan'. Donald was a figure of considerable fame in the history of the MacLeod clan, while Anne, his wife, was the daughter of the 19th chief of MacLeod.[5] Known as the 'Berneray tribe', the eldest of Donald's

opposite

On each linear croft, laid out in the 1830s, an old blackhouse shares the site with a more modern zinc-roofed cottage, gardens and a few cleitean for storage.

Norman MacLeod, University of Aberdeen, 1886, C7186

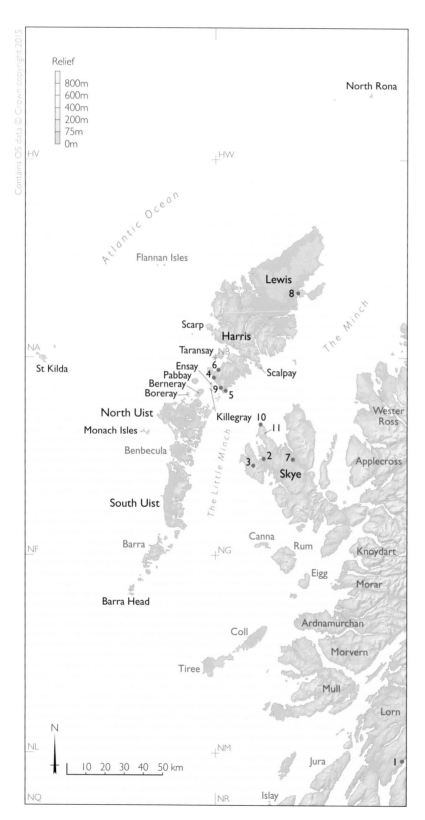

Relief
800m
600m
400m
200m
75m
0m

Atlantic Ocean

North Rona

Flannan Isles

Lewis
8

Scarp

Harris

The Minch

Taransay

Ensay
Pabbay
6
4
Berneray
Boreray
9
5

Scalpay

North Uist

Killegray 10
11

Monach Isles

Benbecula

3
2
7
Skye

Wester
Ross

Applecross

South Uist

The Little Minch

St Kilda

Barra

Canna
Rum

Knoydart

Eigg
Morar

Barra Head

Coll

Ardnamurchan

Morvern

Tiree

Mull

Lorn

Jura

Islay

N

10 20 30 40 50 km

The Western Isles –
sites referred to in this chapter

1   Auchgoyle
2   Dunvegan
3   Durinish
4   Northton
5   Rodel
6   Scarista
7   Skeabost
8   Stornoway
9   Strond
10   Unish
11   Waternish

Captain Alexander MacLeod returned from the East Indies a wealthy man. Purchasing Harris with St Kilda in 1779, he established a new house and harbour at Rodel, complete with a boathouse, storehouses and a net factory.

William Daniell, 1819, SC684186

29 children was Norman, who was described in the 1780s as 'first tacksman in the isles' and is remembered for introducing 'many improvements in the system of farming', as well as a notorious and misguided episode of slaving by which men and women from Harris and Skye were to be transported to the American colonies.[6] The majority of Donald's male children joined the army or navy; and Captain Alexander built up a fortune in the East India trade. Retiring to Harris in 1782, Alexander invested heavily in the parish, restoring the church at Rodel and building a new house nearby.[7] The development of fishing became his primary focus and a new harbour complex was constructed at Rodel, the central node of a scheme that would extend along the east coast of Harris and even out to St Kilda itself.[8]

While Alexander's focus was on fishing, Norman set about introducing improvements to the system of farming in Berneray and took forward the exploitation of kelp, which was burned to produce an alkali used in the production of soap and glass.[9] Both strands of development were to have an important impact on the landscape and the Hebridean economy, helping to stave off debt for landlord and tenant alike. The development of crofting began in the middle of the 18th century on the MacLeod estate. Each tenant was allocated a small plot of land and settlements were re-planned to reflect a pattern of linear holdings. The historian James Hunter has argued that the estates during this period preferred to maintain a high population as a source of labour, but this needed other forms of income given the small size of their crofts. Thus, the croft and the kelp industry in particular, were inextricably linked.[10] Indeed, it was crofts, rather than large specialised farms, that became the typical agricultural unit throughout most of the Outer Hebrides before the mid 19th century. As is explained below, crofting on St Kilda may have developed for different reasons.

Captain Alexander MacLeod's son, Alexander Hume MacLeod, inherited Harris in 1790, but he appears to have left much of the running of the estate to his factor and his tacksman.[11] Returning from India in 1802, he rejoiced that the shores of the estate were 'lined with silver' due to the boom in the kelp trade caused by the Napoleonic Wars.[12] It was perhaps the lack of a kelp industry on either Pabbay or St Kilda that led Hume to sell these elements of the estate in 1804 to Colonel Donald MacLeod of Auchgoyle, the owner of a small estate on the shore of Loch Fyne and formerly of the Madras Army.[13] His son, Sir John Macpherson MacLeod, inherited St Kilda in 1813 just two years after he arrived in Madras and was thus the owner during many of the key developments that subsequently occurred in its architectural and landscape history.[14] In 1871, he sold St Kilda back to the MacLeods of Dunvegan, finally severing the archipelago's long-standing connection with Pabbay and bringing to an end the influence of a tacksman jointly over Pabbay and St Kilda.[15] Unfortunately, there are no estate records known for St Kilda or Harris between 1779 and 1871 that cover this most important period in the archipelago's evolution.[156] The result of this historical mishap is that an understanding of St Kilda's development in the 19th century has been disproportionately distorted by visitors' accounts and, in particular, by that published by the minister, antiquarian and photographer, James Bannatyne Mackenzie, who disseminated in 1911 the notes that had been made by his father Neil some eighty years earlier. Whether by design or accident, the Reverend Neil Mackenzie has thus been elevated to the status of prime mover in the history of St Kilda, especially in the initiation of architectural and agricultural reform.[17]

Before Neil Mackenzie's incumbency as minister, St Kilda and Pabbay came under the management of a succession of tacksmen for whom little documentary

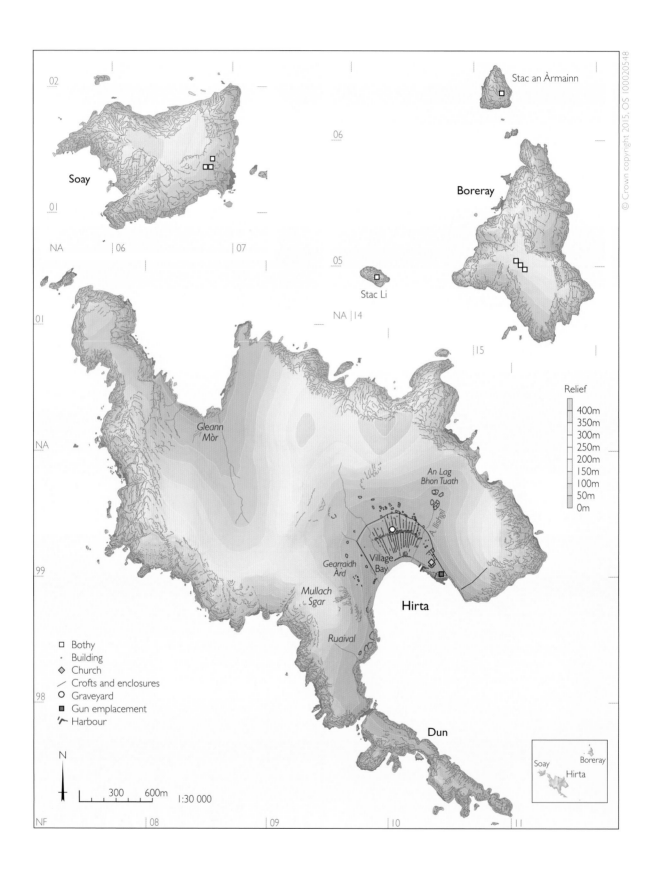

Soay

Stac an Àrmainn

Boreray

Stac Li

Relief

400m
350m
300m
250m
200m
150m
100m
50m
0m

Gleann
Mòr

An Lag
Bhon Tuath

Gearraidh
Àrd

Village
Bay

Hirta

Mullach
Sgar

Ruaival

□ Bothy
· Building
◇ Church
／ Crofts and enclosures
○ Graveyard
■ Gun emplacement
🜨 Harbour

N

300   600m   1:30 000

Dun

Soay   Boreray
        Hirta

evidence has been recovered. The McNeil family of Rodel took over from the Pabbay MacLeods in the 1770s, holding the tack until 1805 when they were relieved of it by a court case that followed the sale of Pabbay and St Kilda to Donald MacLeod of Auchgoyle.[18] Successive tacksmen included Murdo Maclellan of Scalpay (before 1831), followed by Donald MacDonald of Skeabost on Skye – the latter a noted entrepreneur with extensive business interests in Assynt and Skye, including fishing stations and sheep farms.[19] At Skeabost, for example, MacDonald had persuaded many to settle on his crofts hoping that this would induce them to improvements, 'thereby bettering his circumstances and their own'.[20]

The profitable years of the early 19th century were short-lived however, and by the 1820s the kelp market was in sharp decline. This, combined with a high population, caused severe economic and social problems which were exacerbated in later years by the potato famine and the destabilising influence of the sale of the remaining islands in the Outer Hebrides between 1838 and 1844. The search for a new income to replace kelp led most of the estates to establish large sheep farms from early in the 19th century. As a result, many of the surviving townships (thus far little affected by emigration) were now forcibly cleared, including those at Northton on Harris. Bill Lawson, describing Harris in the 1840s, noted that 'there were no people left on the machair except a few sheep farmers and their servants'.[21] He laid much of the responsibility for this on the estate factor, Donald Stewart, who was known even to plough up burial grounds such was his zest for a new model of farming.[22] While St Kilda remained insulated from these changes, the outlying islands of Pabbay, Taransay, Ensay and Killegray were all cleared of large populations at this time. Meanwhile, St Kilda came under the control of Norman MacRaild of Durinish, a factor who managed the island until 1873. He may have been instrumental in the emigration of eight families to Australia in 1852, but it is uncertain whether this was to reduce the number of tenants for economic reasons, or as a result of a continuing disagreement amongst the St Kildans and their factor

The communities on St Kilda and Pabbay were closely linked until the middle of the 19th century when the tenants of Pabbay were removed so that the island could become a sheep farm. Many of the families that once lived in the Pabbay blackhouses found their way to Cape Breton in Canada.
George Geddes RCAHMS. 2011, DP138288

over the Disruption within the Scottish Church that had occurred in 1843.[23]

The second half of the 19th century witnessed a continued expansion of sheep farming onto township land in the Outer Hebrides and a growing tension between tenant, factor and landlord, which finally resulted in the land raids undertaken by crofters from the 1880s.[24] The Royal Commission which was set up to enquire into the conditions of crofters and cottars took evidence throughout the north of Scotland, visiting St Kilda in 1883.[25] Their recommendations eventually led to the establishment of the Crofter's Holdings (Scotland) Act of 1886. Despite the additional efforts of the Congested Districts Board, which had built the quay on St Kilda by 1901,[26] it was only following further legislation after the Great War that conditions began to improve. The majority of the sheep farms that had been established in the Hebrides during the first 60 years of the 19th century were replaced by new crofting settlements – just at the moment when the crofting community on St Kilda was reaching an economic crisis.

While the landscapes of Pabbay and Waternish that were considered in the previous chapter were no longer part of a MacLeod estate in the 19th century, elements of their history and archaeology bear close comparison with St Kilda, yet diverge in certain ways

opposite
St Kilda – sites referred to in this chapter.
RCAHMS. 2015, GV005729

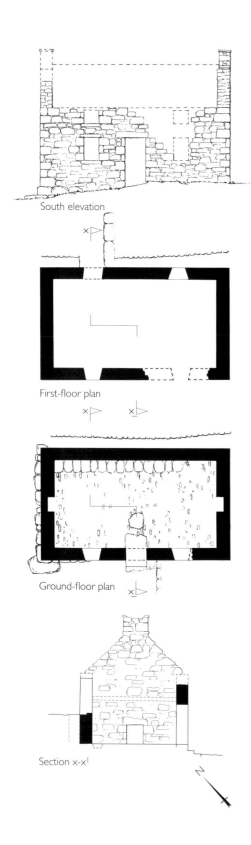

South elevation

First-floor plan

Ground-floor plan

Section x-x¹

This storehouse and tackman's house, constructed sometime after 1779, was the largest and most modern building on Hirta for a generation. It was the nodal point of the islanders' trade, but also played host to religious sermons and the occasional ceilidh.
left RCAHMS, 1983, GV005705
above Steve Wallace RCAHMS, 2008, DP042208

that require explanation. Despite the emigration of the tacksman Alexander MacLeod and the sale of the estate in the 1770s, the archipelago continued to form part of the principal Pabbay rental of McNeil of Rodel. Improvement on Pabbay is attested by a group of blackhouses of large size and regular construction, introduced as small individual farmsteads or associated with regular crofts.[27] At about the same time, lazy bed cultivation was extended to cover much of the upland on the south side of the island. However, a dramatic shift to sheep farming in the 1840s is reflected not only in the pattern of drystone dykes and the construction of a shepherd's cottage, but also in the condition of the blackhouses themselves: each had its roof removed and the heavy stone lintels knocked off its walls.[28] Waternish, too, was disposed of piecemeal by the MacLeod estate during the 18th century, leading to major changes on the peninsula over the following century. By 1853, 156 crofters farmed only 500 acres (202ha) of arable, and much of the peninsula had been cleared for sheep farming. The farm and house at Unish, once the home of Donald MacLeod, the 'Old Trojan', was abandoned during this period and now stands at the centre of a rich and complex landscape of abandoned buildings and fields.[29]

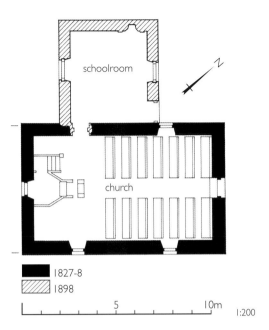

1827-8
1898

5 10m
1:200

The Reverend John MacDonald of Ferintosh first came to St Kilda in 1822 as a representative of the Society in Scotland for Propagating Christian Knowledge. His most enduring legacy on Hirta was the construction of a new church and manse in 1827–8, which replaced the pre-Reformation chapels that had long fallen into ruin. The manse is now the base for the activities of the NTS.
left RCAHMS, 1983, GV005706
above National Trust for Scotland, c1900, SKA733

St Kilda's tacksmen were encouraging agricultural experimentation from the 1750s,[30] but the first major sign of Improvement came with the construction of a storehouse and tacksman's house combined into a two-storey building built between 1779 and 1795.[31] The circumstances that led to its introduction are unclear because there is no primary documentation, but it is certainly different from the vernacular style prevalent on the island, while also denoting a dramatic departure from the more usual methods of storage and distribution that had been practised on St Kilda up to that point. Illustrations from the period show that the storehouse once dominated the bay and, by virtue of its size, it also provided a useful venue for celebrations or sermons. It was here that the Reverend John MacDonald of Ferintosh spoke on one of his visits in the 1820s. MacDonald was a close adherent of Improvement in both religious and agricultural realms, but as Iain Campbell has noted he 'is not unknown to the historians of modern Scotland [although] few of them … are hospitable to his Calvinism or his evangelistic fervour'.[32]

MacDonald also provided the impetus for the construction of the new manse and church on St Kilda, built in 1827–8.[33] The architect was Robert Stevenson, who had been the Engineer to the Northern Lighthouse Board since 1808. His works, which can be seen around Scotland, include the famous Bell Rock Lighthouse, as well as those on Scalpay and Barra Head in the Outer Hebrides, but this church is the only religious building he is known to have designed.[34] Close analogies can be found in the Parliamentary churches designed by Thomas Telford in 1824–5 and in the new church that was built at Scarista (Sgarasta) on Harris in about 1840.[35] The new church and manse on Hirta were established at the south-east extremity of Village Bay and the tacksman, Murdo Maclellan, assigned 1.5ha of land to the Church of Scotland in order to provide the minister with a glebe. This was marked out in late 1827 and subsequently established the regular framework for the fields around the manse, which remain set apart from the crofts and the head dyke to this day.[36] The construction of the church provided the St Kildans with a replacement for the medieval building that had fallen into disrepair more than 60 years earlier,[37] but the use of the earlier burial ground continued. The Reverend Neil Mackenzie recalled the building of the massive stone wall around it before 1844: 'it was the portion of the work in which I took the greatest personal interest, as there I buried three of my children that died in infancy'.[38] Mackenzie came to the island in the summer of 1830, and was the

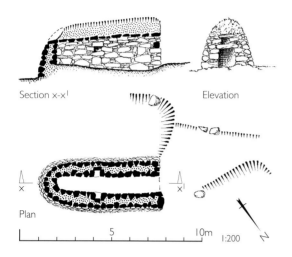

Section x-xˡ   Elevation

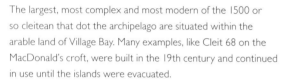

Plan

x   xˡ

5   10m 1:200

The largest, most complex and most modern of the 1500 or so cleitean that dot the archipelago are situated within the arable land of Village Bay. Many examples, like Cleit 68 on the MacDonald's croft, were built in the 19th century and continued in use until the islands were evacuated.

above RCAHMS, c1984, GV005712

right John Keggie RCAHMS, 1986, SC1463864

first minister to occupy the new manse.[39] In the initial years of his ministry, he seems to have limited himself to spiritual and educational matters, although there is little doubt that he undertook the clearing and walling of much of the glebe himself, leading to a number of archaeological discoveries.[40] Contemporary works in the glebe included the construction of a saw pit 'so that driftwood might be cut up and for other uses', as well as the building of a uniquely proportioned cleit that was used to store timber for coffins amongst other things.[41] It seems likely that Mackenzie was also responsible for the creation of the deepest cultivation plots on Hirta, a series of three small fields between Cleitean 3 and 8. Clearly marked as 'glebe' in 1860, these plots are revetted by a wall more than 2m high on the downslope side.[42]

In 1834, four years after Mackenzie arrived, the islands were visited by the Conservative politician Sir Thomas Dyke Acland and on this, his second call, he chose to intervene in the progress of the settlement's evolution by making a large charitable donation. In a journal entry, Mackenzie noted that 'Sir Thomas and his lady' left 'twenty sovereigns to help them build new houses, as soon as they could get their ground allotted',

while the 1911 publication of Mackenzie's memoirs described how 'the tenants resolved to build better houses and wished to have their land divided among them'.[43] The St Kildans would have been well aware of the improved blackhouses and crofting settlements that had been established on Pabbay and elsewhere in the Outer Hebrides.

Mackenzie acted on behalf of the islanders to gain the agreement of both the proprietor, Sir John Macpherson MacLeod, who 'readily consented', and the tacksman Donald MacDonald, whose father came out to divide the land, probably in the summer of 1835.[44] The tenants, dissatisfied with this allotment, took it upon themselves to redistribute the croft land before beginning the construction of the new houses the following winter. A total of nineteen blackhouses survive in the township, while a further four have been removed by later developments. Each was effectively a small farmstead arranged along the metalled trackway known as the Street and each was provided with at least one cleit, a midden and walled kale yards or cultivation enclosures.[45] These and other cleitean built along the Street, or in close association with the blackhouses, can also be ascribed to the same period. In practice, many of the cleitean in Village Bay have been constructed or remodelled in the period since 1886,[46] and there is little doubt from historical references that the use of the largest to store hay and crops within the arable ground is a relatively recent phenomenon.[47]

The blackhouses which survive date to the period after 1835 and at least one was built after 1860, when a plan was taken by Henry Sharbau.[48] Each of the

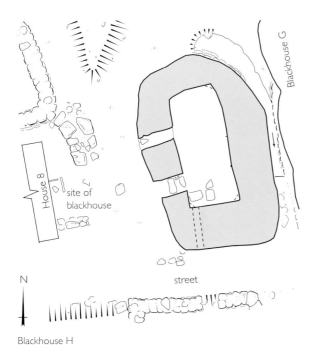

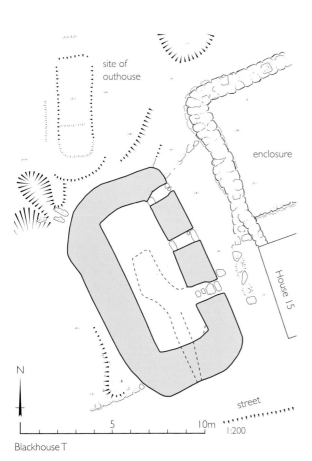

Blackhouse H

site of blackhouse

House 8

Blackhouse G

street

N

site of outhouse

enclosure

House 15

street

5   10m
1:200

N

Blackhouse T

Most of the blackhouses on St Kilda were constructed in the 1830s. While their architecture is a legacy of traditional building techniques, they also included novelties such as glass-paned windows. Each follows a basic pattern that would have combined a living area centred upon an open hearth with a small byre in the same room, but there is a wide degree of variation in size and most have been subject to numerous alterations over the years.
left RCAHMS, 2014, GV005710 and GV05711
above George Geddes RCAHMS, 2014, DP197757

surviving blackhouses has been subject to a detailed survey by RCAHMS and two, including one that is still standing, have been explored by archaeological excavation.[49] As a group they exhibit a wide degree of variation in both their size and form, but not in their general arrangement, as all are laid out up-and-down the slope. In addition, each has been altered and adapted since they were first built. However, their apparently rude construction disguises a carefully thought-out design that extends to the preparation of each plot, for all were supplied with their own drainage system. The buildings themselves contained stone-lined hearths, low partitions between the dwelling and the byre and sometimes wooden tumbler locks on the doors; and although each of these structures was new, some may have included elements of earlier buildings that had stood upon their site.[50] There is little doubt that the process of transition from the earlier houses that had been arranged in a huddle, to the linear arrangement of the new crofts, must have taken several years. Although the work began in 1835, each of the earlier buildings will have needed to be taken down and their materials sorted for re-use. Moreover, the family would have required

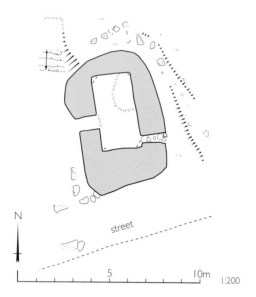

While the crofting tenants of St Kilda each lived in a blackhouse, the landless poor or infirm were provided with smaller, more rudimentary accommodation. Rachel Macrimmon's home (P) is characterised by a rough build and its compactness.

above RCAHMS, 2014, GV005715

right George Geddes RCAHMS, 2014, DP197697

temporary accommodation, as the plot was prepared and additional supplies of stone, turf and thatch were gathered.

While Neil Mackenzie had initially noted the need for 'wood for roofs, small glass windows, and a mason to help them build houses', he later described how the size of the new houses was limited by the availability of timbers that could be re-used from their predecessors.[51] A typical example is the blackhouse of the MacDonald family (H), located near the centre of the township; but other little-altered examples include the houses of the MacKinnon and Gillies families (R and T), both of which are larger than average and lit with two windows rather than one.[52] As many as seven of the blackhouses betray evidence for the rebuilding of the northern gable, probably reflecting the original position of a wall-bed (crùb), an architectural feature that captured the interest of Frederick Thomas in 1860 and is related to the bed neuks and alcoves that are commonly found in vernacular buildings throughout Scotland and Ireland.[53] While in the 19th century the wall-bed was considered an archaic tradition of interest to antiquarians such as Thomas, it was also denoted an

insanitary arrangement that should be discouraged.[54] Mackenzie's intention was that 'the beds were to be no longer recesses in the thickness of the walls', but this was not accepted. However, he met with agreement when promoting the discontinuation of 'the custom of spreading over the floor the ashes and all kinds of filthy rubbish which they used to accumulate for manure, and which before they removed it in the spring had risen as high as the wall, so that no one could stand upright even in the floor'.[55] Manure houses and stone-lined midden pits were introduced at this time. Nine buildings are assigned to this usage on Sharbau's plan of 1860, while six stone-revetted midden pits were recorded by RCAHMS in 1983.[56] The soot-impregnated thatch of the blackhouses would also have supplied more manure, following regular maintenance and repair.

Subsequent alterations made to the blackhouses initially reflected the growth of St Kilda's population and the inability of the regimented system of crofts and houses to allow for expansion. Thus, small annexes for family members or related kin have been added to most of the buildings, and a pattern of alteration and expansion is clearly linked to the known history of those who occupied them.[57] Other alterations were later brought on by the relegation of the blackhouses for use as byres or storage after the cottages were introduced. In some instances the byre drains were extended and tethering rings were added in the area that had formerly been the dwelling.[58] Subsequently,

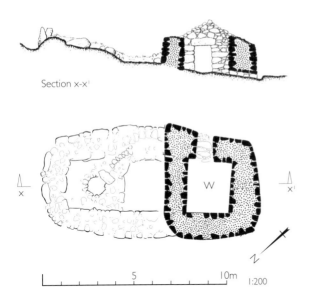

Section x-x'

W

5   10m   1:200

One building of 'blackhouse type' was identified as the site of a
kiln-barn in 1985. The building houses a circular kiln (right) where a
peat fire would dry the grain and a barn where the oats and barley
would have been threshed. It is overlain by a cottar's house (W).

above RCAHMS, 1985, with additions taken from Emery 1996, GV005713

right Steve Wallace RCAHMS, 2008, DP043536

a shortage of timber and the re-use of zinc and wood
in the later 19th century resulted in alterations to their
roofs. Indeed, most had been changed from a hipped
arrangement to one with a stone gable by the late 19th
century.

The variations in the size and layout of the
blackhouses are further illustrated by a group of
smaller examples that were occupied by the poorest
members of St Kildan society – the landless cottars.
Bill Lawson noted the presence of at least four cottars
in the later 19th century and one of their houses (W),
dating from the 1830s, was still occupied in 1886 when
it was recorded in a photograph.[59] A second example
(P), formerly the house of Rachel Macrimmon, is
characterised by its rough build and small size, while a
third (Z) was the home of Roderick Gillies.[60]

Another building that may have been used
eventually as a cottar's house began its life as a kiln barn
in the 19th century. In the past, this has been described
variously as a Viking house or a blackhouse,[61] but its
true identity was recognised during the RCAHMS
survey of 1985. Subsequent excavation by Norman
Emery in 1989 uncovered the well-preserved remains

of the kiln and the flue, close to which a peat fire
would have been lit to allow the hot air to dry the grain
supported on a timber floor. A small barn under the
same roof would have been used to store the grain and
the fuel; and this is also where the barley would have
been threshed and winnowed by hand.[62]

In some parts of the Hebrides, blackhouses with
thatched roofs and walls of field stone were occupied
well into the 20th century and a few were built after
1900. However, a new design began to appear in the
Outer Hebrides from the middle of the 19th century,
which banished the cattle to a separate byre. These
cottages were often shorter and wider than their
predecessors and they sometimes contained a half or
full storey above. Moreover, they used novel materials
such as imported slates, lime-mortar and corrugated
iron. They also had fireplaces and chimney stacks.
This design was not influenced by local culture and
tradition, but rather by wider practices and novel ideas
about healthy living conditions.

A new suite of sixteen cottages was constructed
from 1861. These cottages set the St Kildans apart from
many of their crofter contemporaries in terms of both
the amount of natural light they admitted and the
cleanliness of their homes.[63] While the sheep farms and
shepherds' cottages in the Outer Hebrides were often
of this same modern form, the houses of the crofters
themselves tended to stay true to tradition. The catalyst
for change on St Kilda resulted from the destruction
wreaked by a hurricane on 27–28 September 1860

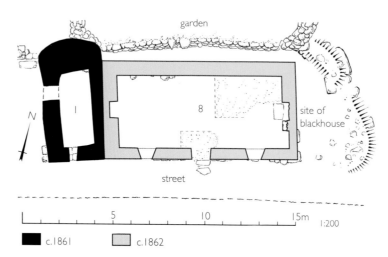

garden

N

1

8

site of
blackhouse

street

5   10   15m
                              1:200

■ c.1861   ☐ c.1862

The MacLeod estate took steps to improve the islanders' living
conditions in the 1860s, constructing a suite of sixteen cottages
of mainland type.
RCAHMS, 1985, GV005708

and, perhaps more importantly, from the response
this elicited from Captain Henry Otter of the Royal
Navy, who happened to be on the island at the time
'to see what progress some masons employed by the
Highland and Agricultural Society [sic] had been
making in the landing place'.[64] When the hurricane
removed the thatched roofs, it was Otter who provided
emergency supplies and swiftly organised a fundraising
campaign for further aid with the assistance of
John Hall Maxwell, the Secretary of the Highland
and Agricultural Society of Scotland (HASS), who
had visited St Kilda with Otter in June that year.
This hurricane, the emergency responses and the
consequent press coverage seems to have prompted St
Kilda's owner, Sir John Macpherson MacLeod, to pay
for the construction of the new houses; and shortly
afterwards four were built with the help of masons
brought from Skye.[65]

For the most part, the sites of the cottages
were chosen to fit between existing buildings and
enclosures, but in a few instances blackhouses were
taken down and replaced. Houses 8 and 10 (and also
possibly 16) were constructed on the site of earlier
blackhouses, while others necessitated the removal
of cleitean. The excavations at House 8 revealed
evidence that this process was relatively circumspect,

One enduring element of the village on Hirta is the burial ground,
once the location of a medieval chapel.
John Keggie RCAHMS, 1986, SC1445323

with significant elements of the earlier structure
remaining, while the drain inserted along the rear
of the cottage was only roughly made. However,
the procedure of creating a level site involved the
formation of platforms, which were produced by
cutting into the old cultivation terraces that lined the
northern edge of the Street and then constructing a
new stone revetment in order to shore these up. The
old yards and enclosures were modified wherever
possible, but where this was unworkable, a new
rectangular yard was built behind the house on the
level of the fields.[66] One interesting by-product of
all of this construction work might have been an

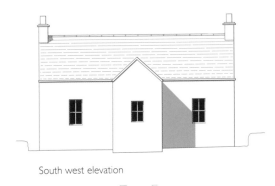

South west elevation

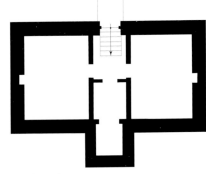

First-floor plan

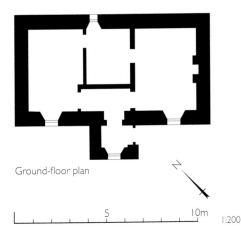

Ground-floor plan

5   10m
                    1:200

St Kilda's factor was provided with a neat new house around the same time the cottages were constructed and he subsequently shared this with many writers and photographers.
left Based on a survey by the Nature Conservancy, 1971, GV005707
above Steve Wallace RCAHMS, 2008, DP042235

alteration to the line of the Street, which appears to have been moved slightly north in the area around Houses 8 and 9. The later addition of a low wall on the south side of the Street, opposite the front doors of five of the cottages, seems to have been a novel way of consuming some of the unused stone by providing a bench.[67] Uniquely, a platform was constructed beside House 5 and this supported a small corrugated iron shed that acted as the Post Office.

The new arrangement, with each cottage set along the slope and facing the sea, not only provided a level site upon which it was easier to build a regular cottage, but also helped amplify the availability of light to the interior. Internally, the cottages typically measured about 9m by 4m which, when compared with the area of a blackhouse, represented a significant increase in the living quarters.[68] They generally contained a kitchen and a bedroom flanking a central entrance-lobby, together with a back room opening off the kitchen; while externally they were gable-ended and built of lime-mortared stone, some of which was neatly dressed. The increase in size provided more privacy and space for the looms with which the islanders wove Harris Tweed, but the cottages were colder and in some instances damper than the blackhouses, not least because of disturbances to the carefully laid out drainage of the 1830s.[69] However, in eschewing the use of thatch, the roofs of zinc proved a liability for they were difficult to repair and in later years they were completely replaced by a cover of tarred felt – the model followed by the NTS in its restoration of six of the cottages between 1964 and 1994.[70]

The building known as the factor's house was probably also built in the 1860s, for Norman MacRaild, factor to Sir John Macpherson MacLeod, as part of the investment by the estate in the island's

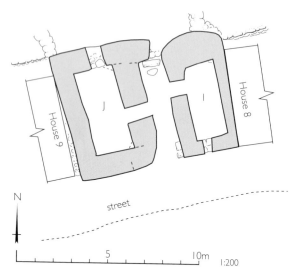

Plans to install an 'American hand-milling machine' in the 1860s came to nothing, but the remnants of a building set up to house it can be found within these two small dwellings used by the MacDonalds. For generations, milling was done by hand with rotary querns, but as John Mathieson 'could not persuade the women to pose', two men were happy to demonstrate the technique.

top left RCAHMS, 1986 and 2014, GV005714.

top right John Keggie RCAHMS, 1986, SC1463902

right taken by John Mathieson, National Trust for Scotland, c1927, 1002015

accommodation. While the construction of the new cottages had been prompted by the hurricane and the pressure subsequently exerted on MacLeod by Captain Otter and the press, the factor's house is more likely to have resulted from MacRaild's petition for a residence that properly reflected his status in the new architectural context. The building is of a conventional mainland type, purposefully situated on the common land that had been abandoned through emigration in 1852. As well as hosting successive factors during their short sojourns on the island, the building provided more permanent accommodation for those who stayed longer – at times a schoolteacher and at others a nurse, as well as visitors of note.[71]

Although Sir John Mackenzie MacLeod funded the construction of the cottages in the 1860s, Captain Otter and the HASS combined forces to help the islanders further by buying foodstuffs and a new boat, as well as funding specific building projects. One such was the construction of a mill in the centre of the township, which was intended to house an 'American hand-milling machine'.[72] Although the machine was never purchased, a rectangular building was erected for it on the Street, only to be subsequently converted into two small dwellings (Blackhouses I and J). The St Kildans continued to use rotary querns until the evacuation, despite the fact that small horizontal mills were well-established in parts of the Outer Hebrides, while more powerful estate mills were also a relatively ordinary part of the 19th century landscape.[73] Otter also funded attempts to improve the facilities for landing. Both the breakwater and the capstan installed beside the storehouse may well reflect his efforts.[74] It is not known whether the village barn erected in the 1860s was also conceived by Captain Otter, but its location near the mill and the idea of a communal building might suggest he took a hand in it.[75]

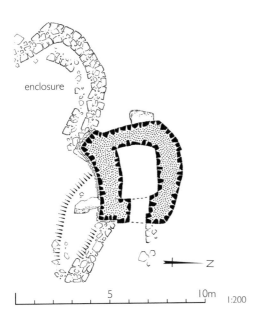

enclosure

5   10m
1:200   Z

This diminutive hut of apparently 'rude' construction was used to shelter a bull provided to the St Kildans by the Congested Districts Board. In the years since 1886 the adjacent enclosure has been reduced to footings, as its stone was robbed and recycled into other structures.

left RCAHMS, c1985, GV005709
above John Keggie RCAHMS, 1986, SC1463854

While the 1830s and the 1860s witnessed planned programmes of Improvement, smaller building projects continued to be set in train throughout the 19th and into the 20th century. The manse was altered and repaired during the 19th century and a significant extension was added in 1903, while a schoolroom was attached to the church in 1898.[76] The school was funded by the Highland Committee of the Free Church of Scotland and constructed through a contract with a Mr Bain of Carnan, South Uist, who had 'to take with him the whole of the building material, with the exception of the stone', which was presumably quarried from the shore.[77] Other small islands like Scarp, the Monach Islands and Boreray (North Uist) had already been furnished with better schools within a few years of the Education Act of 1872.[78]

One of the small drystone buildings beyond the head dyke can also be ascribed to this period. Known as the 'Bull's House', it was used in the early 20th century to shelter a beast provided by the Congested Districts Board. Confirmatory evidence in the form of 'small pieces of dried cattle dung' were identified in its walls in the 1980s.[79] The building, shown thatched in an 1886 photograph, was once associated with an enclosure which was later largely removed for the construction of Cleit 141.[80] Comparable structures have been recorded on Skye.[81]

Hitherto, efforts to construct a breakwater on St Kilda had failed. The structure that was established in

the 1860s by Captain Otter and the HASS had been washed away. In its stead, the Congested Districts Board finally built a substantial quay in Village Bay after the minister, Angus Fiddes, in conjunction with the owner, petitioned them for assistance.[82] Construction was organised by the Works Department of the Scottish Office between August 1899 and September 1901; and the St Kildans, who worked as labourers on the project, later described it as 'the greatest benefit that has been conferred upon us'.[83] While the quay addressed one of the longstanding complaints of the community, communications were further improved in 1913, when the *Daily Mirror* sponsored the construction of a wireless station on the island following a story that the islanders were starving. This consisted of two 75ft [23m] masts and a 1.5kW Marconi radio set which was installed in the factor's house.[84] However, the newspaper was soon keen to bring an end to the provision of the wireless set due to the running costs and it was reportedly packed up in cases by 1915. Nevertheless, the Great War brought a reprieve, as the Admiralty asked Marconi (who had retained ultimate ownership of it) for permission to use it; and so St Kilda became one of two wireless telegraph stations in the area – the other being at Stornoway on Lewis. In addition, there were

25 telegraph stations, more than 30 coast-watchers and a group of ships on patrol in the northern part of the Outer Hebrides.[85] On Hirta, the small garrison running the wireless station constructed two wooden barrack huts, a store hut, a cook house, together with a food store, latrine and ablutions block, most of which stood in the land immediately behind the manse. At least one and probably two cleitean were altered for use as watching stations.[86]

On 15 May 1918, the German submarine *U90*, commanded by Walter Remy, entered the bay in search of this military base. After issuing a warning, the crew fired 74 shells from a deck gun, causing significant damage to a number of buildings and almost demolishing the storehouse, which they took to be a power station. Only 16 days after the attack, *U90* took the largest victim of its career by sinking the Navy Troop Transport, the USS *President Lincoln*. On the way back from that same patrol she stopped off at the remote island of North Rona, in order to catch sheep for provisions.[87]

Repairs were eventually undertaken to most of the buildings, but the storehouse was abandoned. The armaments of the garrison, which simply consisted of rifles and pistols, were now considered inadequate; and so, in late 1918, a gun emplacement and a nearby magazine were constructed just east of the storehouse to prevent any such event occurring again.[88] The gun, reclaimed from a warship, is now one of only three that remain in place from the Great War in Scotland, the others being at Vementry on Shetland.[89] Comparable magazines also survive at Hoxa Head on Orkney.[90]

As well as a large number of buildings that can be confidently ascribed to the 19th century, Village Bay is covered in the remains of a field system, elements of which date to this period. The change of the agricultural regime from one in which a series of small

The Congested Districts Board constructed a quay on Hirta between 1899 and 1901, finally ameliorating the severe difficulties of landing in a southerly swell. Communications were further improved in 1913 following the introduction of a wireless and two tall masts to the island – a system that provided the basis for that used by the military garrison during the Great War. The timber huts of the garrison provided accommodation and storage space.

National Trust for Scotland, c1899, 1002290

National Trust for Scotland, c1915, 1002287

National Trust for Scotland, c1915, 1002495

In May 1918 a German submarine opened fire on the garrison and, as a response, a gun emplacement and magazine were installed later that year. The gun is now one of only three in Scotland that belong to this period and still remain in place. Levelling, quarrying and construction reflect activity here dating from at least the 18th century.

above Steve Wallace RCAHMS, 2008, DP042232

bottom GV005435

fields and enclosures allotted every few years were cultivated by the whole community, to one where each family had a specific croft is reflected in the construction of a fan-like set of boundaries that survive as a series of straight banks dividing the arable ground into eighteen long, thin, rectilinear plots.[91] The croft boundaries delineate holdings that vary between about 0.5ha (1.4 acres) and 1ha (2.3 acres), the largest of which tend to be located in the centre and the smallest in the eastern quotient. In places, the boundaries incorporate clearance cairns, edge-set boulders and cleitean, but there is no reason to think they were ever carried to a height that would have prevented the free grazing of animals after the harvest.

While each croft is ostensibly similar in size, there are large variations in the character of the enclosed fields, some including more rocky and uneven ground, while others include areas of peat and turf stripping. However, three of the boundaries have been developed into massive stone consumption dykes designed to absorb the excess stone cleared from the fields and removed from earlier buildings; and it is no coincidence that they are found near the area of the pre-Improvement township. The croft boundaries, which climb over and bend around the earlier buildings and terraces, have in their turn been dug out and built over – in some instances providing an indication of their relative chronology.

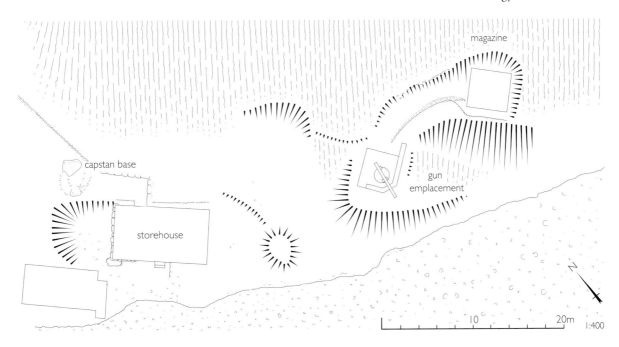

The St Kildans divided their agricultural ground into a series of eighteen long, thin, rectilinear plots known as crofts. Each croft was farmed by a particular family whose house and ancillary buildings stood on the Street that split the croft land in two. A pair of huge consumption dykes divides three of the crofts, reflecting the removal of earlier buildings and the clearance of the fields.

Steve Wallace RCAHMS, 2008, DP044780

The crofts were enclosed within a new head dyke that is carried unbroken across burn gullies, although it is pierced by openings in a number of locations to permit access between the cultivated land and the rough grazing. Mackenzie's memoirs included a note relating to the construction of this 'ring-fence', which must have been completed during his thirteen year tenure. He described how it was continued along the coastline in order to provide a windbreak that could offer a little protection to the sown seed, the growing crops and the harvest.[92] The construction of this dyke and related features, such as the Street and the revetment of the Abhainn Ilishgil, represent a significant investment of time and energy by the community.[93]

In addition to the croft land, the group of smaller walled fields beyond the head dyke were also in use during this period, providing a measure of continuity between the new arrangements and the pre-Improvement system. As mentioned above, one enclosure was associated with the Bull's House, while another small group to the north-east of Blackhouse Z and abutting the head dyke was used by one of the cottars at the time Sharbau undertook his survey.[94] The condition of the walled enclosures at An Lag Bhon Tuath and at Ruaival also suggests that they remained in use during the 19th and 20th centuries, although it is not certain whether they were utilised to fold animals, grow cereals, or produce grass for fodder. At least two of the walled enclosures contain evidence for cultivation in the form of raised beds, which may have been used for the cultivation of potatoes, although the principal crop in the middle of the 19th century was barley, with a little oats.[95] A handful of much smaller enclosures known as planticrubs, found within the croft land and on the lower slopes of Mullach Sgar, were also cultivated. These are clearly recent, but no explanation has yet been suggested for their

Many of the better preserved cleitean on Hirta date to the 19th and 20th centuries. These three are situated on the lower edge of a well defined trackway leading into Gleann Mòr that takes the most direct route from Village Bay.
Steve Wallace RCAHMS, 2008, DP051768

appearance so far from their normal dominion in the Northern Isles.[96] It seems likely that the St Kildans must have learned of their value as a protection against high winds, either directly, or indirectly, from their fellow islanders.

Photographs taken by Norman MacLeod in 1886 for the George Washington Wilson studio show that the ground in front of the factor's house was divided into numerous rectangular plots, which survived until 1957 when they were destroyed during the construction of the military base.[97] Very similar plots were recorded by RCAHMS in the western half of the township, particularly on the crofts abandoned in 1852; and the current St Kilda Archaeologist, Kevin Grant, has suggested that their layout reflects the apportionment of this new common land among the families as an echo of the former system. A photograph

dating from about 1920 shows rectangular patches of cultivation above and below the Street (page 194). These have left virtually no archaeological trace, but they demonstrate that the islanders cultivated small plots within the crofts. The traces of cultivation surveyed in 1983 seem to match exactly those shown in the 1886 photographs, especially in Crofts 2 and 6, while an undated image shows cultivation extending across the area above the Street, between the burial ground and the glebe.

One striking feature of St Kilda's 19th century fields is the paucity of lazy beds, which presumably results at least in part from the apparent failure of the trials in the mid 18th century. Nevertheless, it was the common form of cultivation in those parts of Scotland where populations were high and the terrain was both rough and poorly drained. The explanation may lie with the soils, which are not of the heavy peaty type that is dominant throughout much of the Hebrides. The richest areas on Harris are characterised by light soils and these were ploughed in the late 18th century on large farms like Rodel and Strond with 'a common Scotch plough and feathered sock drawn by four

Animal husbandry continued to play an important role in the St Kilda economy until 1930. Cattle were a fundamental part of island life, each family having at least one cow with which they shared their daily lot. During the summer months, the cows were let out to graze on Hirta's pastures.

horses'.[98] This method of cultivation was also employed on the islands of Pabbay, Killegray and Ensay; but the heavier soils there were cultivated as lazy beds – the expansion of which into the more inhospitable areas often corresponds with the high watershed of population. Thus, on Pabbay, the lighter soils which were once so rich are encircled by a large acreage of lazy bedding on the higher peatier ground, which may have been part of the common grazings.

Animal husbandry continued to play a significant part in the agricultural economy of St Kilda and there is no reason to doubt that many of the dykes in Gleann Mòr were maintained and used throughout this period. Records suggest that up to 50 cattle could be pastured there throughout the summer,[99] although now the women had to walk twice daily from Village Bay in order to milk the cows.[100] The milk was usually turned into cheese rather than butter, while beef was salted to preserve its longevity.[101] In the late autumn the cows were driven back to Village Bay, where they would be overwintered in the blackhouse byres. However, the St Kildans were keen to improve their stock, and bulls were imported occasionally from both the Outer Hebrides and Skye from the late 1860s.[102]

All four of the islands carried sheep, and records suggest that up to 2,000 might be supported.[103] The gathering folds in Gleann Mòr remained in use, while the sheep on Soay were reserved to the owner in the 1830s, who also held the sheep on Dun.[104] The tups were isolated here until required for breeding and it is possible that the iron chain hanging off the cliff at the north-west end of the island was supplied to facilitate access from Ruaival when the tide was low, in order to allow them to be inspected. The sheep, which were sometimes overwintered in cleitean, provided wool, mutton and milk, which was usually made into more cheese. Those on Hirta were cross-bred with blackface sheep from at least the 1830s,[105] but the islanders were forbidden to cross-breed those on Soay.

The exploitation of peat and turf continues to be well attested throughout this period and the use of these resources as the primary fuel of the islanders persisted until the island was evacuated in 1930. The dating of features relating to the winning, drying and storage of fuel is particularly difficult, but much of the identifiable peat cutting on Hirta may well be relatively recent. Certainly, peat and turf were removed from An Lag Bhon Tuath *after* cultivation there ended. It is equally difficult to date the fragmentary remains of the paths and tracks that the St Kildans used as they drove their cattle to grazings, or made their way to the fowling cliffs, whether in this period or at an earlier date. By far the most conspicuous old track outside Village Bay is on the route to Gleann Mòr. It runs for about 250m from Cleitean 478–555, while another shorter section cuts diagonally across the slope of Gearraidh Àrd. Elsewhere, there are fragments of a well-worn track running from the village to the fields at St Brianan's; and there are also the remains of a revetted path crossing the steep slopes of Dun.[106]

The fowling element of the economy was also pursued intensively throughout the 19th and early 20th centuries; and the rentals paid to Donald MacLeod and his son, Sir John, suggest that the harvesting of bird feathers in particular, was of especial importance to the St Kildan economy in both the early and mid 19th century. Feathers are mentioned specifically from the 1790s and again in 1814, when they comprised the only rent, although one year later cheese and wool were also included.[107] However, they continued to dominate the rental between 1814 and 1841, comprising almost the entire tariff in the 1820s and 1830s.[108] Feathers were used at this time for a variety of purposes, including bedding, meal brushes, fishing lures, sewing materials and the manufacture of golf balls;[109] and they remained a key component of the rental until the 1890s, when their value dropped significantly due to cheap imports from elsewhere. The factor still received 200 stone (1.25 tons) in feathers in 1894 and Kearton noted how they were then being used for soldiers' pillows.[110] The other principal contemporary source of this commodity in Scotland was the Bass Rock in East Lothian, where the feathers were described in 1839 as 'valuable and skilfully prepared for use'.[111] There is less information about the value of the other products of fowling, but the export of 32 barrels of bird oil in 1847 gives some indication of the importance of that commodity.[112]

The success of the fowling economy ensured the economic well-being of St Kilda's crofting community at a time when many comparable settlements in Harris and the Outer Hebrides were being abandoned, due at least in part to the failure of the kelp industry and the strengthening value of sheep for the factors and the estates. The change in the focus of estate economies from kelp to sheep resulted in the widespread abandonment of townships, but the particular economic value of St Kilda's harvestable resources contributed to its survival as a crofting community. By contrast Pabbay, which for centuries had been the dominant component of the tack with St Kilda, was cleared and transformed into a sheep run.[113]

While the fowling economy may have been expanded, or perhaps otherwise simply refocused on feathers, it is not yet possible to determine whether this is reflected in an increase in the number of cleitean and whether this went hand in hand with a programme of reconstruction and maintenance. In some instances, buildings that were employed in the 17th and 18th centuries, such as the bothies on Soay, Stac Lì and Stac an Àrmainn, appear to have continued in use. However, there are three bothies on Boreray, that seem to have replaced those that were utilised in the 18th century;[114] and at least one of these was still in use up until the evacuation. In the more remote parts of Hirta, the bothies described in the previous chapter appear to have been abandoned before the 19th century.

Although St Kilda continued to share much in common with other island communities during the early 18th century, its economy and landscape gradually became increasingly distinctive. This was in no small part due to the investments made in the islands throughout the 19th century and to the survival of its community when most elsewhere were failing. The old clan system may have broken down, but the island's new owners and tacksmen inherited both a tenantry with few options but to stay and the immense seabird colonies which represented a valuable commodity with a growing market value. If the historical records for the islands' rental and management are notable by their scarcity, the archaeological evidence is compelling. The growth in the number of cleitean from the 500 or so reported

In later decades, three turf and stone bothies on Boreray were used by the St Kildans during their seasonal visits to harvest the seabirds and manage the sheep left on the island. Each provided accommodation for a few people. Although their interiors offered only basic comforts, they were lit by lamps burning fulmar oil. The bothies have collapsed completely in the 80 years since the evacuation.

Alexander Cockburn, National Trust for Scotland, c1927, 1002071, 1002115

by Martin at the end of the 17th century is at least in part a measure of this,[115] while the investment reflected in the new storehouse and tacksman's house in Village Bay is a further reminder of the islands' role as a producer for an external market. The general absence of lazy bedding, which is such a common trait elsewhere, reflects a relatively stable population reliant upon a largely traditional form of mixed subsistence agriculture. The wholesale introduction of the new crofting landscape, the replacement of the blackhouses by cottages and the introduction of the new quay, all reflect a complex interaction between outside influences and internal demand. Emigration even to the Outer Hebrides remained relatively rare and so the shock to the community when eight families chose to travel to Australia in 1852 must have been immense.

While Pabbay's tenants were removed and the island was turned over to sheep, the community on St Kilda was transformed into crofters with a continued specialisation in fowling. Returns on investment were relatively high in the 1840s, but there is little doubt that continuing change during the following decades was not always positive. Although tourism provided another strand to the economy through which the islanders could gain some benefit, these and other activities leave little archaeological trace. Outsiders continued to bring the idea of the wider world to the islanders and the possibilities that this might afford; and eventually these ingenious people, worn down by difficulties extending from their health to problems consequent upon a dwindling of their population, finally elected to leave. And once they had taken their leave, all that they and their antecedents had achieved on their islands slipped away into the past; and the physical traces of the infrastructure that had supported their lives slowly began to fall to ruin and so became grist to archaeology's mill.

But this did not bring the story of St Kilda to a close, because after a shadow-filled hiatus, changing circumstances led to the renewed occupation of the islands and a new kind of inhabitant.

Chapter Seven
Rockets Galore – 1930 to the present day

The landscape archaeology and the architecture of St Kilda since the evacuation of 1930 encompass more than simply the abandoned houses and crofts of the islanders. Recent land use reflects a wide range of activities, including the scientific study of the bird population and the breeds of sheep, the management and conservation of the historic landscape, the maintenance and operation of the radar station and the administrative requirements connected with the growing number of visitors. Each of these elements has had its effect on the physical landscape and the way it is perceived; and each has led to the introduction of new elements, or has otherwise reconfigured the old.

The abandonment of many of the smaller Outer Hebridean islands is a common thread throughout the 19th and 20th centuries, as the changing nature of the national economy induced communities to coalesce and made permanent habitation of those that were economically more fragile less tenable. The construction of causeways to communities on Berneray (Harris), Eriskay and Vatersay has helped

The Hebrides Range has an important node at Balivanich on Benbecula from where the helicopters that supply Hirta depart each Tuesday and Friday.

Robert Adam RCAHMS. 2005, SC1013221

opposite

'The first wheeled and tracked vehicles to land on St Kilda. 40 tons of high explosives were used to make a beach-head for landing craft.' This was the caption written by the mountaineer, surveyor and author Tom Weir, who visited St Kilda in 1956 and 1957, recording the biggest change on the island for 27 years.

Tom Weir, National Trust for Scotland, 1957, 1002366

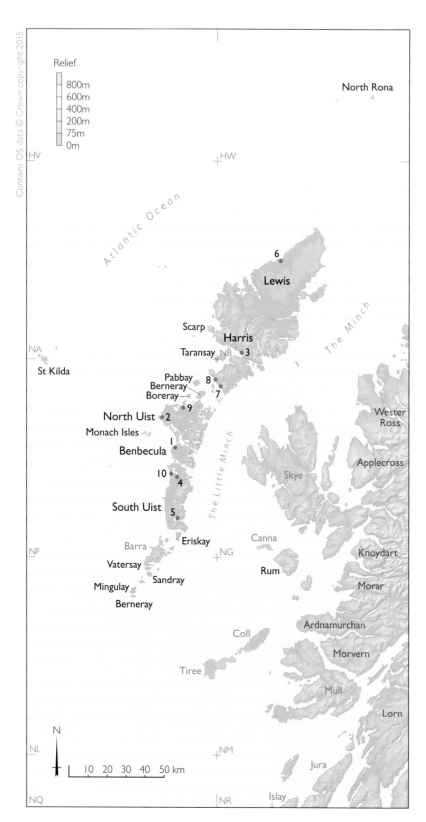

Relief

800m
600m
400m
200m
75m
0m

Contains OS data © Crown copyright 2015

North Rona

Atlantic Ocean

HV

HW

Lewis

6

The Minch

Scarp

Harris

Taransay NB 3

NA

St Kilda

Pabbay
Berneray
Boreray

8

7

9

North Uist 2

Monach Isles

1

Benbecula

10

4

Wester
Ross

Applecross

Skye

The Little Minch

South Uist

5

Eriskay

Barra

NF

NG

Canna

Knoydart

Vatersay

Sandray

Rum

Morar

Mingulay

Berneray

Coll

Ardnamurchan

Morvern

Mull

Tiree

Lorn

N

NL

NM

Jura

10 20 30 40 50 km

NQ

NR

Islay

The Western Isles –
sites referred to in this chapter

1   Balivanich
2   Balranald
3   Bunavoneader
4   Drimore
5   Lochboisdale
6   Loch na Muilne
7   Leverburgh
8   Northton
9   Sollas
10 West Geirinis

RCAHMS, 2015, GV005725

In the years following the evacuation and before the outbreak of the Second World War, Hirta played host to regular visitors including tourists, researchers and a handful of St Kildans. Mrs Ann Gillies, her son Neil and Finlay MacQueen await the steamship for the return journey on 9 August 1938.

Robert Atkinson, School of Scottish Studies, 1938, S354

to ensure their survival, as has the establishment of a more regular and reliable ferry infrastructure in recent years. However, many islands were abandoned after 1900, including examples at the southern end of the Outer Hebrides, such as Berneray (Barra), Sandray and Mingulay, as well as those closer to St Kilda, such as Taransay, Scarp and Boreray (North Uist). Most abandoned islands are now used for the grazing of sheep, while others such as Pabbay, play host to holiday homes or small sporting estates.

Although abandonment is a recurrent theme when analysing the history of the smaller islands, the Outer Hebrides more generally witnessed a dramatic resurgence in the establishment of crofting communities in the early 20th century, as government policy altered to support the re-occupation of the land that had been lost to the sheep-farms of the 19th century – so reversing one of the main economic themes of the previous 100 years. In one example, the township at Northton on Harris was re-established in the 1920s having been made redundant some 80 years earlier. The contemporary development of nearby Leverburgh into a small town and fishing station, although eventually seen to be over-ambitious, added to a sense of investment and growth. Whaling, too, was practised from the station at Bunavoneader (Bun Abhainn Eadarra) on Harris between the 1920s and 1950s; and sometimes Hirta's Village Bay was used as a temporary depot for carcasses.[1]

As with other outlying islands, the evacuation of St Kilda in August 1930 did not sever the links of the outgoing community with their former home, and the regular steamer visits of the 1930s provided some of the islanders with an opportunity to visit again and again. A few stayed for lengthy periods, acting out their lives in much the same way as before – catching birds, collecting eggs, carding and spinning wool – only packing up again to leave on the last boat of the annual service, as the summer gave way to autumn

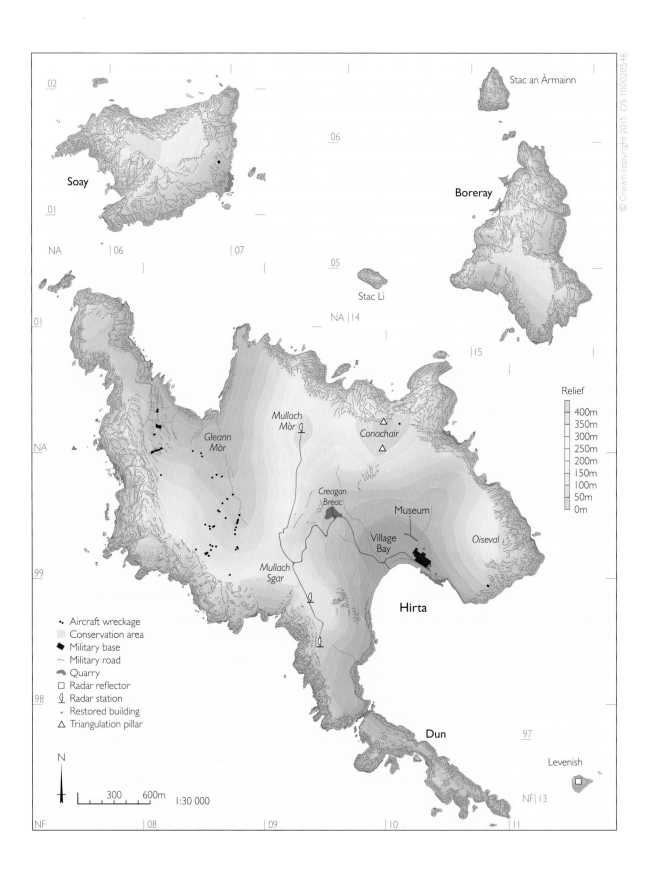

Soay

Stac an Àrmainn

Boreray

Stac Li

NA | 14

Relief

400m
350m
300m
250m
200m
150m
100m
50m
0m

Mullach
Mòr ⚲

Gleann
Mòr

Conachair △

△

Creagan
Breac

Museum

Village
Bay

Oiseval

Mullach
Sgar

⚲

Hirta

⚲

• Aircraft wreckage
▨ Conservation area
◆ Military base
~ Military road
🦪 Quarry
□ Radar reflector
⚲ Radar station
· Restored building
△ Triangulation pillar

Dun

Levenish

□

NF | 13

N

300   600m   1:30 000

Three plane crashes on St Kilda during the Second World War left their impact sites strewn with wreckage. Even now, pieces of highly engineered aluminium from the Sunderland ML858 that crashed in Gleann Mòr on 7 June 1944 litter the slopes.
The Scotsman, c1957, Licensor Scran

and poorer weather began to set in. The photographs taken by Robert Atkinson in 1938 capture Finlay MacQueen, Neil and Ann Gillies living in their old houses among the semi-abandoned detritus of the island as the agricultural land became fallow.[2] All three had appeared at the Glasgow Empire Exhibition that same year, where they had demonstrated the weaving of tweed within a section devoted to Highland Industries.[3]

The outbreak of the Second World War finally put an end to the regular steamer service to St Kilda, effectively terminating seasonal occupation by the islanders. While the archipelago was not inhabited

opposite
St Kilda – sites referred to in this chapter.
RCAHMS, 2015, GV005730

during this period, three military aircraft on routine training sorties were lost during bad weather; one crashed into the east flank of Soay and two into the upper slopes of Gleann Mòr and the east flank of Conachair on Hirta respectively.[4] Despite efforts being made to clear up the debris on Hirta, sections of all three planes survive and those elements that were readily accessible were mapped by RCAHMS in 2007–9. It is also likely that the islands were used as a stop-off point for water and fresh food (in the form of the Soay sheep) by both Allied and Axis forces. Alexander Ferguson, who visited in 1942, reported the presence of a flag with a swastika fluttering in Village Bay.[5] In the years preceding and following the war, St Kilda was visited on a number of occasions by notable scientists including David Lack, John Morton Boyd and Max Nicholson; and an increasing number of published papers emphasised the importance of the islands' natural heritage.[6]

However, it wasn't until the mid 1950s that major changes were to take place on St Kilda. Although the military were already beginning to make plans that might potentially affect the islands, the decision by the 5th Marquis of Bute to bequeath the archipelago to the NTS was also to have a profound impact[7] and it was the designation of St Kilda as a National Nature Reserve in 1957 that largely set the agenda for the following half century. The Nature Conservancy, a much larger body than the NTS, took over the day-to-day management of the islands, providing wardens and acting as the principal negotiator with the forces. Several National Nature Reserves were later established on abandoned islands in the Outer Hebrides, including North Rona and the Monach Isles, while there are also smaller reserves at Drimore on South Uist, Balranald on North Uist and Loch na Muilne on Lewis. These reserves are all important, but the only island with a programme of ecological research comparable to that of St Kilda is Rum in the Inner Hebrides.

In the same year that St Kilda became a National Nature Reserve, it was drawn into the wider geo-political context of the Cold War when it became the outermost component of a prospective missile testing range, which was to be constructed by the United Kingdom Government in the Outer Hebrides, principally on the islands of Benbecula and South Uist. As the military's plans began to solidify, their logistical support made the activities of the Nature Conservancy and the NTS very much easier. Originally conceived as a joint-services project to be used by the Army, the Navy and the Air Force, the budget was set at £25 million to allow for the testing of ground, sea and air launched weaponry. After a reconnaissance in 1956, the military concluded that 'Hirta would make an ideal site for air and sea surveillance radars, giving good coverage of air space down-range and being well situated to locate shipping'.[8] Described as 'one of the most memorable projects attributed to the Airfield Construction Branch', the building of the military base on Hirta was undertaken by RAF 5004 Squadron between 1957 and 1958.[9]

A requirement for County Council planning consent had been introduced to Britain in 1947, but the Air Ministry's demand for 'service lands' in the Outer Hebrides (as they were then known) entailed agreement with other agencies.[10] These included the Ministry of Works, which was to orchestrate the programme of survey and excavation in advance of the proposed Range's construction,[11] the Department of Health, the NTS and the Nature Conservancy. This was a lengthy and complex process, but the survival of the historical landscape on Hirta owes as much to this laborious

procedure, as to the minor decisions that had to be made from day to day after the work was set in hand, when representatives of the Nature Conservancy and the Ministry of Works were often present to offer advice.[12]

In June 1956, a multi-disciplinary team of 20 military staff and civilians travelled to St Kilda to undertake a reconnaissance. This included Roy Ritchie, the Regional Inspector of the Ministry of Works, as well as representatives of the Air Ministry, the Ministry of Supply, 22 Helicopter Squad, the Nature Conservancy and two St Kildans who acted as guides.[13] Four months later, the Air Ministry submitted their proposals, which included a plan to use Hirta's township as a convenient quarry for stone, together with an outline of the route of the road that was required to service the installations of the new base.[14]

On 7 November 1956, an article appeared in *The Scotsman* which discussed the proposed development, explaining how only one of the St Kildan houses was to be retained, as it had 'a cross of religious and archaeological interest'.[15] In fact, Roy Ritchie and the Ministry of Works had already conceived a plan of mitigation. This was to include a detailed survey of Village Bay making use of available aerial photographic coverage, a programme of monitoring as the work continued (this would now be termed a 'watching brief') and the possibility of excavation – all underpinned by a close liaison with the several interests involved.[16] Among the many meetings convened in Edinburgh and London, that held at St Andrew's House, Edinburgh, on 17 January 1957 stands out, as it was on this occasion that Ritchie and Jamie Stormouth Darling of the NTS put forward the case for the preservation of even the most recent remains.[17] Thereafter, the consultation was further extended to include other agencies, such as the Ministry of Transport, Inverness-shire County Council, RCAHMS and eventually the School of Scottish Studies at Edinburgh University.[18]

On 12 February 1957, planning consent was granted, but with a series of hard-won conditions that were outlined in a memorandum issued the following day.[19] These specified that the Air Ministry should 'not demolish the houses or erections within the village wall [i.e. the head dyke] or the village wall unless the wall requires to be breached by the Ministry's road' and that they should align the road 'to avoid the village area'. In addition, they were also to consult

The military originally thought of using Hirta's abandoned buildings for construction material, but lengthy negotiations and a realignment of the road saved most of them. Instead, the rock was quarried at Creagan Breac and fed into a crusher by dumpers.
National Trust for Scotland, c1957, 1002540

with the representatives of the Ministry of Works and the Nature Conservancy in the course of these works and were to make a record of any 'cletes, walls and erections' which it was necessary to demolish.[20] The second of these conditions was to prove critical when the representatives of the Nature Conservancy and NTS sent a telegram to the Air Ministry from St Kilda on 19 April 1957, only three days after the arrival of the Advance Party.[21] In this, the writers formally alerted the Air Ministry that the 'line of the proposed road … will cause greater destruction and disturbance to village amenities and wild life than previously anticipated'.[22] Their alarmed interjection was also supported by the construction team on the island and following the Air Ministry's agreement the road was finally re-routed through the lower parts of the croft land, causing minimal damage.[23] Roy Ritchie limited his own work

to creating an annotated plan of the field system in Village Bay and making records of features that might be disturbed before the arrival of members of the School of Scottish Studies, who had been invited by the Ministry of Works to undertake this aspect of the work. He undertook a second visit before July, in order that 'an inspector might be present when the roadway was constructed across ground adjacent to St Columba's Church', recording two short lengths of wall just in case they might prove to be part of its enclosure.[24]

While it is clear that every effort to mitigate was made by representatives of the NTS, the Ministry of Works, and the Nature Conservancy, inevitably some elements of St Kilda's historic landscape were damaged during the construction of the military base. The use of the existing water supply issuing from Tobar a' Mhinisteir led to the loss of the original well head, but in the main it was simply the drystone dykes around the minister's glebe, the nearby croft boundaries and the evidence for 19th century cultivation that were removed in the lower reaches of the croft land. Both the route of the road and the source of the stone to make it were bones of contention throughout the planning

above

This pair, among a collection of some 750,000 images taken by the RAF, illustrates the dramatic effect of Operation Hardrock on Hirta. Taken one month apart, the first shows a handful of tents belonging to the Advance Party, while the second captures the full complement when some 300 airmen occupied the island.

RAF, 1957, SC1453627 and SC1453629

below

Plans for the military base chopped and changed between 1957 and 1958, as budgets were reduced and practical difficulties overcome. Early plans (left) were laid aside, while temporary Nissen huts (right, in blue) were unexpectedly left to withstand the winter gales for twelve years.

National Records of Scotland, May 1958 and March 1959, DD27/3231

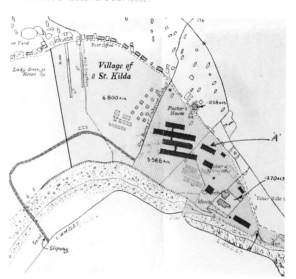

phase, but the final execution avoided damage to the majority of the features along its route. Instead of using the upstanding buildings and dykes as rubble for hardcore, the Air Ministry were permitted to open a large quarry at Creagan Breac, where a rock crusher was employed.[25] It has been suggested that this quarry obliterated the remains of earlier evidence for stone extraction, although this interpretation is reliant solely upon aerial photographs taken in 1947 and 1957.[26]

The initial layout of their temporary camp was captured in an aerial photograph taken just nine days before the arrival of the main work parties on 3 and 5 May.[27] However, moves were afoot by July 1957 to dramatically reduce the budget of the project from £25 million to £16 million and this led to the abandonment of the airfield planned for Sollas on North Uist. Nevertheless, work continued on St Kilda and by the end of August 1957, when construction finished for the year, the 350 airmen who made up the party had achieved significant progress in constructing the road network and the erection of both the temporary and permanent buildings located north-west of the manse.[28]

Another less remarked element of St Kilda's 20th century landscape are the triangulation pillars and survey marks that were set out by five staff of the Ordnance Survey during a visit to the island that same year. The pillars and the slight remains of an adjacent tent stance survive on the summit of Conachair, but it is unclear how many of the remaining surface blocks and bolts may remain beneath the turf elsewhere.[29]

The Air Ministry's plans for 1958 were drastically revised in April, when the financing of the project stalled for about a month and the decision was taken to delay the construction of permanent replacements for the Nissen huts that had been erected the previous year. Instead, work concentrated upon the raising of the concrete buildings that were intended to house the plant and machinery.[30] In addition, the roads created in 1957 were re-surfaced and the networks supplying hot and cold water, together with drainage and electricity, were installed. A series of drawings made the following year not only illustrate the layout of the Nissen huts and the concrete ranges, but also the refurbishment that had been undertaken at the manse and the factor's house.[31] The five Nissen huts that had been built in 1957 had now been refitted to provide kitchens, storerooms, messes, officers' accommodation, a drying room and a library, together

While all the Nissen huts erected in 1957–8 (top) have now been replaced, the contemporary concrete structures have fared better. The technical hub, known for many years as 'Red Square', is now some 57 years old and the radar sites have developed piecemeal as surveillance equipment has evolved.

When the military arrived in 1957 an effort was made to render the church, school and manse (left) wind and watertight. The restored manse, seen on the right beside the new officers' mess, was then maintained by the military, before returning to the National Trust for Scotland in 2009.

Roy Ritchie, Historic Scotland Collection, 1957, SC1463066
Steve Wallace RCAHMS, 2008, DP043440

with communication and recreation rooms. The concrete buildings included a pump house, a boiler house, a power house, septic tanks, ablution blocks and a section given over to military transport. By the summer of 1959 a Decca Radar had been erected on the southern flank of Mullach Sgar,[32] and a Marconi Radar on the summit of Mullach Mor, while a radar reflector had also been installed on Levenish.[33] Soon afterwards, a Corporal missile, the first of Britain's guided missiles capable of carrying a nuclear warhead, was fired from the range at South Uist and tracked using this facility.[34]

While the military were primarily focused on setting up and readying their base for active service in 1958, the NTS began to invite work parties of volunteers to come to St Kilda and take part in the repair of many of the historic structures. The first parties, led by George Waterston and Alex Warwick respectively, concentrated their efforts on rebuilding the collapsing wall circumscribing the graveyard and 'tidying up' other structures lining the Street.[35] The programme thus initiated in so small a way would in

the long run have as profound an effect on the island's archaeology and architecture as that of the military, for the bulk of the conservation work which was undertaken in the years that followed was concentrated within the head dyke.

Accommodation on the island was extremely limited. In early 1957, only the manse was partly habitable, but despite the stringency of the Air Ministry's budget, this building was refurbished, while the factor's house was repaired the following year. Although the factor's house was handed over to the Nature Conservancy in 1962, the erection of a small ablutions block outside its front door in 1957 even now recalls its role in these early years. The initial work parties camped in the glebe in tents supplied by the Army, but a programme to restore some of the croft houses on the Street, beginning with House 1 between 1964 and 1966, eventually provided more salubrious lodgings.[36]

Ongoing maintenance and improvement continued at the military base, with as many as 120 contract staff stationed on Hirta within five years of the re-occupation.[37] In 1962 a new officers' mess was constructed immediately against the manse, while the factor's house returned to civilian use.[38] Three years later, the fields below Houses 1–9, once so full of tents and

opposite
The military base, initially laid out in 1957, includes structures that are now between 30 and 58 years old.
RCAHMS, 2015, GV005716

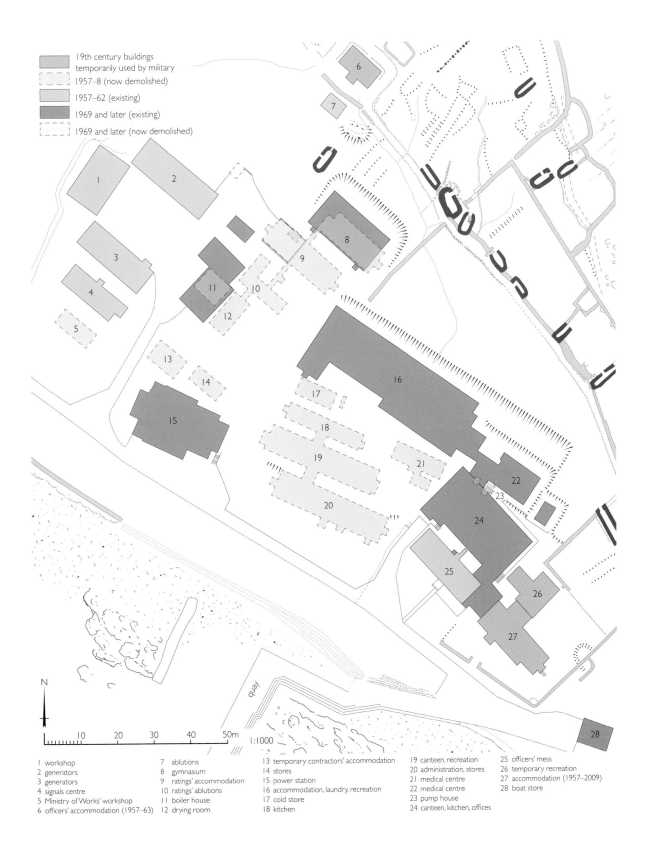

19th century buildings
temporarily used by military

1957–8 (now demolished)

1957–62 (existing)

1969 and later (existing)

1969 and later (now demolished)

N

10   20   30   40   50m

1:1000

quay

1 workshop
2 generators
3 generators
4 signals centre
5 Ministry of Works' workshop
6 officers' accommodation (1957–63)

7 ablutions
8 gymnasium
9 ratings' accommodation
10 ratings' ablutions
11 boiler house
12 drying room

13 temporary contractors' accommodation
14 stores
15 power station
16 accommodation, laundry, recreation
17 cold store
18 kitchen

19 canteen, recreation
20 administration, stores
21 medical centre
22 medical centre
23 pump house
24 canteen, kitchen, offices

25 officers' mess
26 temporary recreation
27 accommodation (1957–2009)
28 boat store

temporary buildings, were almost entirely deserted, the footprint of the base having contracted to the area covered by the terms of a long-term lease granted by the NTS. However, construction continued with more buildings being added up to 1968, when the decision was finally taken to extend the life of the range so that it could be used for testing air defence missiles and unmanned aerial vehicles.[39] This required an investment of some £7 million and an increase in staff.[40] The British, American and West German armies retained an interest at this time, but there was a period of relative inactivity the following year due to the Government's reluctance to commit to either the Sergeant or the Electric Blue Water missile.[41] A major revamp of the base followed in 1969–70, which included the removal of the remaining Nissen huts, the refurbishment of some of the existing concrete buildings and the construction of three new blocks in Siporex – a lightweight precast-concrete building material. In addition to a boiler and generator house, the two domestic blocks were to house new medical facilities, kitchens, offices, storerooms, ablutions, recreational facilities and sleeping quarters for sergeants and staff.[42] This major programme of work also included an extension to the quay and the provision of 100,000 litres of bulk fuel storage, both of which required major earth-moving.[43] Indeed, these earthworks, which were mapped by RCAHMS in 1983, are by far the largest man-made features of their type on the island. Improvements also took place to the radar systems: an upgraded Plessey AR1 was installed on Mullach Mòr in 1970, a Decca HR25 on Mullach Sgar in 1976 and a NIDIR tracking radar in 1978, while the tall telemetry mast on Mullach Mòr was installed in the early 1980s.[44] One other notable introduction before 1977 was a Romney Hut sited south of the factor's house, which was to serve as a large gymnasium.[45] The lower radar site on Mullach Sgar was later abandoned and its concrete footings were mapped by RCAHMS in 2007.[46]

Meanwhile, the NTS and their staff of volunteers expanded the programme concerned with the restoration of the buildings in Village Bay, while

The hub of modern St Kilda is a mix of restored buildings dating from the 19th century, amongst which those of the military base find a place. Both groups of buildings are of their time and each reflect particular episodes in the islands' evolving story.
Steve Wallace RCAHMS, 2008, DP043443

continuing to undertake maintenance. The completion of the work on the church and school, together with the 50th anniversary of the island's evacuation, were marked by a commemorative service on 27 August 1980, while House 3, the former home of the Gillies family, was re-roofed the following year and opened as a museum in 1983.[47] The storehouse, unrepaired since being damaged by enemy gunfire in 1918, was their next project, completed by 1986, the same year that RCAHMS brought its first survey to a close.[48] House 6, which was restored between 1994 and 2000, was the last of the buildings on the Street to be re-roofed. Now used as accommodation, it was intended to provide an illustration of a croft house in the 19th century.[49]

Far from being a landscape frozen in time, change still remains the watchword on St Kilda, although the focus of conservation work now is on the less-invasive programme of maintenance. The manse, used by the military since 1957, was handed over to the NTS in 2009, thereafter undergoing a sensitive restoration as a centre for the Trust's activities.[50] The factor's house, perhaps the least altered of St Kilda's modern buildings, was also sympathetically renovated in 2012.[51] Moreover, changing attitudes towards the visual impact of the concrete buildings on the base has led to their external re-decoration in green; and at the time of writing, there is an intention to completely revamp this yet again in the coming years, so adding yet another layer to the continuing story of St Kilda.

opposite
One of the steepest roads in Britain provides access from the base to the surrounding hills, where the radars survey the sea and air during missile testing.
Royal Navy, 1977, Open Government License v3, SC1484568

Conclusion

Visitors have always found it difficult to gain a perspective on St Kilda and its people without reference to various preconceptions. These include the idea of singularity that appears as far back as Martin Martin's writings and which has since continued as a bold thread running through much of the literature describing the islands and their history.[1] This quality of distinctiveness has also been informed and strengthened by notions of remoteness and isolation, which have often been served up as explanations rather than descriptions. It is as if the same evolutionary processes that are at work in the natural environment were also acting upon the islanders and their culture. Moreover, the exaggerated emphasis on difference and distance, in conjunction with the ruggedness of the physical geography of the islands, has also excited emotive responses that belong properly only to the utopias envisioned through the lenses of romance or the sublime.[2]

What little is known of the islands' prehistory or early history hardly suggests that the people who inhabited the archipelago were uniquely different from their neighbours on the Outer Hebrides, or

living elsewhere along the Atlantic coast of Scotland. Such differences as there were are likely to have been influenced by the same factors as in more recent times – the overall size of the islands, the difficulties of communication over the winter months and the harshness of the climate. The varied relief, the drainage and the soils will all have contributed their own constraints to food production; while the absence of timber will have forced a greater reliance upon stone, turf and peat as raw materials. However, these were not novel limitations and they will not have fostered a distinctive St Kildan culture.[3] What did begin to make a dramatic difference to the landscape, possibly from medieval times, was the establishment of a social and economic network that encouraged the inhabitants to exploit the one extraordinary natural advantage of the archipelago – the vast seabird colonies that nested around the islands and stacks. This demanded not only extraordinary courage, but intelligence and ingenuity – the latter expressed in the location and architecture of the cleitean that were central to the endeavour. Far from being primitive or rude, these elegant and sophisticated drystone and turf constructions were perfectly fitted to their tasks of drying and storage.[4] So rich was this resource that the infrastructure supporting the fowling economy was already dominating parts of the island when Robert Moray and Martin Martin first described them towards the end of the 17th century.[5] Thereafter, the cleitean,

For hundreds of years, Boreray and the stacks were at the centre of the St Kildans' way of life – the seabird harvest providing a focal point each summer. For some 85 years the birds have been protected from hunters, but there is little doubt that fishing and climate change may affect their future.

Jill Harden, 2010

representing the quintessential expression of this economy, appear to have greatly increased in number.

However, the St Kildans were unlucky in comparison with some of their neighbours. The growth of tourism, especially in the second half of the 19th century, meant they often had to contend with a curious, but relatively naive visitor, who was sometimes also tactless, condescending, ill-informed and uncomprehending. Indeed, even the most congenial, courteous and knowledgeable amongst them could hardly help but perceive island life through anything but a series of preconceptions. Some were still informed by notions of romance or the sublime born of a late 18th century sensibility, while others focussed instead upon technological and social evolution, with the idea of progress at its heart. This way of thinking, which had been developing since at least the 1830s, was increasingly influential amongst the well-read from the 1850s.[6] Just as the public had been introduced to a new way of contemplating the past through the classification of implements and weapons according to the materials from which they were made, so they were gradually becoming aware that societies might be similarly classified according to a wider set of criteria that marked out several stages of development in an ascent from the 'savage' to the 'civilised'.[7]

In broad terms, little of this was applicable to the St Kildans. They were simply one amongst a number of peripheral communities in Britain that were relatively poor, barely literate, possessed of limited freedoms and spoke a language that differed from the majority. However, for the educated observer, the islands held much that was fascinating, especially at the boundary where the newly minted mid-Victorian disciplines of archaeology, ethnology and anthropology all intermeshed. No visitor was perhaps more receptive to these new frameworks than Captain Frederick Thomas. His report on the antiquities of Orkney published in 1851 had been essentially descriptive and factual, although it is clear that he was already interested in ethnography.[8] However, his later work was differently coloured, quite possibly under the influence of Daniel Wilson, his correspondent and a fellow member of the Society of Antiquaries of Scotland, who was also the foremost advocate for these new disciplines and the light they might throw upon Scotland's past.[9] Thomas himself was especially interested in 'rudely built' structures that were still in use in the Outer Hebrides (or had only recently fallen into ruin), which appeared to be essentially unchanged from those of prehistoric times.[10] He believed that by recovering contemporary information as to how these were constructed and used, an insight could be gained into the ancient society that had built similar dwellings. Indeed, the general proposition that it was still possible to see aspects of the past in the everyday life of traditional communities became hugely popular in the latter part of the 19th century, especially in relation to their technologies. This enthusiasm is encapsulated in the series of influential lectures prepared for the Society of Antiquaries of Scotland by Sir Arthur Mitchell, which were subsequently published in 1880 with the title, *The Past in the Present: What is Civilisation?*[11] It is no surprise to find not only that Mitchell accompanied Thomas to inspect the beehive shielings at Làrach Taigh Dhubhastail, Ceann Reasort, Uig, on Lewis in 1866,[12] but that the latter subsequently took a hand in the proofreading of his friend's seminal study which devoted part of a chapter to such buildings.[13]

It was and has remained very easy to see St Kilda through this same prism – a quaint society situated somewhere between the past and the present. However, to do so is to ignore their well-adapted technologies, early adoption of a crofting system, the modernity of their cottages and those aspects of their ideas, beliefs and values that fully conformed with those held elsewhere. It was and remains very easy for them to become victims of an erroneous exceptionalism. This was something RCAHMS was well aware of when conducting their first study of the Outer Hebrides after 1914.[14]

Just as the plans for the RCAHMS re-survey of St Kilda began to take shape in 2006, two major studies were published that have made an important contribution towards the development of a new perspective of the islands' archaeology. The first of these, Andrew Fleming's *St Kilda and the Wider World,* represented the final summary of a series of substantial papers in which he sought to challenge the conventional orthodoxy that has so mythologised the islands by firmly rejecting exceptionalism, instead situating them and their inhabitants in a much wider geographical and cultural context. This he achieved by presenting a careful re-analysis of the documentary and archaeological evidence, whilst simultaneously arguing that Hirta, especially in Village Bay and Gleann Mòr, retained extensive fragments that survived from both early and later prehistoric times. Although his perception of the landscape as having chronological depth was perhaps not entirely new, his observations were based upon a great deal of skill and experience in unravelling such complex topographies. Moreover, his willingness to put forward a series of research hypotheses that were testable by excavation was almost unprecedented. A number of these he undertook himself and if the evidence he obtained was often equivocal and did not perhaps always fulfil expectations, this was as much a result of the small scale of the cuttings as of difficulties in interpretation.

The second work, Michael Robson's *St Kilda: Church, Visitors and 'Natives'*, also attempts to demythologise the islands' history. This he achieves through a rigorous examination of original documentation and a critique of the perspectives of those who have sought to write about the community. It is a work of painstaking research, careful commentary and encyclopaedic breadth. As such, it deserves to be much better known.

Both of these far-reaching studies have influenced the outlook of this book. They have helped shape its overall framework, while confirming that it is no longer acceptable to study the islands without reference to the accomplishments of similar communities on the Outer Hebrides. However, we do not necessarily accept their findings in every respect, especially Fleming's notion of a particularly rich early prehistoric landscape in Village Bay, while the very idea of Pictish survivals in Gleann Mòr is simply unsupportable. Instead, we have recognised a rich medieval period. This can be identified in the chapels, altars, field systems, shielings and other structures scattered across the whole of the archipelago – although inevitably, the attribution of some of these elements to this era will remain

contentious until they have been adequately dated. This, in its turn, has affected our readings of the landscape at both earlier and later periods.

It has been persistently stressed throughout this book that the physical geography of the islands and the comparatively limited ground that was suited to settlement, the growing of crops and the grazing of animals, led to intensive land-use in some areas. This has resulted in the gradual depletion of elements in a landscape that was constantly evolving under social and economic pressures. The rhythm of recycle and replacement occurs everywhere, but on St Kilda it is especially problematic, as it is so hard to recover the earlier constituents of the process and frame them in the islands' chronology. What little excavation that there has been has proved invaluable and there can be no doubt that further work addressing the many issues and ambiguities that remain will help clarify the story. Novel methodologies and more searching questions need to be applied to ensure a robust and fuller narrative, while contributions from other disciplines will add colour, texture and depth.

Yet in spite of the difficulties in unravelling what is evidently an exceptionally complex landscape, it is the features associated with the fowling economy that are the most striking and unusual. This transformed the islands and the lives of the St Kildans from at least the 17th century; and it still has an arresting impact upon the visitor contemplating the scenery to this day. Although its origins and development are still largely unexplored, it bears testimony to a remarkable and resilient people who forged a living in very difficult circumstances from a handful of tiny islands on the fringes of the Atlantic Ocean. A people who not only shared a rich culture with their neighbours, but one to which they also made their own unique contribution.

Images of
St Kilda

Taken from an RCAHMS survey
aeroplane, this bird's-eye view reduces
the archipelago to two monoliths: Hirta
on the left and Boreray on the right.
These islands survive as a remnant of an
ancient volcano, linked by a rim traversing
the ocean floor.
Dave Cowley RCAHMS, 2012, DP134231

Landscape

Landscape

Some 9,000 years ago, the earliest occupants of Scotland reached the western shore of the Outer Hebrides. In the distance, they would have seen two cloud-capped silhouettes interrupting the Atlantic horizon: Hirta and Boreray.

These people were well used to navigating coastal waters in their pursuit of food and resources. Had they risked the treacherous journey across the open sea, they would have sailed into the edge of an ancient volcano, whose collapse and erosion has created the dramatic scenery so familiar today. The granites, gabbros, breccias and dolerites that make up the St Kildan archipelago forced their way to the surface over 55 million years ago. Although much younger than the surrounding gneiss of the Outer Hebrides, they have been scoured fiercely by glaciers, frost and coastal erosion over the millennia. Roaring winds of over 70mph regularly blast the islands and, perhaps every 50 years or so, waves of more than 35m smash against their cliffs and shores.[1]

Around 10,000 BC, St Kilda was released from the grip of the last Ice Age, resolving into four main islands and several sea stacks. The first visitors would have likely made their journey in the summer, to hunt and fish. On approach, and as they sought out a place to land, they would have been surrounded by a wheeling mass of gannets, fulmars and puffins. The islands are encircled by impressive cliffs. Those of Conachair are the tallest in Britain at 430m high, while Stac an Àrmainn, which rises to 190m, is the highest sea stack. In places, the lower coastline is pierced by natural arches and tunnels through which a small boat could pass. These original explorers – just like those visiting by sea today – must have settled for one or other of the two large bays on Hirta; each is provided with freshwater springs and small streams, a pre-requisite for any continuing human presence.

St Kilda's climate during the period of human occupation has not been constant, but its oceanic character has remained much the same. The islands themselves encourage the formation of clouds that attract blustery and squally winds and increase the rainfall which sweeps off the steep slopes surrounding the bays. Compared with the rest of Britain, temperatures are relatively warm in the winter (5.6°C) and relatively cool in the summer (11.8°C).[2] Despite the effects of wind and salt spray, soils and vegetation have developed over most of the rocky islands, except on the steepest cliffs and stacks. In the main, the soils are boggy and acidic, although the growth of peat across the islands has been limited by the steepness of the ground. The vegetation cover is peculiarly rich in salt-tolerant plants and lichens, but within Village Bay the well-drained and relatively fertile soils encourage a rich mix of common bent grass and Yorkshire fog. Where the ground is manured by seabirds or animals, it responds with denser growth and in particular an abundance of sorrel. Flatter ground tends to be marshy and is characterised by sphagnum moss and moor grass, but the drier slopes of the hills are dominated by a heathland of ling and crowberry. The archipelago's

St Kilda has the second biggest northern-gannet colony in the world and their numbers circling the boat grow to hundreds as you approach, occasionally peeling off to dart the water's surface in search of fish. One gannet, in a summer in the 1680s, was said to have struck the tacksman's boat so hard that its beak pierced the hull and lodged in a plank.[3]
Benjamin Dürig, 2013

Looking across Hirta's Gleann Mòr, the
island of Boreray, 8km away, is capped
by a tuft of white cloud. The towering
cliffs of Stac an Àrmainn and Stac Lì stand
to its left, playing host to thousands
of nesting gannets now safe from the
seasonal hunts of the St Kildans.

Dave Cowley RCAHMS, 2008, DP046583

only species of tree, the dwarf willow, grows to no more than a centimetre or so in height.

Such an exposed and varied landscape has been colonised by numerous insects and has been a stop-over for migrant and non-resident bird species for millennia. But it is its importance as a breeding site for seabirds that brings St Kilda to the notice of the world's ornithologists. At present, the nesting pairs number 23,000 Common Guillemots, 45,000 Leach's Storm Petrels, 60,000 Northern Gannets, 63,000 Northern Fulmars and an astonishing 142,000 Atlantic Puffins.[4] Burrow-nesting species like the puffin and the Manx Shearwater find shelter in the steep grassy slopes, while others cling to rocky ledges.

The natural landscape of St Kilda is cloaked in placenames of Norse, Gaelic and English origin which describe both physical elements such as form, character and colour, as well as functional elements, relating to history and myth.[5] Of the former, there is *Gleann Mòr*, 'the Big Glen', *Cnoc na Gaoithe*, 'the Knoll of the Wind' and *Tobar Ruadh*, 'the Red Spring'; of the latter, *Àirigh Mòr,* 'the Big Shieling' and the Norse cum Gaelic *Geàrraidh Àrd*, 'the High Park', reflect the use of parts of the island as summer pasture for cattle and sheep. In some instances, placenames record elements of the medieval Christian landscape, such as *Geodha Chille Brianan,* 'the Cleft of Brianan's Chapel', or *Tobar nam Buadh,* 'the Well of Virtues'; while in others voice is given to places of traditional importance, such as *Clach a' bhainne*, 'the Milk Stone', *Taigh an t-Sithiche,* 'House of the Fairies', and *Liana nan Òr,* 'the Plain of Spells'. In recent years, new names have appeared to describe other elements of the landscape, such 'the chimney', a vertical scar through Clais na Bearnaich, or 'the cleit at the end of the world', for a particularly remote and exposed cleit.

Although the earliest visitors to St Kilda have left little lasting impact on the landscape, the islands today are the product of thousands of years of co-existence between people and the natural environment. The sheer density of archaeological features across all the islands and many of the stacks is testament to the intensive exploitation of the archipelago's resources over thousands of years. Seemingly inaccessible places, such as the steep boulder field of Carn Mòr on the west coast of Hirta, or the precipitous faces of Stac an Àrmainn, each provide the setting for at least 80 structures relating to the hunting of seabirds for flesh, oil and eggs. More than 1,300 cleitean have been recorded on Hirta alone, reflecting not simply the storage required for fowling, but also for the drying of peat and turf. While these provided the main sources of the islanders' fuel, they were also used for walls and roofs, as well as being added to the fields. Indeed, the human occupation of Hirta has resulted in the massive removal of the surface sward from the slopes of the hills and its transfer into the fields and terraces of Village Bay. Grazing cattle and sheep have been present on St Kilda since they were introduced in prehistory. Each animal has been fed by the land and in return has provided manure as fertiliser, promoting, nourishing and adapting components of the soil and the vegetation. Village Bay itself hosts a complex of archaeological features stretching back at least 2,000 years and possibly very much further still. Despite its apparent remoteness, almost no part of St Kilda has been left untouched or unaltered by people.

above
The great sea stacks of Stac an Àrmainn, in
the foreground, and Stac Lì in the distance.
Robert Atkinson, School of Scottish Studies,
1947, S562

opposite
The jagged eastern coast of Boreray
stutters to an end before Stac an Àrmainn.
Robert Atkinson, who took these two
photographs from an aeroplane on a sunny
day in July 1947, described how 'the Stacs
were a sun dazzle of gannets from above'.[6]
Robert Atkinson, School of Scottish Studies,
1947, S563

The northern cliffs of Boreray present a
terrifying aspect to this photographer, who
is standing on Stac an Àrmainn after having
pulled and cajoled his unwieldy glass plate
camera into position. Such is the height of the
Atlantic swell that a landing on Boreray or the
stack can only be attempted in calm weather
National Trust for Scotland, c1886, 1002062

Norman MacLeod's photograph, taken in 1886, shows the jagged northern coast of Hirta leading to the island of Soay in the distance. This view was taken from Àird Uachdarach, the high promontory near the summit of Conachair, from where the cliffs plunge over 400m to the sea below. Many of MacLeod's photographs were subsequently used by George Washington Wilson and Co.[7]

opposite
The steep slopes of Boreray are rarely visited by even the most adventurous nowadays. This grassy sward is dotted with more than 60 structures, while evidence for a system of fields and enclosures is testimony to an attempt at permanent occupation. During a ten day trip by RCAHMS in 2010, a massive storm kept the team confined to their tents for more than twelve hours.
Dave Cowley RCAHMS, 2012, DP134197

right
Mist catches the rocky knoll of Clagan na Rusgachan at the western tip of Boreray.
Ian Parker RCAHMS, 2010, DP099629

The 240 acre island of Soay, rising to some 340m above the sea, is the last and outmost isle of St Kilda itself. While it was used by the islanders to graze the famous Soay sheep, and as a base for fowling expeditions, the survival of a simple altar on the higher ground suggests that it may have also been included in a medieval pilgrimage route around the archipelago.

Dave Cowley RCAHMS, 2012, DP134117

Dropping nearly 300m to the sea below, the steep grassy and rocky eastern flank of Oiseval is now left to the Soay sheep. A few cleitean cling to the rocky spines, some with stacked turves still inside. No longer used, a ledge along this slope once provided access to the cliffs to the north and to places where grass could be plucked for fodder.

Dave Cowley RCAHMS, 2012, DP134160

The western flank of Oiseval, with Levenish in the distance. Dotted with the remains of cleitean, the hill once provided much of the islanders' supply of turf, which was used for fuel and for the creation and maintenance of the cultivated ground down in the village below.
Dave Cowley RCAHMS, 2102. DP134134

Barely distinguishable from numerous glens in the Highlands and Islands, the rich grasses of Gleann Mòr played an important role in the St Kildan economy. Often seen by visitors and writers as a place apart, the landscape here was once filled with the lowing of up to 40 cattle and the bleating of hundreds of sheep
Dave Cowley RCAHMS, 2012, DP134174

Between the highest summit of Conachair and the heather-clad slopes of Oiseval beyond, lies the little valley of An Lag Bhon Tuath. While the enclosures at its centre were used for growing winter fodder, the ground nearby provided summer grazing and another source of peat and turf for the islanders' fires.

Dave Cowley RCAHMS, 2012, DP134208

Four boats are just visible hugging the coastline of Village Bay – the best shelter in a generally exposed and ragged coastline. Rowing or sailing out of this bay to Soay or Boreray was a serious undertaking, even in relatively good weather.
Dave Cowley RCAHMS, 2012, DP134184

Village Bay on a summer's day. A cleit
stands sentinel, its turf roof (originally
cut from around the building) being
slowly removed by the ever-present
wind. This bay has provided the shelter
and fresh water necessary to sustain
a permanent occupation on Hirta for
thousands of years.

Steve Wallace RCAHMS, 2008, DP044808

Ann Gillies, then about 21 years old, leans against the souterrain knitting socks. She later married Norman MacKinnon and the couple went on to have eight children on the island. Ann survived the devastating effect of tuberculosis on her family after they left St Kilda in 1930, but eventually she moved to Ferintosh on the Black Isle where she died in 1963.

taken by R M R Milne, National Trust for Scotland, c1909, 1002523

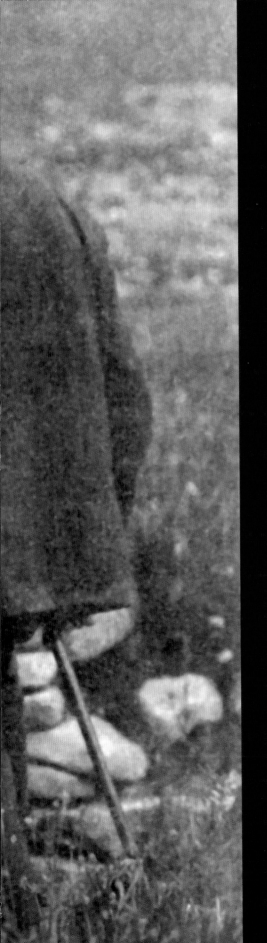

St Kildans

St Kildans

From the moment they established their first settlement, most St Kildans played out their whole lives on the islands, passing on their knowledge and practical experience through more than a hundred generations.

Shared stories of daring exploits scaling cliffs and crossing seas were part and parcel of everyday life, no doubt recounted time and time again by firesides in Village Bay. Long before written records began, these were the ways that people connected with their past and the personal lives of their ancestors, perpetuating myths, legends and achievements.

Martin Martin's account of St Kilda at the end of the 17th century acknowledges the islanders as a homogenous group, referring to them as 'the inhabitants' and setting the tone for almost every account that followed. Martin gave voice to only one individual, an infamous character known as Roderick the Imposter, who exploited his fellow islanders by feigning a meeting with John the Baptist, and subsequently shaping their religious and personal lives to his advantage. Martin portrayed the St Kildans as a unique and distinctive community, adding to his title page a paean to their 'beauty and singular character; (fornication and adultery being unknown among them) their genius for poetry, music, dancing; their surprising dexterity in climbing the rocks and [also the] walls of houses … their extensive charity; [and] their contempt of gold and silver as below the dignity of human nature'.[2] While this description undoubtedly promoted the sale of his book, there is little evidence to support the assertion that St Kildans were somehow different. Taken as individuals, every islander has a story to tell.

From the middle of the 19th century, government bureaucracy finally made the journey across the sea to St Kilda to record births, marriages and deaths and, once a decade, to conduct a census of the population. To this we can add accounts of visitors like the Duke of Atholl, who came to the island in 1860, staying a night with the islander Betty Scott and her 'husband, son and daughter, 3 dogs, 1 puppy and 3 cats'.[3] Betty was born in the parish of Assynt around 1816 as the illegitimate daughter of a farmer Thomas Scott and his mistress Rachel Campbell.[4] She came to St Kilda to work as a servant to the minister and married the islander Malcolm MacDonald in 1834.[5] Betty was the only islander with English and Gaelic. She was also recognised as 'intelligent and superior', sometimes being dubbed 'the Queen of St Kilda'.[6] On 3 April 1863 she boarded the *Dargavel* to sail from St Kilda to the Sound of Harris 'in a favourable wind' to sell 'cloth, salt-fish and other native produce'. The boat, 'when last seen from the heights of the island', was 'careering onward at rapid speed', but was never seen again.[7] Although her untimely death in her forties was a tragedy, she had lived a remarkable life and was later described as 'the best head, indeed the ruling spirit of the island'.[8]

In the year before her death, Betty was introduced to a baby boy who would grow up to epitomize the St Kildan cragsman: Finlay MacQueen.

The men who built the quay pose with their tools after their work was complete. At the back, the minister Angus Fiddes, wearing a fine hat, stands beside the engineers of the Congested Districts Board. Second from the left, fixing the photographer with a steely gaze, is Donald Ferguson, the ground officer and a church elder.

National Records of Scotland, c1901

Perhaps the most famous photograph taken of the St Kildans. The men of the island posed for Norman MacLeod in 1886, creating an image that was sold a thousand times over by the George Washington Wilson studio. Depicting an apparently egalitarian scene, the photograph in fact relays the hierarchy of St Kilda – Donald Ferguson, soon to be the ground officer, stands at the front of the right hand row.
Norman MacLeod, University of Aberdeen, 1886, C7107

Finlay, who would become the only islander to be the subject of a biography,[9] was born next door to Betty in 1862. In his early twenties he was captured in Norman MacLeod's photograph of the St Kilda 'Parliament' (sixth from the right). He married Mary Gillies two years earlier, and inherited his grandfather's croft at No. 2. The couple went on to have eight children between 1885 and 1903, seven of whom survived their early years. By the time of the evacuation in 1930, Finlay was a formidable 68-year-old and was clearly reluctant to leave the island of his birth, a place he knew intimately. He corresponded frequently with the Government after the evacuation, writing with the help of a translator in 1931, that 'I was promised everything before I left St Kilda and now I find myself stranded'.[10] Although he went to live with his daughter Mary and her husband Neil Ferguson near Stromeferry and then Kincardine, Finlay took every opportunity to revisit St Kilda. He died in 1941 at Tulliallan in Fife.[11]

Just a year after Finlay's death, another redoubtable St Kildan, Alexander Gillies Ferguson, also returned to St Kilda.[12] By then 70 years of age, Alexander was brought up at No. 5, Hirta, the eldest surviving son of Donald Ferguson, the 'ground officer' who dealt with the affairs of the estate on the island.[13] Born on Harris on account of his mother's poor health, Alexander left St Kilda as a young man of about 20, perhaps following the advice of the schoolmaster who noted his aptitude for learning. He went on to become a successful merchant of wholesale Harris Tweed and also sold cloth produced in Ireland, as well as his native island. Even after his marriage to Catherine Sinclair from Glasgow in 1901 and the birth of four children, he never forgot his roots and returned to St Kilda whenever he could. In 1897, when the Kearton brothers visited the island, Alexander was able to act as one of their guides and posed for a photograph on the cliffs of Boreray. He was captioned as 'the ex-fowler in the holiday war-paint of Buchanan Street'.[14] After purchasing the *Colonsay* for £8,000, Alexander began sailing to Hirta regularly, including a trip to erect a headstone for his brother Neil in 1953.[15] In 1956, at the age of 74, he worked with the Royal Air Force on the island, acting as one of their 'native guides'.[16] He died four years later in 1960.[17]

Together, these lives illustrate the fascinating story of individual St Kildans. Although all were poor in today's terms, there is no correlation between economic and cultural poverty. Their narrative during the latter part of the islands' history and specifically in the time before the 1930 evacuation, was as much a tale of ingenuity, adventure and entrepreneurship, as it was of gradual economic decline. While their lives told of hardship, they were also inextricably part of a rich Gaelic tradition; and as such, they enjoyed an appreciation and intimate knowledge of their island environment that only a handful of people can now hope to attain. The St Kildans were an adept and educated people, but their knowledge and experience were situated within a local and regional context, set apart from the skills in literacy and numeracy which have become the hallmark for learning in modern times. For archaeologists interested in St Kilda's more remote past, it is rarely possible to consider the islands in terms of the impact and influence of each and every individual. But for those interested in more recent centuries, it is essential to recognise the role that they played. Their lives and the decisions they made have often had a significant and lasting effect upon the surviving landscape.

The St Kildan men, young and old, relax
in the sun outside the home of Neil
Ferguson, senior St Kildan, third from the
right. Neil was born in 1876 and took over
from his father Donald as ground officer,
becoming postmaster on St Kilda in 1905.
Neil died in Tulliallan, Fife, in 1944.[18]

A group of St Kildan women and children. Second from the right sits a young Ann Ferguson (b1865), eldest child of the senior St Kildan Donald and his wife Rachel who lived at No. 5.[19]

National Trust for Scotland, c1886, 1002043

above

This apparently similar composition of two St Kildan women (both featuring Ann MacKinnon née Gillies on the left) captures two very different scenes, one with the girls preparing to sell socks and gloves to tourists, the other as married women attending church in their Sunday best.

above left
Michael Stevenson, National Records of Scotland, 1913, Licensor Scran
above right
Lachlan MacDonald Collection, National Trust for Scotland, c1920, 1002640

opposite

This rare shot of a group in Gleann Mòr shows the women busy knitting, with a climbing rope lying on the ground ready to be used. In contrast the majority of group images depict men in Village Bay.

opposite top
National Trust for Scotland, 1002524
opposite bottom
R M R Milne, National Trust for Scotland, c1910, 1002552

The schoolchildren and their teacher, George Murray, pose with the island of Dun in the background. Murray came to the island for only one year, nonetheless managing to 'try the rope' on Boreray, catching twenty fulmars and two gannets. His relationship with the islanders was not always easy and on one occasion he had a furious row with Donald Ferguson over the supply of peats for his fire.[20]

taken by Norman MacLeod, University of Aberdeen, 1886, C04251

Posed and less formal photographs of St Kilda's children became a common subject from the 1860s. In this selection of images taken between c1900 and c1910, there is only one in which the subjects have been identified. The six pictured in the bottom left lived in Nos. 2 and 3 and were the children of Finlay and Mary MacQueen, and William and Mary MacDonald. The eldest of the eleven MacDonald children left St Kilda in 1913 and the remaining members of the family followed in 1924. The youngest child pictured, Calum, went on to become butler to Lord Dumfries and worked at a hotel in Park Lane.[21]

top left
National Trust for Scotland, c1900, 1002165
bottom left
R M R Milne, National Trust for Scotland, c1910, 1002551
opposite top
National Trust for Scotland, c1900, 1002164
opposite bottom
National Trust of Scotland, c1900, 1002488

Finlay MacQueen features in numerous photographs of St Kilda between 1886 and 1938, sometimes pictured with one or other of his eight children or in deep conversation with the MacLeod factor John Mackenzie. Robert Atkinson described how Finlay aged 74 was 'insensitive to heights. He perched on the Lover's Stone, a slice of rock sticking up into thin air from the cliff top. He liked to roll boulders over the edge and to watch their frightful plunge and bounce'. When Robert followed Finlay to the Carn Mòr screes 'he insisted on roping us together, which was alarming'.[22]

top left
National Trust for Scotland, c1910,
Licensor Scran
bottom left
Neil Ferguson Collection, c1910
opposite top left
National Trust for Scotland, c1920, 1002012
opposite top right
taken by Alasdair Alpin MacGregor, National
Museum of Scotland, 1930, Licensor Scran
opposite bottom
Robert Atkinson, School of Scottish Studies,
1938, S323

Posed by the 'the leading photographer of the north' this group includes nurse and teacher Ann MacKinlay (centre) and her successor Kenneth Campbell (far left). Donald Ferguson, senior St Kildan, is fourth from the left.[23]

taken by David Whyte, National Trust for Scotland, 1884, 1002344

More than 1,500 cleitean dot the archipelago of St Kilda, each one sited in the best place for its intended use. Whether storing birds, fish, hay, peat or manure, the cleitean provided a safe haven for each family's stores, seeing them through the long winter months.

Angela Gannon RCAHMS, 2009, DP212658

Seasons

Seasons

Huge flocks of noisy seabirds arrive on St Kilda every spring, their incessant calls heralding the beginning of a new breeding season. Thousands upon thousands of puffins and gannets descend upon the islands and stacks to nest, accompanied by improved weather conditions and, soon after, by numerous landings of tourists and researchers. For the St Kildans in earlier times, the beginning of spring released them from a reliance on the food and fuel stored over winter in their many cleitean. Fowling tackle would be brought out and tested for strength, while the boats – used only very occasionally in winter to reach the outer isles and stacks – would be checked over for seaworthiness.

The success of lambing on Hirta, Boreray and Soay in April relied a great deal on good weather, as did the movement of sheep to and from the island of Dun, where some were overwintered. Preparation of the land for cultivation began in the spring with the manuring of the fields by the addition of muck, mixed with old thatch, ashes, peat dust and seaweed. Crops of barley, oats and potatoes were planted after the fields were turned over manually with the cas-chrom, caibe and racan (spade, hoe and rake),[1] or in later years by 'the English spade'.[2] Each crofter was largely reliant on the labour of his family to undertake these tasks. In contrast, the fowling expeditions were a community enterprise – particularly when the islanders could muster only one boat: 'about the middle of March, a select band of adventurers put to sea in this boat, and go to the neighbouring isles, upon an expedition that to them is of very great importance. This is the season for catching the old Solan-Geese before they begin to lay; they hunt them in the night time, through steep and (to all other men inaccessible) precipices'.[3] Back on Hirta, the cattle, weakened by a winter in the byre, were brought out to feast on the fresh growth around the beginning of May. Both cattle and sheep were driven out to summer pastures in the high ground and did not return until months later.

It was common for many different activities to run concurrently, especially if the weather provided good opportunities. On 28 May 1887, George Murray recalled the 'lively times' when the islanders went to Soay for adult fulmars, returning with a haul of some five hundred. That same week the islanders took the lambs and ewes over to Gleann Mòr and began the collection of their winter fleeces.[4] Some of the requisite wool processing could be done by hand on the move and many images capture the St Kildans knitting or spinning whilst in conversation. In August and September, the islanders took in the harvest of barley and oats. Macaulay noted in 1764 that 'the harvest is commonly over in this place before

Rising some 172m above the sea, Stac Lì was a hunting ground of the St Kildans each August from at least the 17th century. A small bothy clings to the rock face to provide some shelter during the harvest of the young gannet (or guga). The mutton and wool from the Boreray sheep in the foreground were used by the islanders for food and clothing.[5]
Stuart Murray, 2011, DP099634

Mrs Ann MacKinnon (née Gillies) and her son Finlay are captured bringing fulmar back from the north side of Hirta. The harvest of young fulmar was one of the main events of the St Kildan calendar, occupying between ten and twenty days in August each year. Young Finlay died of tuberculosis in 1935.[16]

National Trust for Scotland, c1925, Licensor Scran

the beginning of September, and should it fall otherwise, the whole crop will be almost destroyed by the equinoctial storms – all the islanders on the western coast, have great reason to dread the fury of the autumnal tempest'.[6]

The busy agricultural cycle had to fit around the principal events of the fowling calendar which included, in particular, the main fulmar harvest. In the 1830s, Mackenzie recalled that by 'the beginning of August the young fulmars are about fully fledged and ready for killing. During the preceding week an unusual excitement and alertness pervades the village'.[7] In preparation 'every rope was tested, every oil dish cleaned, and every barrel emptied. The twelfth arrives, the rope is made fast round the waist of the heavier party, whilst the lighter party is let down the perpendicular rock several hundred feet. Here work of destruction goes night and day for a given space; the St Kildan man has nothing to do but to take the young Fulmar, wring his neck, and then suspend him by a girth he wears round his loins'.[8] Once all the fulmars were gathered, 'plucking off the feathers, disposing of the internal fat, and salting the carcases for winter use, goes on until far into the night'.[9] The same scene had greeted John MacCulloch some twenty years earlier when he found that 'the town is paved in feathers, the very dunghills are made of feathers, the plough land seems as though it had been sown with feathers, and the inhabitants look as though they had been tarred and feathered, for their hair is full of feathers and their cloths are covered in feathers'.[10]

By October there was still plenty of work to do: bringing in the hay, lifting potatoes, thatching roofs and slaughtering sheep for the winter stores.[11] The sheep catch, known as *Ruagadh* – the chase – was a great day full of excitement.[12] The succeeding winter months were a much quieter time. Most of the seabirds had left the islands by the end of November, and the last of the late crops had been taken in that same month.[13] Peat and turf for fuel, and grass for fodder, continued to be gathered piecemeal throughout the winter; and George Murray remembered how on a snowy day 'the people in single file carrying peats home across the white hills present a curious spectacle'.[14] Winter was also the time for repair work, and for the processing of wool. Carding, spinning and an intense period of weaving began in December and carried on until the spring.[15]

There is little doubt that the St Kildan way of life described here was affected by the vagaries of the weather, as well as by the life-cycles of the seabirds, cattle and sheep. However, it is equally true that there was a great deal of change over the centuries. Fluctuations in the market value of feathers and tweed, for example, had a profound influence on the seasonal round. Indeed, the summer visits of the tacksman and factor, as well as the ever-growing influence of tourism – itself seasonally confined – were to have a major impact. Nevertheless, the transitions between seasons still provided the basis for the St Kildan calendar, affecting every element of a life that was firmly rooted in the resources to hand. This theme continued throughout the 19th and 20th centuries, as the nature of the economy changed and the building blocks of society altered. Even now, St Kilda shares much in common with other parts of rural Scotland; it is the seasons that continue to control so many aspects of daily life.

A 74 year-old Finlay MacQueen demonstrating the use of the fowling rod to catch puffins. Adult birds were usually taken in June and July of every year. A skilled fowler could take several hundred in a day. On this occasion, Finlay caught only a 'small-purchase of sea-fowl for breakfast the next morning'.[17]

taken by Robert Atkinson, School of Scottish Studies, 1938. S331

From the 18th century until 1930, it was part and parcel of the summer season for the St Kildan cragsmen to demonstrate their skills to visiting tourists. The majority of the photographs and film footage created since the 1860s captured the islanders descending these cliffs at the Gap, the closest area to the village.

opposite left
J Lupton Collection, National Trust for Scotland, c1890, 1002534
opposite top right
National Trust for Scotland, c1920, 1002119
opposite bottom right
National Trust for Scotland, c1900, Licensor Scran
left
National Trust for Scotland, c1920, 1002614

Young St Kildan men plucking wool from their sheep, a task usually undertaken each June. Lachlan MacDonald, second from right, holds a knife to ease off stubborn clumps. Lachlan's reminiscences of St Kilda made an important contribution to David Quine's *St Kilda Portraits* published in 1988.[18]
taken by Alexander Cockburn, National Trust for Scotland, c1927, 1002025

Neil Ferguson carrying a sack of sheep wool. This image was taken on the day of the evacuation.
taken by Alasdair Alpin MacGregor, National Museum of Scotland, 1930, CLA 39

Norman MacQueen with a young Soay lamb, probably on the island of Soay in April (top). A few years later, in June 1932, Calum MacDonald helped transport 107 Soay sheep to Hirta by rowing boat to establish another flock (bottom). Before the evacuation, trips to Soay were not limited to the summer months and the islanders made occasional excursions for sheep during the winter – an arduous 18km round trip by boat.[19]

National Trust for Scotland, c1927, 1002030
National Trust for Scotland, 1932, 1002388

opposite

While wool was sometimes packed for export to the mainland,[20] when intended for island use it was cleaned, carded, spun and then woven or knitted into cloth and made into clothing. Most households in 1907 had a gathering where a group of friends and family would card all of their wool in January. The majority of spinning was undertaken on wheels like that owned by Alice MacLachan. Hand-made looms were taken down from the lofts and there was a period of intense weaving for two months during the dark winter days and nights.[21]

opposite top left
taken by R M R Milne, National Trust for Scotland, c1910, 1002507
opposite top right
taken by S MacLachan Collection, National Trust for Scotland, 1908, 1002556
opposite bottom
taken by R C MacLeod, School of Scottish Studies, c1900, 2131

Steam trawlers first came to St Kilda in the 1890s and during the winter months, for the next 40 years, the fleets of Aberdeen and Fleetwood in particular became a common site in Village Bay. One day in 1907 Alice MacLachan recalled in her diary that she was brought goods from Aberdeen, a case of Scotch, copies of the *People's Friend* and newspapers, postcards, letters and 'a splendid turbot'. The trawler pictured here (centre), the *Glenbervie*, was launched in Glasgow in 1915 and foundered after a collision in the Thames in 1940.[22]

The establishment of a Norwegian whaling station at Bunavoneader on Harris in 1904 created another regular connection for St Kilda, even providing employment for some of the men. In August 1907, the founder of the station, Karl Herlofsen, came to St Kilda with a view to setting up a possible outpost. Lachlan MacDonald recalled how the Norwegians would moor up to four whales on a buoy in Village Bay and that, if left for a few days, the whales would blow up like a 'great balloon' and smell terribly.[23]

Scores of cleitean in Village Bay were used to house the islanders' produce, providing a safe place for storage through the winter. Each one was owned by a particular family. The ground to the left of the head dyke was used in the summer for grazing cattle and sheep, keeping them away from the crops that grew in the croft land to the right.

John Keggie RCAHMS, 1986, SC1463951

St. Kilda Bay and Island of Dune

Village, St. Kilda, from E.

opposite top
Cattle graze outside the enclosures in An Lag Bhon Tuath, let out from the byres to enjoy the new growth of grass. Within the enclosures grass was protected from animals so that it could be gathered for winter feed. A few tourists wend their way up to the Gap for a stunning view of Boreray.
National Trust for Scotland, c1920, 1002143

opposite bottom
Few photographs of St Kilda's Village capture the rectangular plots where each crofter and his family cultivated their barley, oats and potatoes. Sown in April, oats would be harvested the following September, and the islanders' sheep and cattle would be kept outside the head dyke during that time. The maintenance of the buildings in Village Bay was, and indeed still remains, a continual year-round task.
National Trust for Scotland, c1920, 1002277

right
Rachel Ann Gillies with a scythe at the harvest in the fields behind the Street. Rachel became briefly famous in the newspapers in the summer of 1928 when she followed her employer, the minister's wife, from St Kilda to Lancashire. 'I would not like to go on that' she exclaimed when she saw the Big Dipper at Blackpool.[24]
National Trust for Scotland, c1927, 1002582

Tourists outnumber gannets in a view from the foredeck of a cruise ship. Cruises to St Kilda became commonplace from the 1870s and, after a hiatus between 1939 and 1959, started up again. The cruise around, and sometimes between, Stac Li and Stac an Armainn is now an obligatory part of the trip.

National Trust for Scotland, c1970, 1002581

Tourism

Tourism

In the summer of 1758, just twelve years after three Royal Navy warships had visited St Kilda in search of Bonnie Prince Charlie,[1] the Reverend Kenneth Macaulay became one of the archipelago's first tourists during an official visit. He recalled standing petrified as the St Kildans demonstrated their prowess on the crags:

> Two noted heroes were drawn out from among the ablest men of the community: One of them fixed himself on a craggy shelf: His companion went down sixty fathoms [110m] below him; and after having darted himself away from the face of a most alarming precipice, hanging over the ocean, he began to play his gambols: he sung merrily, and laughed very heartily. The crew were inexpressibly happy, but for my part, I was all the while in such distress of mind, that I could not for my life run over half the scene with my eyes.[2]

This is the earliest description of a St Kildan deliberately trying to impress a visitor with a display of their climbing skills: it was a performance that would be witnessed by many over the next 180 years. Macaulay and his fellow adventurers portrayed a visit to the islands as an experience of high drama and romance. In the aftermath of the Jacobite Rebellion, the political temperature of the Highlands and Islands cooled, opening up the opportunity for what Elizabeth Bray has called the 'Discovery of the Hebrides'.[3] Visits to St Kilda for the most intrepid became more common from about 1800, but notable early travellers, including Thomas Pennant and Samuel Johnson,[4] never reached St Kilda, and we often need to turn instead to accounts produced by lesser known writers.

In 1831, George Atkinson set a precedent when he chartered a boat specifically for the trip. Just three years later, the *Glenalbyn* became the first steamship to reach Village Bay, causing 'excitement and astonishment' among the islanders.[5] The reaction of Sir Thomas Dyke Acland that same summer is recorded in his journals and letters, which betray both a recognition of the St Kildans' abilities – one islander was noted as 'rather intelligent' – and a pressing need to judge them.[6] Tourism, even at this early date, was mixed up with morality and philanthropy.

The sharp-witted St Kildans seized the opportunity to capitalise upon the chance to sell souvenirs such as cheese, brooches and even apparently dogs.[7] At the same time, Acland provided the St Kildans with 20 sovereigns 'to help them build new houses'.[8] The impact and intervention of tourists could be both dramatic and well-intentioned, in this case providing the catalyst that brought about the wholesale redevelopment of Hirta's housing and farmland in Village Bay.

The first visit by a scheduled commercial vessel came in 1877. The steamer *Dunara Castle* arrived from Glasgow, carrying about 40 passengers on a tour of the west coast that included Skye and Harris. At this time the

Landings on St Kilda have always been a tricky business. Before the 1902 summer season, visitors to Hirta disembarked onto the rocks of Village Bay, climbing from the jolly boats of the *Hebrides*. Visits to the outer islands still require the same leap of faith.
National Trust for Scotland, c1925, 1002256
National Trust for Scotland, c1920, 1002129

St Kildans themselves, as well as the romantic landscape, were the subject of a pervasive and perverse interest. Their community was cast as an example of an evolutionary backwater – a survival of 'the past in the present'.[9] For their part, the islanders looked forward to more prosaic advantages, such as 'regular post and communication'.[10]

The *Dunara Castle* and other steamers continued to ply the route to St Kilda until the outbreak of the Great War. Some of the best-known memoirs of the islands come from this time, such as Richard Kearton's *With Nature and a Camera*, and Norman Heathcote's *St Kilda*.[11] As in the years before the war, after 1919 the steamers not only brought an influx of visitors, but also the opportunity to import foodstuffs, as well as export the islanders' own produce.[12]

Some of the most evocative material comes from a small collection of films held at the Scottish Screen Archive. Footage dating to around 1929 captures a voyage by the *Hebrides* and features rare demonstrations by the islanders of spinning wool and abseiling on the cliffs for birds.[13] After the evacuation of 1930, the steamers continued to visit during the summer, although now their only purpose was to bring the tourists, including some St Kildans, to the islands. Colour film of a trip in the 1930s shows the *Dunara Castle* in Village Bay more than 50 years after her first visit, with smoke rising from the chimneys at No. 11.[14]

A major hiatus occurred after 1939 when, for the first time in over 60 years, there were no regular trips to St Kilda. The era of modern tourism began about 20 years later, with the first visits of the NTS cruise ship SS *Meteor*. Short trips, although not a new invention, are now far more commonplace, with as many as five boats coming to the island on any one day. Some 5,000 visitors can now reach the islands each summer.

The effect of tourism on the archaeology of the island is important in two respects. Before the re-occupation in 1957, the practice of archaeology on the island was sporadic and piecemeal, being often undertaken by tourists and 'sightseers'. In this context, it is perhaps less of a surprise that a visitor like Captain Patrick Grant of the Indian Army, should have been asked to report on the souterrain for RCAHMS in 1924.[15] Early excavators like the ecclesiologist Thomas Muir were only on the island for a short time, while later archaeological studies, such as those of John Mathieson, were represented as a secondary concern. The second effect of tourism has been on the landscape. While crofts were established over much of north-west Scotland by estates and their factors, the catalyst on St Kilda came from Acland, a tourist. Furthermore, the advent of work parties on St Kilda from 1958 has itself created a continuing link between tourism and the active management of St Kilda's landscape – the sites within Village Bay now being kept in a state of arrested decay.

Looking back to the beginnings of tourism, the old steamships that once provided such a crucial link for the islands also offered trading opportunities and connections. The very existence of the community became enmeshed with seasonal visitors and, even now, their demands continue to have a great impact on both the modern and historical fabric of the islands. On today's St Kilda, it is seldom clear where tourism begins and ends, and which of us is a visitor.

It was common for the islanders to sell souvenirs to tourists from at least the 1830s. By the early 20th century this avenue was an important part of the St Kildan economy, allowing the islanders to circumvent the estate and sell their products directly. Demonstrations of their skills included prosaic tasks, such as the spinning of wool, as well as daring exploits on the cliffs.

Newsquest, 1930, Licensor Scran

National Trust for Scotland, c1920, 1002278

This apparently typical scene of tourists and islanders on Hirta during the summer of 1890 tells an unusual story. Hearing of the intended wedding of Ann Ferguson (seated centre), John Gall Campbell (in the deerstalker, standing seventh from left) came to St Kilda on a privately hired steamship with an entourage of 'north of England Whitsuntide holidaymakers' and a chosen minister, Mr Rae of Sunderland. In the 'St Kilda Fiasco', as it was dubbed by the *Hartlepool Mail*, Campbell's plan to orchestrate the wedding was rejected by Ann's father Donald (standing, second from left) and the resident minister Angus Fiddes.

National Trust for Scotland, 1890, 1002174

This unusual panoramic view was captured
by James Davie, a photographer with
an office at 19 Gordon Street, Glasgow.
Only the forenames of four of the tourists
are known – Jamie, Phoebe, Jeannie and
Alexander.

taken by James Davie, National Trust for
Scotland, c1910, 1002619

Two St Kildans, Finlay MacQueen (standing centre) and Finlay Gillies (sitting left), pose as fowlers among a group of tourists. Displaying their rods, ropes and some captured puffins, the islanders are the only identified subjects in this vignette. The two Finlays were featured in a contemporary volume, Richard Kearton's *With Nature and a Camera*, in 1897. Some 32 years later, during the great catch of sheep before the evacuation, even 'the two old men of the island' were out on the hills.[16]

National Trust for Scotland, c1890, 1002526

opposite

Douglas Scott, mountaineer and photographer, was part of the 1950 Scottish expedition to the Himalayas. Kilted and barefoot he looks out over the cliffs of Hirta, with fulmar wheeling around him. In the distance, the stacks off Boreray shine brightly with thousands of nesting gannets.

taken by Tom Weir, National Trust for Scotland, 1956, 1002264

right

A group of tourists explore the 'Mistress Stone' at Ruiaval. More than 250 years earlier, Martin described how 'every Batchelor-Wooer is by an ancient Custom obliged in Honour to give a Specimen of his Affection for the Love of his Mistress'. By bowing out from the rock over the cliffs while standing on one foot, the suitor was 'accounted worthy of the finest Mistress in the World'.[17]

National Trust for Scotland, c1970, 1002263

While rock climbing on St Kilda is largely precluded by the nesting of seabirds, both sea kayaking and diving remain popular ways of exploring the archipelago. The impressive stacks of Biorach and Shoaigh (top left) lie off the Cambir cliffs. Long considered the toughest ascent on St Kilda, Stac Biorach was climbed for seabirds in the 17th century and later as a display for tourists. The islanders' technique prefigured the modern form of rock climbing known as deep-water soloing; 'if he misseth that footstep, (as oftentimes they do) he falls into the Sea, and the Company takes him in by the small cord'.[18]

Douglas E Wilcox, 2011

The *Dunara Castle* (left) and HMS *Harebell* quietly moored in Village Bay on 28 August 1930. Launches can be seen carrying people and their belongings back and forth. The *Dunara Castle*, with Alasdair Alpin MacGregor and other visitors on board, set sail for Oban that day. The *Harebell* followed with the islanders the next day, allowing them to 'spend the last moments on the Island in calm'.[1]

Alasdair Alpin MacGregor, National Museum of Scotland, 1930. C15520

Evacuation

Evacuation

St Kilda is best known – in the popular consciousness at least – for its evacuation. More famous even than its remoteness, or the supposed specially 'evolved' big toe of its inhabitants,[2] the evacuation has become legendary.

This 'Fall of Man', often portrayed as the final act in St Kilda's history, is now entrenched in the literature describing the archipelago and an urge to explain it has become central to the historical narrative.[3] The abandonment of smaller islands was, in fact, a common response to changing circumstances – in particular, the decline in the ability of communities to remain largely self-reliant. Having said that, formal evacuation only occurred in cases where islanders petitioned the Government. Eight years after the departure from St Kilda, twelve people were taken from the tiny island of Eilean nan Ron off the coast of Sutherland.[4] In 1953, 27 people from Soay, off Skye, petitioned the Government for resettlement on Mull, leaving only Tex Geddes, the author of the *Hebridean Sharker*, on the island. The islanders were picked up by the old west coast steamer *Hebrides*, some fourteen years after her last trip to St Kilda.[5]

While the evacuation of St Kilda took place in August 1930, the size of the community had ebbed and flowed throughout the historical period. A sizeable influx of people followed the 1727–8 smallpox epidemic but 1852 saw a large exodus, as about one third of the population emigrated to Australia, partly as a response to disputes within the Church of Scotland.[6] Historical records in later years recall the continual movement of younger people in search of work. An individual croft was never likely to support parents with as many as twelve children – children who would, in turn, go on to have families of their own. Set in the wider context of the Outer Hebrides, these movements of people were not particularly unusual for the time. Indeed, a limit on the amount of available land, houses and jobs meant that emigration, of one form or another, was inevitable.

While the impetus for St Kilda's tacksman Alexander MacLeod to emigrate to America in 1773 may have been financial, the decision by 20-year-old Alexander Ferguson (son of the senior St Kildan) to leave in 1892 was surely centred on the opportunities that Glasgow had to offer.[7] The years after the Great War proved to be a tipping point on St Kilda, where the number of able-bodied people declined to such an extent that handling the boat, cultivating the fields and harvesting the cliffs became more difficult. The remoteness of the community from improving healthcare and burgeoning job opportunities was stark. Another islander, Reverend Donald John Gillies, left in 1924 to pursue a religious career. For Donald, it was the lure of far off places that was so appealing, not to mention the opportunity of an easier life.[8] That same year, the MacDonald family left for Harris, father William following his sons who had gone before him.[9] For Lachlan MacDonald, 'life had become pretty well impossible', healthcare being a particular issue as much as the difficulty in making a livelihood.[10] A brief read of Bill Lawson's family history shows

John Gillies and Rachel Ann Gillies carrying their belongings down to the quay on the day of the evacuation. John was aged 33 at the time. He had celebrated the birth of his second child Annie in early 1930, an event made bittersweet with the death of his wife Mary MacQueen in May of that same year.
Newsquest, Licensor Scran 1930

that the last generation of St Kildans found their way to various places across Scotland, from Lewis and Aberdeenshire to Glasgow, as well as to more far-flung communities in America, Canada and Australia.[11] Indeed, there were probably more St Kildans living in the outside world by 1930 than still resided on the island.

News of the evacuation brought a flurry of letters to the office of the Secretary of State for Scotland asking for permission to join the Government boat. Applications from Alasdair Alpin MacGregor, Seton Gordon, the *Daily Mirror*, the *Daily Express* and numerous press agencies were summarily refused, the Admiralty being 'hostile to the idea of publicity', while Under-Secretary of State for Scotland, Mr Tom Johnston, was 'strongly of the opinion that the utmost effort should be made to avoid the miseries of the poor people being turned into a show'.[12] The file in which these applications can be found also holds enquiries as to the possibility of buying, leasing or settling St Kilda in the event of the evacuation, as well as an offer to sell the Government '100 acres with buildings' near Guelph, Ontario, by a Canadian – 'Why not send them all here', he suggested.[13] Among these more unusual requests were two from islanders who wished to return to St Kilda to witness the evacuation. Christina (Kirsty) MacQueen wrote that she 'would like to see my brother and sister, and be present when the last remnants of my race bid the old home goodbye'.[14] A week later, she wrote again, adding that 'I am anxious to tell my people something about mainland life that has not been told them, and further, to appeal to them to make Governments, of whatever colour, do their duty and save the home that was mine and my father's', continuing with the statement that 'the whole business from start to finish has been the work of despairing Sassenachs'.[15] Christina wrote in the *Oban Times* that 'governments for the last forty years have been unheeding for our plea of better facilities during the winter', while another correspondent argued that the answer was 'fast motor boats … [that] could dash to St Kilda, choosing the best days in winter, in a few hours'.[16]

Despite a refusal from the Government to provide travel, MacGregor managed to make his way St Kilda on the *Hebrides* arriving on 23 August 1930. Acting as special correspondent to *The Times*, he captured the final days before evacuation, publishing a lengthy description in 1931.[17] In his summing up, MacGregor noted that 'Hirta will now be devoid of human interest', and it was perhaps difficult for him to imagine or realise that those St Kildans with the time and money to return would in fact come back to the island on many occasions in the following years.[18]

The evacuation of St Kilda had a profound effect on the islands' history and archaeology. This 'final' act provided ideal grist to the mill of journalists and historians, but it also created a new opportunity for archaeologists and other researchers, who could now study the abandoned landscape and the islands' natural environment. A joint expedition from Oxford and Cambridge seized their chance and arrived to undertake detailed fieldwork only a year later, but the first dedicated archaeological research was not set in motion until 1956.[19] The evacuation has created an artificial chronological horizon, which has usually been seen by archaeologists as the critical point when change, development – and in effect St Kilda's entire history – abruptly stopped.

An article in *The Scotsman* newspaper on 1 August 1930 noted that 'one of the representatives of the Department of Agriculture, along with two shepherds and their dogs, are remaining on the island'. Their assistance was helpful in gathering up 'something like 1300' sheep on Hirta and 'between 350–400' on Boreray. Sheep and cattle were taken away from Hirta by the *Dunara Castle* throughout the month of August.

Newsquest, 1930. Licensor Scran

Finlay MacQueen on his way down to the quay with his personal belongings. Lachlan MacDonald recalled that 'the older people agreed to leave but when the case came to push and they knew they were going, well, they would rather stay, but they had signed the petition and what was the good of them staying anyway'.[20]
Newsquest, 1930, Licensor Scran,

opposite
The writer Robert Atkinson's study of the kitchen in No. 10 captures the decay of ropes and twine, shoes, mousetraps and old boxes. Donald MacQueen, a St Kildan who had eighteen children between 1862 and 1894, used to warm himself by this fire.[21] His second wife Marion MacDonald died after him in 1921, but following a brief occupation by her son-in-law John Gillies, the house was abandoned in the years before the evacuation.
Robert Atkinson, School of Scottish Studies, 1938, S262

Some 27 of the 36 St Kildan evacuees
were landed at Lochaline on the Morvern
peninsula in Argyll. Some were later
installed nearby in the old workers'
cottages at Larachbeg built in 1875 to a
design by Samuel Barham. Three of the
cottages were occupied by St Kildans in
the 1930s.[22]

Newsquest, 1930, Licensor Scran

Finlay MacQueen returned to St Kilda
repeatedly during the 1930s, taking part in
the sheep transfer from Soay to Hirta in
1932 and providing demonstrations of his
fowling skills to visitors. Robert Atkinson
captured Finlay relaxing outside his home,
smoking a pipe and using his binoculars to
survey the happenings of the bay, much
as residents of the Street do now.
Returning a decade later, a few years
after Finlay's death in 1941, Atkinson
found a scene of decay and destruction,
but chose to write nothing about it
in his book *Island Going* published the
following year, perhaps intending to
write more in the future.

above
Robert Atkinson, School of Scottish Studies,
1938, S267
opposite
Robert Atkinson, School of Scottish Studies,
1948, S529

following two pages
In 1929 Malcolm MacDonald died leaving
his bed and the byre (top left and right)
to become grass-grown, while the home
of Neil Ferguson crumbled into ruin
(bottom left). As ground officer, Neil's
home and the tin-roofed Post Office he
ran were a central point of the village.
Another house (bottom right) was
abandoned in the 1920s when the widow
Marion MacQueen passed away.

top left and right
Robert Atkinson, School of Scottish Studies,
1938, S263 and 273
bottom left and right
Robert Atkinson, School of Scottish Studies,
1949, S745A, 1938, S258

The idea of a house filled with flowers, sunlight and laughter, juxtaposed with a bare, empty window frame, is of particular poignancy. The image on the left was taken in the factor's house, accommodation to the great and good since the 1860s, eight years after the evacuation. Most of the old cottages along the Street had long lost their roofs, windows and doors, leaving the detritus to be cleared up by work parties in the late 1950s.

Neil (left) and Donald Gillies, both born in the 1890s, returned to St Kilda in 1966, providing first hand commentary for the tourists aboard a cruise ship, pictured here off Soay.[23] Many native St Kildans and their descendants have taken the opportunity to visit the islands, whether in the 1930s or after the re-occupation of 1957. Some have chosen to be buried there in the small graveyard.

National Trust for Scotland, 1966, 1002321

L4128 *Arezzo* was one of the landing craft that supported Operation Hardrock and the maintenance of the base for many years. When her companion ship *Abbeville* was 'blown broadside on to the beach' on 22 May 1957, *Arezzo* came to the rescue towing her off and leaving St Kilda at 3.45am the following day. In this shot, an airman in a Caterpillar D6 tows supplies and building materials up the beach.[1]

National Trust for Scotland, 1957, 1002369

Military

Military

Some 27 years after the evacuation of St Kilda, the island of Hirta was re-occupied by a military force tasked with establishing accommodation and technical facilities for a radar station.

When an old St Kildan, Donald John Gillies, visited the island some years later, he noted with surprise that 'the moment the Army came in' there were roads, electric lights, telephones, radios and helicopters. While it may have seemed to Donald that modern technology had been introduced overnight, the military occupation of St Kilda was not without significant challenges.

The beach-landing of the Operation Hardrock Task Force began at about 11am on 16 April 1957. Wing Commander Cookson, known as 'Cookie', recorded in some detail the ensuing difficulties: 'approximately 27 tons were hand lifted over the rock beach. Tents were set up for Senior NCO's and airmen, officers and civilians were accommodated in the top two rooms of the Factor's house and the evening meal was taken on the island. From that date until 1 May 1957 the main consideration of this Advance Party was the construction of the slipway at the beach, over which the whole of the stores, plant and M.T. would in the future be ferried.' [2] Cookson continued: 'this was carried out, in spite of a gale, which lasted for approximately 24 hours, more or less continuous rain and a peat bog immediately inland from the slipway. It may be noted here that some 400lbs of explosives was used in the construction of the slipway.' The beginning of the Operation brought modernity to Hirta quite literally with a bang. Over the next five months, some 300 airmen set to work on construction, leaving a few weeks for 'winterisation' in September. Hirta was left to a skeleton force over the winter months with new advance parties arriving in spring 1958. Progress was delayed by a halt in construction in May, but the full complement was on the island later that month to oversee the completion of the work. On 27 August 'Royal Air Force St Kilda' was officially handed over to the Officer Commanding, Royal Artillery Guided Weapons Range Unit, Hebrides.[3]

In cataloguing every element of the Operation, the official records of Hardrock also touch on the experience of St Kilda for the conscripted airmen. Commander Cookson noted that 'as a correspondent of *The Scotsman* pointed out, the general attitude is one of "one more yard completed is a step nearer finishing the job and a step nearer home"'.[4] The commander also recorded that the opening of a 'wet canteen' during June 1957 'has proved very popular, particularly with the arrival of bottled beer'.[5] This military drinking mess was the origin point of that most famous of modern St Kildan establishments, the Puff Inn. Now housed in a building constructed between 1969 and 1970, the inn has been a hub of St Kildan life for the last 45 years. Although it has not been open to members of the public since 2005, those working on the island are fortunately still allowed access.[6]

The principal technical site on St Kilda was
established on the summit of Mullach Mòr
some 361m above sea level. From this
position, the radars can monitor a huge
sea area used for missile testing, while the
mast also provides for communications
to Benbecula and South Uist. The radars
and masts have been sporadically updated
since the late 1950s and this particular
array was erected in 1980.
George Geddes RCAHMS, 2014, DP197673

Among the records of hundreds of conscripted servicemen that came to St Kilda during the Operation, occasional mention is made of civilians, often representatives of government agencies or the NTS. The relationship between the airmen and the civilians must have been cordial in the main – although only after the thorny issues surrounding the proposed demolition of parts of the village were resolved.[7] The Nature Conservancy's Ken Williamson and Morton Boyd described how 'on calm summer evenings and Sunday afternoons cricket was played in the glebe – the superimposition of the English village green on an alien meadow. The crack of bat upon ball as the batsman belaboured the full toss rang across the quiet glen like a rifle-shot; and the genteel patter of applause which commended a maiden over or saluted a forceful innings might have come from the Members' Enclosure at Lord's, except that it was strangely mingled with the wayward chorus of kittiwakes in the Dun Passage.'[8] Military staff also took an interest in the archaeology and natural history of the islands. Medical officers Peter Saunby, David Boddington and James Mackay undertook small studies and expeditions, two later writing books about the islands, although Mackay's methods may not have always met with official sanction.[9] Boddington, a friend of Ken Williamson, 'effectively functioned as warden' during his time on Hirta.[10]

Every year since 1957 has brought challenges to those working on the island, whether these related to climate, logistics or the forging of compromise between the various interest groups. These have simultaneously reinforced and tested relationships between the modern islanders. By the mid 1960s a significant question mark hung over the continued operation of the range, and other agencies began to consider how they would manage St Kilda in the military's absence. The installation of the first television set on the island in 1966 brought a welcome respite for the staff, and a government decision to reinvest in the late 1960s finally brought a reprieve.[11] The late 1960s also witnessed an effort at conservation of the military gun – the garrison spent several days chipping, scraping and cleaning it, as volunteers do to this day, before finally unveiling it in a bright yellow livery which they had painted overnight.[12] The commanding officer was not amused. Weather was a continual force to be reckoned with. One severe gale in January 1974 'destroyed the sewage outlet and part of the jetty and removed a section of the cliff in front of the Messes. The top of the newly built gabion wall collapsed, the helipad was covered in rocks and the doors were blown off the pump shed by the slipway.'[13]

Life on St Kilda in the present day is conditioned by the close contact of communities with disparate backgrounds, methods and objectives. There is little doubt that the current operations of the principal government agencies and the NTS are predicated on the facilities provided by the military presence – regular helicopter landings, bulk fuel supply, the provision of electricity, drainage and medical facilities. As plans are developed to reconstruct the base once again, there is an increased urgency to record the experiences of those involved in the first days of the re-occupation of St Kilda. Their stories are every bit as valuable and interesting as those of its earlier inhabitants.

Lieutenant James Mackay of the Royal Army Educational Corps at the 'Amazon's House', Gleann Mòr. Mackay worked on St Kilda from 1959 until 1961, and published three books covering different aspects of the islands' military and communications history. In one of many St Kildan romances, he met his future wife on the island in 1959.
The Scotsman, c1959, Licensor Scran

After a lengthy career in East Africa, Dr Joe Eggeling (right) returned to Scotland in 1955 to work for the Nature Conservancy, eventually rising to become Scottish Director. On a visit in early May 1957, Eggeling is seen here petting a Soay lamb held in the arms of a young airman.[14]
taken by Tom Weir, National Trust for Scotland, 1957, 1002532

About 27 tons of material was manhandled across the beachhead in the days following 16 April 1957. The need to move diesel in 45 gallon drums was one of the least-loved tasks facing the airmen and soldiers on the island. There was great relief as bulk fuel storage and a system of pipelines made this unnecessary from 1970.

opposite top left
Newsquest, 1957, Licensor Scran
opposite top right
Newsquest, 1957, Licensor Scran
opposite middle left
National Trust for Scotland, 1957, 1002158
opposite middle right
National Museum of Scotland, Scottish Life Archive, c1957, Licensor Scran

opposite bottom left
National Trust for Scotland, c1957, 1002163
opposite bottom right
National Trust for Scotland, c1957, 1002376
above
Newsquest, 1957, Licensor Scran

Men from the military detachment take
time out to walk among the houses of
their predecessors. For some, St Kilda
occupied only a short spell in their military
or civilian careers. For others, St Kilda has
been a place of work for years or, in a few
cases, decades.
Newsquest, 1957. Licensor Scran

The bulldozer was the trusted friend of
the airmen on St Kilda during 1957–8.
High on the slopes of Mullach Sgar with
the islands of Dun and Levenish in the
background, earth is being moved for the
construction of a technical site. Hundreds
of metres of roller track were used to
move heavy materials around.
National Trust for Scotland, c1957, 1002365

The power station (opposite bottom)
completed in 1970 houses four huge
Mirlees Blackstone generator sets which
still provide power for the accommodation
and the radar sites on Mullach Mòr (left)
and Mullach Sgar (opposite top).

left
Steve Wallace RCAHMS, 2008, DP042246
opposite top
Dave Cowley RCAHMS, 2012, DP134142
opposite bottom
Steve Wallace RCAHMS, 2008, DP043411

More than 50 years after the first landing craft beached in Village Bay, the *Elektron II* is seen here in 2008 supplying the base with fuel, heavy equipment and supplies. Just as the *Abbeville* was washed onto the beach in poor weather in 1957, so the *Elektron II* suffered the same fate in 2000. Badly damaged, she was rescued by a tugboat and taken through appalling weather conditions to Belfast for repair.

George Geddes, 2008. DP212705

Investigative journalism went beyond the day-to-day on St Kilda.
A reporter explores the Iron Age souterrain.
The Scotsman, c1957, Licensor Scran

Expec

Expeditions

The first travellers to St Kilda must have prepared carefully for their trip across the daunting Atlantic waters, readying their boat, gathering food and fuel, and looking out for good weather conditions.

In the 17th and 18th centuries, the journeys made by the islands' tacksman were sometimes transformed into battles for survival – in one case during the 1690s, tacksman Alexander MacLeod and his party were blown off course by some 200km to the island of North Rona, where they were forced to spend the winter.[1] For the St Kildans themselves, careful preparation and good weather were prerequisites for visits to the outlying islands and stacks; even the closest island of Dun presented a significant and treacherous challenge, three men drowning there in 1909.[2]

A sense of danger and adventure has been at the heart of visitor and islander experience on St Kilda since the very beginning. There is little doubt, however, that the evacuation encouraged intrepid scientists, who were more than happy to take on the challenge of living and working on the archipelago without help from anyone else. The 1931 St Kilda expedition, made up of students from Oxford and Cambridge Universities, and led by 'one of the foremost scientists of his generation', David Lack, was a defining example.[3] Visitors after the evacuation also included Robert Atkinson, whose *Island Going* ranks among the best of all Hebridean travel books. Atkinson and his companion John Ainslie began their island adventure in 1935 with a trip to Handa, driving up in Atkinson's mother's car.[4] His interest went beyond ornithology and his photographs, now held at the School of Scottish Studies, form a unique record of St Kilda's archaeology and architecture.

Combining the close study of natural history with a more general description of the islands they visited, Lack and Atkinson paved the way for scientists like John Morton Boyd, for whom St Kilda would be a rite of passage on his way to becoming the Head of the Nature Conservancy. In 1969, Boyd described how 'St Kilda has always been a great event for me. My first visit to the islands in 1952 was my breaking clear of a life where mediocrity provided enough incentive for mediocre achievement. St Kilda has been my emblem of endeavours and I swear that if I were ever to make recognition of one place as having influenced me more than another, I would not choose Canada or Africa or Britain, but St Kilda.'[5] The opportunity to combine adventure with conservation was opened up to a wider community in 1958 when the first of the NTS work parties came to the island, a tradition that has continued to this day. The volunteers, many of whom have returned time and again, were behind the creation of the St Kilda Club in 1976, and the periodical the *St Kilda Mail,* whose first edition described how for 'those who prefer a challenging, strenuous but very satisfying vacation, a visit to St Kilda … is surely a must'.[6]

In that same issue, the warden, George Wood, wrote of how 'early in May Dr Mike Harris and Stewart [sic] Murray were engaged on a Puffin

St Kilda's climate offers every extreme.
Regrouping at the satellite base station,
our staff recover after a long and hot day's
surveying.
Angela Gannon RCAHMS, 2007, DP062834

Boreray has long attracted the adventurous visitor. The islanders came here for birds and eggs, and grazed their sheep on the steep slopes, while most modern visits have been centred around scientific studies, whether of seabirds or archaeology. Some of the most surprising results of the survey came when working out of this tented camp.
Ian Parker RCAHMS, 2010, DP099628

Study and swinging across the Breaches Buoy with them I enjoyed two wonderful days on Dun'.[7] Stuart Murray first came to St Kilda in 1974 and in a few short years he had taken every opportunity to explore the archipelago, reaching all of the outer islands and stacks. Stuart's abilities as a guide and climber were to have a great influence on the survey begun by Mary Harman in 1977. His contribution was no less important to the work of RCAHMS in the 1980s and 2000s, whether on Dun and Boreray, or on islands like North Rona and the Flannans. Our records of archaeological sites on the stacks still rely on the work of Murray and Harman before 1985. In his comprehensive *Natural History of St Kilda* John Love was able to venture that 'no one today … knows St Kilda as intimately'.[8] For Stuart, *Island Going* has become a way of life, where adventure and research are interwoven and inextricably linked.

On 26 February 1908, when RCAHMS first met in Edinburgh at 29 St Andrew Square and discussed how they would 'make an Inventory', they settled upon a fundamental principle – it was essential that the staff should undertake fieldwork, 'personally inspecting each monument so as to satisfy your Commissioners as to its true character and condition'.[9] Expeditions to islands became commonplace, beginning with Fidra in the Firth of Forth in 1913 and many of the Outer Hebridean islands between 1914 and 1926.[10] Adventures by boat reached an apex during the survey of Argyll, when the purchase of a dedicated vessel became necessary. In the 1980s, St Kilda presented a unique challenge, through the complications of the survey, and the uncertainties involved in travel to and from the island. Conditions were much more straightforward during the 2007 to 2009 survey, with the facilities offered by the NTS ever-improving.

Perhaps the only 'true' expedition that formed part of the project was the survey of Boreray in 2010. A team of two RCAHMS staff joined archaeologist Jill Harden, Stuart Murray and ornithologist Sarah Wanlass. Camping among the Cleitean MacPhaidein, the team endured a storm of terrifying ferocity and witnessed the richest sunsets imaginable, while recording in detail the dense archaeological landscape. Three years later, another multi-disciplinary team set out from Leverburgh at 4am with the express aim of landing on Stac an Àrmainn and recording the incredible evidence of fowling that still survives on its craggy slopes. This was sadly prevented by a tremendous sea swell, which was only appreciated when the boat was within metres of the rocks.

Far more than allowing us to assess the character and condition of St Kilda's monuments, our expeditions to the archipelago have provided a remarkable opportunity to understand the nature of living and working on the islands. It has brought into focus what was, for the St Kildan, an everyday experience. Each day presented different and wildly varying weather conditions, each element of the landscape new challenges in understanding and recording. A few areas also remained out of bounds, whether deemed too dangerous without the help of climbers, or because they are protected as the breeding grounds of important seabird colonies. Some 58 years after its re-occupation, St Kilda still offers an opportunity for adventure that is unparalleled in the United Kingdom.

Voluntary work parties have visited the island of Hirta in almost every year since 1958. Over the course of some 57 years, they have made a huge contribution to the upkeep of St Kilda's historic buildings, many of which have been held in a state of 'arrested decay'. These team photos, from 1958 and 1959, capture something of the spirit of the programme.

Led by Stuart Murray, a group reached the summit of Stac an Àrmainn on 18 June 1977. The St Kildans once harvested the seabirds from the stack, which is now out of bounds during the nesting season.
taken by Kenny Taylor, Stuart Murray Collection, 1977, DP167220

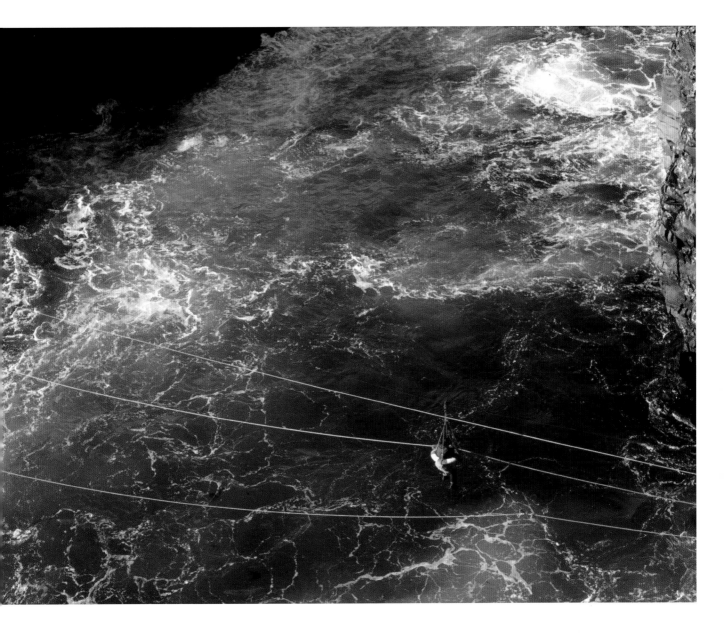

The rough waters in Village Bay rarely
provide an opportunity for a safe landing
on Dun. In 1974, Mike Harris and Stuart
Murray were set on a detailed study of
the island's puffin colony and decided
that 'rigging a cable across the gap and
hanging a breeches buoy from it was the
only sensible method'. The system was
used successfully for four seasons before
it finally succumbed to salt-spray in late
summer 1978.[11]

opposite
taken by Stuart Murray, 1974, DP166322
above
taken by Stuart Murray, 1974, DP166325

No words can express the joy and fun to be had working with the birds and mice of St Kilda. Set in such spectacular scenery, each day feels like a new one, each measurement taken a gift to science – even when a puffin bites back.

left
taken by Mike Harris, Stuart Murray Collection, 1975 DPI66348
left bottom
Newsquest, c1931. Licensor Scran
opposite
The Scotsman, c1959, Licensor Scran

Working with colleagues from the NTS, surveyors, archaeologists and a photographer RCAHMS recorded over 1600 structures on Hirta alone, ranging from the tiniest pile of stones to dykes more than a kilometre long. Each one plays a part in the story of St Kilda's archaeology. This book draws on images of St Kilda taken by RCAHMS photographers Steve Wallace (pictured above) and John Keggie, as well as those taken by the survey team.

above
taken by Ian Parker RCAHMS, 2008, DP208459
opposite top left
taken by James Hepher RCAHMS, 2007, DP037435
opposite top right
taken by Strat Halliday RCAHMS, 2010, DP099635
opposite middle left
taken by Angela Gannon RCAHMS, 2007, DP029265

opposite middle right
taken by Ian Parker RCAHMS, 2008, DP212708
opposite bottom left
taken by James Hepher RCAHMS, 2007, DP212707
opposite bottom right
taken by James Hepher RCAHMS, 2008, DP222286

The dynamic and stunning landscape of
Village Bay is always changing. A century
of decay, repair and new construction
has changed the view. The building of a
quay and successive power stations has
transformed St Kilda into a place where
modern life resembles that elsewhere.
Much the same was true of this landscape
in the 1880s.

Norman MacLeod, 1886, SC1218065

John Keggie RCAHMS, 1986, SC1467643

The St Kilda World Heritage Site

The archipelago of St Kilda was one of the first Sites in the UK to be inscribed on to UNESCO's World Heritage List (in 1986). World Heritage Sites are exceptional places of Outstanding Universal Value 'belonging to all the peoples of the world'. St Kilda was added to the List initially for the global significance of its landscape and natural heritage, which includes sheep, field-mice and wrens unique to the islands. This inscription was extended in 2004 to take account of the outstanding marine environment that includes the largest colony of seabirds in northern Europe. The quality of the islands' rich and valuable natural heritage is hardly surprising, as even by today's standards St Kilda is remote and is largely unspoilt by modern development.

In 2005 St Kilda was, unusually, inscribed as a World Heritage Site for a third time, to recognise the additional importance of its cultural heritage and historic landscape. The story of the evacuation of its last few inhabitants in 1930 is well-documented and the image of the abandoned central Street of the main island of Hirta is iconic, evocative of an isolated way of life lost in the relatively recent past. However, as illustrated within this volume, it is likely to be far less well-known, and more surprising to most people, that the islands have a rich and distinctive cultural heritage, some of it unique to St Kilda, that spans a period of more than 4,000 years.

St Kilda was the first World Heritage Site in Scotland, and remains the only natural Site. However, it has since been joined by a further five cultural Sites. The Old and New Towns of Edinburgh, one of the world's most beautiful cityscapes, was inscribed in 1995 for the contrast between the medieval Old Town and the planned Georgian New Town. The Heart of Neolithic Orkney (1999) is one of the richest surviving Neolithic landscapes in Europe, a high-quality collection of prehistoric stone monuments. New Lanark (2001) is an impressive group of 18th century cotton mills and associated mill village synonymous with Robert Owen's social reforms. The Frontiers of the Roman Empire: The Antonine Wall (2008) once marked the most northerly boundary of the Roman Empire and now forms part of an extensive transnational Site. The most recent inscription, The Forth Bridge (2015), has been recognised for its innovative design that marked a milestone in the evolution of bridges and steel construction.

These Sites represent some of the most significant aspects of Scotland's heritage and collectively highlight key points in its history. With the accolade of World Heritage Site status, they have joined a select family that attracts international interest and affection. As World Heritage Sites, they have to be protected, conserved and presented for future generations, and to achieve this each Site has a group of partners who work together under the umbrella of a holistic management plan. For St Kilda, its owners, the National Trust for Scotland, leads the way in its sustainable management, conserving its iconic structures, promoting new research and telling its unique story more widely.

St Kilda is still one of only a handful of World Heritage Sites inscribed for a combination of natural and cultural heritage. Each aspect is outstanding in its own right, but the inter-play between them is also special, with the harsh natural environment honing the human instinct for survival in a particular direction that has left its unique mark on the islands, and on Scotland's history.

Dr Lesley Macinnes
Head of World Heritage Site Co-ordination
Historic Environment Scotland

The human history of St Kilda, played out against the dramatic backdrop of the islands and sea stacks of the archipelago, continues to fascinate and beguile, drawing an increasing number of visitors to the islands. Today the main attraction is the abandoned settlement in Village Bay, which is a poignant reminder of the final phase of indigenous settlement of the island. This book, based on extensive surveys and research, brings together recent archaeological studies to depict a fuller picture of life throughout the millennia on the most remote islands of the Outer Hebrides. Of particular interest is the setting of St Kilda within the wider context of the Western Isles, drawing out the similarities where they exist, yet highlighting the unique developments to reveal a more complicated and nuanced landscape and history. The inclusion of later 20th century settlement is to be welcomed, recognising the impact of the military and the National Trust for Scotland in the continuing story of St Kilda.

When the Marquis of Bute bequeathed St Kilda to the National Trust for Scotland, the concept of World Heritage was in its infancy and no-one could have imagined that these far-flung islands would become one of only 32 World Heritage Sites inscribed for both natural and cultural criteria. As Scotland's leading conservation charity the NTS is well placed to manage the complexities of this site and has done so through a management partnership with Historic Scotland, Scottish Natural Heritage, Comhairle nan Eilean Siar and the Ministry of Defence. The Trust is mindful that it owns St Kilda on behalf of the nation and bases all management decisions on the Trust's core policies of conservation, access, enjoyment and education.

Through working with RCAHMS on this extensive archaeological survey, we have not only enhanced our own understanding of the islands to ensure best conservation practice, but we hope that we have also contributed through this publication to the wider public knowledge of these iconic islands and the small community that called them home. This book also highlights the areas where our knowledge is wanting. It is an exciting prospect that with further work we can continue to gain insight into the everyday life of those on 'the last and outmaist Ile'.

Susan Bain
Western Isles Manager
National Trust for Scotland
www.kilda.org.uk

End Notes

Introduction

1 Bellenden 1821 xlvii, trans. Boece 1527 fo. xiv, 32–3

2 Maclean 1996; see Scottish Executive 2003 for a selected bibliography; see Harman 1997, 18–37, for a discussion of the map evidence

3 Placenames within this book include examples derived from English, Gaelic, Old Norse and anglicised versions thereof, but we have generally used the name that is most commonly found in the archaeological literature, supplying the Gaelic equivalent where necessary on the first occasion that each arises

4 Secretary of State for Scotland 1985; there are now 32 sites with Mixed World Heritage Status, whc.unesco.org (page consulted 28 August 2015)

Chapter One

1 RCAHMS 1928, v

2 *Ibid*

3 RCAHMS 1997; 2007

4 RCAHMS 1928

5 RCAHMS 1928, v; while the introduction to that volume suggested that fieldwork finished in 1925, a small number of sites were recorded in 1926 eg 1928, 178

6 RCAHMS Minute Book No. 1, held in RCAHMS Library

7 RCAHMS 1928, xx, xxi, liv

8 Fox 1928, 537; Wheeler 1929, 381

9 RCAHMS Minute Book No. 1, 28 July 1914, 22 October 1914, held in RCAHMS Library

10 RCAHMS 1928, vi

11 RCAHMS 1928, 46, No. 158, figs 74–5; photographs RCAHMS IN792–4 (SC1467660–2); drawing RCAHMS IND88/1 (DP222511); Captain Charles John Patrick MacAlpine Grant (1880–1961) was born at Chinsurah, West Bengal, the son of Lieutenant Charles Grant of 102 Royal Madras Fusiliers and Agnes Georgina (née Isaacs), his wife. He was the grandson of Sir John Peter Grant, 11th of Rothiemurchus (RCAHMS MS7641/1); Captain Grant had joined RCAHMS on fieldwork in North Uist on 18 July 1928 (RCAHMS MS36/70); **9697**

12 Sands 1878, 187; reference is also made to information added by Richard Kearton (1897, 13)

13 **3960**, **9650**, **9657**

14 RCAHMS 1928, 46–7; special mention was also made of beehive shielings in the introduction (1928, xli), perhaps due to the interest of the Secretary William Mackay Mackenzie who had published a paper on this subject some fourteen years earlier (Mackenzie 1904); **3968**, **3969**

15 House of Lords Debates, 27 October 1955, vol 194 cc75–108

16 Peter Roy Ritchie b.1926 Auchtergaven; d.2006 Edinburgh

17 The sites excavated by RCAHMS staff were **9925**, **9945** and **9946**

18 Parker Pearson *et al* 2004, 18; Sharples (ed) 2012, 11

19 *Glasgow Herald*, 11 June 1956, 5; 16 June 1956, 7; RCAHMS MS7273

20 NRS DD27/3231

21 Programme of Work dated 16 April 1957, RCAHMS administrative file 102/3/I; Macaulay 2011; RCAHMS Minute Book No. 1, 27 April 1910, held in RCAHMS library

22 RCAHMS MS7273

23 Alastair MacLaren's St Kilda File, RCAHMS Batch 359/462/7

24 *Ibid*

25 *Ibid*

26 Letter from Geoffrey Stell to Mary Harman, 23 December 1976, RCAHMS administrative file 161/1 Western Isles Area, Prehistory; Harman 1977; email from Mary Harman to George Geddes, 8 May 2015, RCAHMS MS7641/1

27 Bennett's request resulted from an enquiry the NTS had received from Andy MacMillan of the Glasgow School of Art on behalf of one of his students (Gordon Fraser) for information on the buildings

in Village Bay. This revealed the dearth of information then to hand; email from Alexander Bennett to George Geddes, 12 May 2015, RCAHMS MS7641/2; letter from Alexander Bennett to John Dunbar, 29 March 1982, RCAHMS administrative files 161/1, Western Isles Area, Prehistory

28   *Ibid*

29   Letter from John Dunbar to Donald Erskine, 12 September 1983, RCAHMS administrative file 161/1, Western Isles Area, Prehistory

30   Correspondence within RCAHMS administrative file 161/1, Western Isles Area, Prehistory

31   Stell 1995, 30

32   *Discovery Excavation Scot* 1983, 42; 1984, 53

33   Stell 1995, 30

34   *Ibid*, 37

35   *Ibid*, 34

36   RCAHMS 1998

37   For example RCAHMS 1990; 1993; 1995

38   Islands subject to archaeological mapping in the years following the publication of *Buildings of St Kilda* included Canna, Eigg, Mingulay, Muck and North Rona; RCAHMS 1999; 2003; 2010

39   RCAHMS Project Plan 316 v2, dated 13 September 2006; minutes of meeting between RCAHMS and NTS, 16 June 2006

40   Jamie 2012, 131–64

41   Gannon and Parker 2012

42   Halliday 2013

43   Thomas 1862

44   The results of these projects are included within the relevant Canmore entries and noted in brief *Discovery Excavation Scot*; see also Geddes 2014 and Benjamin *et al* 2014

Chapter Two

1   Bray 1996

2   Withers 1999, 2–3

3   Martin and Monro 1999, 22, 33; **3960**, **3968**

4   eg Macaulay 1764, 50, 54

5   *Glasgow Journal*, 7–14 May, 1767; Graham-Campbell 2008, 193–204; Manville 1993, 91–113

6   Mackenzie 1905; 1911

7   Muir 1885; Muir and Thomas 1862, 225–32

8   Armit 1996, 8; see also Parker Pearson *et al* 2004, 15

9   Geddes and Grant (forthcoming); for an obituary of Sharbau (1822–1904), see Anon 1904

10   Thomas 1862; 1869, 153–95; see Dalglish 2002 for a critique; Geddes and Grant (forthcoming)

11   Carmichael 1900

12   Robson 2005, 497–8; Sands 1876; 1878, 186; John Sands died on 20 March 1900 at the age of 75 and was recorded in his death certificate as a 'retired writer' NRS Statutory Registers, Deaths, 283/00 0005; **9697**

13   Sands 1878, 190

14   Sands 1882

15   Kearton 1897, 13–16

16   The factors were John Tolmie Mackenzie (c1829–1910), followed by his son John Ferguson Mackenzie (1866–1933); MacLeod 1915

17   Heathcote 1900

18   Mackenzie 1905

19   See volumes 32, 34, 35 and 43 of the *Proceedings of the Society of Antiquaries of Scotland*; RCAHMS Photographic Albums PA186–188

20   Mathieson 1932

21   Mathieson 1925; **4972**

22   Mathieson 1928b; Ordnance Survey 1928

23   Print copies of a selection of Robert Atkinson's photographs are held at RCAHMS (H85079PO–H85215PO), and the original negatives are held by the School of Scottish Studies at the University of Edinburgh; see Atkinson 1949; Harman 1992

24   Boyd 1952; 1957; Love 2009; Poore *et al* 1949, 83

25   House of Lords Debates, 27 October 1955, vol 194, c93; MacDonald 2011, 319

26   Love 2009, 306

27   RCAHMS MS7273

28   Fairhurst 1969; **5682**

29   Notes from the School of Scottish Studies for a press conference March 1957, RCAHMS MS7272

30   Macgregor 1960; 1989

31   Love 2009, 306–8; Williamson 1946; eg Williamson and Boyd 1960

32   Williamson and Boyd 1960, 67

33   See Love 2009 for a detailed history of the study of the sheep, mice and wren

34   Williamson nd; Williamson and Boyd 1963, 140

35   MacDonald 2011

36   At this time it was the Nature Conservancy through Morton Boyd that wrote the management plan of the islands (NRS DD12/2102); the NTS took over the management of St Kilda in 2003

37   Harden and Lelong 2011, 10; Geddes 2011b

38 Mackay 1959; RCAHMS MS6339; **9700**

39 A massive clearance operation removed the remaining fixtures and fittings of the houses during the late 1950s, and subsequent consolidation and repair were often undertaken without record in line with the procedures of the day (eg NTS JD/1472/3). However, a 1968 report by a Ministry of Works' Architect commended much of the conservation work undertaken by the NTS and also suggested that invasive archaeological work was kept at a minimum due to the requirement to gain consents to work in Scheduled areas (RCAHMS MS7272)

40 Celoria 1966; Harden and Lelong 2011, 12; NRS 0027/1017; NTS 1966 Work Party Report

41 See papers in Frodsham et al (eds) 1999

42 This is held in RCAHMS collection of Ordnance Survey Archaeology Division maps and a digital copy is available as DP207928

43 This is held in RCAHMS collection of Ordnance Survey Archaeology Division maps and a digital copy is available as DP207930. The original record cards are held by RCAHMS, and much of the material, including the supporting photographs, has been added to Canmore. Jimmy Davidson's report is held within RCAHMS MS7272

44 RCAHMS MS7273

45 Cottam 1979, 36; Rutherford's contribution is probably the '1:500 plan of the village street' referred to by John Dunbar in a letter to Alexander Bennett, 14 April 1982, RCAHMS administration file 161/1, Western Isles Area, Prehistory; a Thomas Rutherford is recorded as a member of the St Kilda Club in St Kilda Mail 1987

46 Cottam 1979, 36; a copy of Tom Hetherington's report is filed in the papers of Alan Small, RCAHMS MS7256; see Hetherington 1984; 1985

47 Photocopies of Cottam's reports of 1973 and 1974 are held in the papers of Graham Ritchie, RCAHMS MS7375 and MS7393/1–3

48 Cottam 1979, 39, 61; RCAHMS MS7256; http://canmore.org.uk/c14sample/SRR-316; **9664**

49 Harman 1977; 1978; 1979a; 1982; email from Mary Harman to George Geddes, 8 May 2015, RCAHMS MS7641/1

50 Proposed Archaeological Projects on St Kilda, Recommendations by SDD, January 1984 (RCAHMS administrative file 161/1, Western Isles Area, Prehistory)

51 T A Quine 1983; D A Quine 1988

52 John Dunbar wrote to Rosemary Cramp 'at the suggestion of Donald Erskine, deputy director of the National Trust for Scotland … in the hope that you may be willing to consider the possible investment of your department in a proposed archaeological project on St Kilda', 6 February 1984 (RCAHMS administative file 161/1 Western Isles Area, Prehistory). That the universities of Bradford, Edinburgh and Glasgow were also considered in the preliminary discussions is shown by a letter from Geoffrey Stell to John Dunbar, 24 January 1984, and another from Donald Erskine to John Dunbar, 21 December 1983 (RCAHMS administrative file 161/1 Western Isles Area, Prehistory)

53 The committee comprised Colleen Batey, Alexander Bennett (followed by Philip Schrieber), Meg Buchanan, Rosemary Cramp, Norman Emery, Mary Harman, Chris Morris and Geoffrey Stell (Emery 1996, xi)

54 Emery 1988; 1990; 1991; 1996, ix; Emery and Morrison 1995; Harden and Lelong 2011, 13–14; Morris and Emery 1987

55 Harden and Lelong 2011, vii, 15; Emery and Morrison 1995, 48

56 Discovery Excavation Scot 1995, 106; 1996, 105, 1998, 100; Fleming 1995; 1997; Fleming and Edmonds 1999

57 Meharg et al 2006

58 Harden and Lelong 2011

Chapter Three

1 Armit 1996, 33–40; Gannon (forthcoming); Hardy and Wickham-Jones 2000; Wickham-Jones 1990; Wickham-Jones and Hardy 2004; see also the 'Paleolithic & Mesolithic Panel Report', Scottish Archaeological Research Framework, www.scottishheritagehub.com/content/palaeolithic-mesolithic-panel-report (page consulted 28 May 2015); **11349**; **181536**; **22202**

2 Edwards 1996; see also 'The Holocene', Scottish Archaeological Research Framework, www.scottishheritagehub.com/content/holocene (page consulted 28 May 2015)

3 Bishop et al 2011; 2013; Church et al 2012a; 2012b; 2012c; Holderness 2007, 202; Snape-Kennedy et al 2013; **10502**; **72700**; **296389**

4 eg Beveridge 1911; Scott 1935

5 Henshall 1972, 500–3; RCAHMS 1928, 73–5, No. 224; **10236**

6 Henshall 1972, 506–11; RCAHMS 1928, 78–9, No. 233; **10106**

7 Henshall 1972, 514–5; RCAHMS 1928, 77–8, No. 231; **9981**

8 Henshall 1972, 429, 504; RCAHMS 1928, 40–1, 43, 70, Nos. 126, 134, 217; **10394**; **10480**; **10491**

9 The majority of the cup marks recorded in the Outer Hebrides are of questionable date and character eg RCAHMS 1928, 56–7, No. 182; **10321**; **10395**

10 Ashmore 1981, 49–50; Ashmore 2002a, 29; **4156**

11 Armit 1996, 43–57; Branigan and Foster 2002, 33–40; Crone et al 1993; Downes and Badcock 1998; Parker Pearson et al 2004, 38–40

12 Armit 1996, 55–6; Crawford 1980; 1981; 1983; 1984; 1986; Simpson 1966; 1976; Simpson et al 2006; **10069**; **10319**; **10330**; **10502**

13 Branigan and Foster 2002, 40

14 Armit 1996, 61; Sheridan 1992; **71061**

15 Walker 1984, 103, 107–8; Radiocarbon Sample SRR-2362

16 Fleming 2005, 38–9

17 Meharg et al 2006, 1826; the most recent palynological study on St Kilda (Donaldson et al 2009) adds little to the summary presented here as to the beginning of agriculture on Hirta

18 Fleming and Edmonds 1996, 105; 1999, 152–3; **108328**

19 Classification confirmed by emails; Alison Sheridan to Angela Gannon 28 May 2015; Ann MacSween to Angela Gannon 31 March 2015; RCAHMS MS7641

20 Clarke in Harden and Lelong 2011, 67; Harden and Lelong 2011, 58–9; **347914**

21 Ballin in Harden and Lelong 2011, 135; Harden and Lelong 2011, 171

22 Fleming 2005, 43–51; for a useful summary of the evidence for modern usage of stone tools on St Kilda, see Fleming and Edmonds 1999, 152–4

23 Sands 1878, 187

24 Fleming 1994; 1995; 1997; 2005, 40–2; Fleming and Edmonds 1995, 106; 1999; **92181**

25 Harden and Lelong 2011, 37–42

26 Clarke in Harden and Lelong 2011, 38–9, 66–7, 134, 147, 150–1; Fleming and Edmonds 1999, 119, 121

27 Fleming 2005, 44, 48; Fleming and Edmonds 1999, 131–2

28 Clarke 2006; Clarke in Harden and Lelong 2011, 39

29 Fleming 2005, 44; Fleming and Edmonds 1999, 132

30   Clarke 1992, 245, Table 18.1; Saville 1994, 103–4; **1663**, **2790**, **2717**, **3422**, **3576**

31   Clarke 1992, 257; Clarke in Harden and Lelong 2011, 151

32   Clarke 2006; Clarke in Harden and Lelong 2011, 171

33   Fleming and Edmonds 1998, 100; 1999, 126; **138030**

34   Fleming and Edmonds 1999, 119

35   Fleming and Edmonds 1999, 148, 150

36   Simpson 1976; Simpson *et al* 2006; **10502**

37   Crawford 1980; 1981; 1983; 1984; Crawford and Switsur 1977, 128, 134; **10319**

38   Branigan and Foster 2002, 69; **69639**

39   Armit 1996, 91; Cowie 1987; **4288**

40   Armit 1996, 92; Sharples 1983; 1984; **4206**

41   Shepherd and Tuckwell 1976, 35; 1977, 18; **10197**

42   Sharples 1998; **140904**

43   Close-Brooks 1978, 34; 1995, 254–7; **4003**

44   Simpson 1976, 224–6

45   Meharg *et al* 2006; Walker 1984

46   Mathieson (1928a, 127) noted the existence of *Tigh na Faire* (watching house) but provided little detail, while Ritchie interpreted it as a platform (RCAHMS MS7273), and Davidson as a hut circle (1967); **9648**

47   Davidson 1967; Fleming 2005, 51–4; Macgregor 1960; **9654**

48   Davidson 1967; **3963**; **3970**

49   Fleming 2005, 54–6; **244228**

50   See Harman 1997, 92, for a comment on the authorship of Macaulay's *The History of St Kilda*, 1764

51   Macaulay 1764, 58; **3969**

52   Gibson (ed) 1695; Macaulay 1764, 54, 57–61; Stukeley 1740; Toland 1814

53   Curtis (2010, 176) also relates that Keith Payne drew what he took to be the one surviving stone of Macaulay's stone circle on the slopes of Sunadal in the mid 1980s; Sharkey and Payne 1986, 157–8; **3969**

54   Mathieson 1928a, 130; Sands 1878, 189

55   Davidson 1967; **9642**

56   Curtis and Curtis 2007, 198–9; 2008, 178

57   Crawford and Switsur 1977, 129, 135; http://canmore.org.uk/c14sample/Q-1458; **10319**

58   Close-Brooks 1995, 263; http://canmore.org.uk/c14sample/GU-1174; Dunwell *et al* 1995, 284; http://canmore.org.uk/c14sample/GU-3488; **4003**

59   Mackenzie 1905, 398

60   Mackenzie 1905, 398; 1911, 6

61   Mackenzie 1905, 398, 1911, 7; Davidson (1967) thought this might be another souterrain; **9694**

62   Mackenzie 1911, 7

63   Ordnance Survey 1928

64   Ordnance Survey 1928; **9695**

65   Stell and Harman 1988, 49; **9684**

66   Simpson 1976, 224; **10502**

67   Crawford 1964; 1979; **10196**

68   Close-Brooks 1995, 261–4; **4003**

69   Feachem 1964

70   Davidson 1967; **9664**

71   Cottam 1979, 39; http://canmore.org.uk/c14sample/SRR-316; **9664**

72   Fleming 2005, 38–9; Harden and Lelong 2011, 101; Harman 1997, 60

73   Harden and Lelong 2011, 165–7; the 1995 excavation at The Gap did not provide conclusive results, although the excavator preferred a prehistoric explanation (Turner 1996); **9665**

74   Harding and Dixon 2000; **4020**

75   Harding and Gilmour 2000; **4100**

76   Parker Pearson and Sharples 1999; **9825**

77   Fojut 1982; Sharples (ed) 2012, 27; **108290**

78   Lawson 1994; MacLeod 1927, 34; **10474**

79   Campbell 1991; **10337**

80   Young and Richardson 1962; **9949**

81   Fairhust 1971; **9947**

82   **9957**

83   Armit 2006; **4009**

84   Interim reports on The Udal are held in RCAHMS Library; Crawford and Switsur 1977, 129; Crawford and Selkirk 1996; **10319**

85   Sharples (ed) 2012; **108290**

86   Geddes forthcoming; Thomas 1869; **10151**; **10155**; see also Taigh Talamhanta (Young 1955); **9721**

87   Sands 1878, 186; Sharbau 1860; **9697**

88   Sands 1878, 186

89   Kearton 1897, 14, plate

90   MacLeod 1939, 94

91   Kearton 1897, 14; see digital images related to **9697**

92   Mathieson 1928a, 125–6, figs 2–3; RCAHMS 1928, 46, No. 158; see end note Introduction 11

93   Compare RCAHMS photographs SC1453652 (1957) and SC1463872 (1986) related to record **9697**; RCAHMS MS7272; *contra* Harden and Lelong 2011, 157

94   Stell and Harman 1988, 48–9

95   Harden and Lelong 2011, 139–58

96   *Ibid*, 157–8; Harman 1997, 64; Stell and Harman 1988, 48–9; see also Miket 2002

97   Clarke in Harden and Lelong 2011, 147

98   *Ibid*

99   MacSween in Harden and Lelong 2011, 151

100   *Ibid*

101   Armit 2006, 112, 115; Campbell 1991; MacSween in Harden and Lelong 2011, 153; Parker Pearson and Sharples 1999, 210–11

102   Harden and Lelong 2011, 47; http://canmore.org.uk/c14sample/GU-9816; **302991**

103   *Ibid*, 21–9

104   MacSween in Harden and Lelong 2011, 35; **9825**; **10337**

105   Harden and Lelong 2011, 55–74; Sands 1878, 188; **9650**

106   Harden and Lelong 2011, 69; Sands 1878, 188

107   For information on the name, see Harman 1997, 336

108   Martin 1749, 22; Martin and Monro 1999, 251; **3968**

109   Martin 1749, 22; Martin and Monro 1999, 251

110   Macaulay 1764, 54–5

111   Kennedy and Thomas 1875, 705

112   Kennedy and Thomas 1875, 705, 710–1

113   Geddes forthcoming; RCAHMS 1928, 116–18; Thomas 1869, 165–7; **10151**

114   Thomas 1869, 173–5

115   Fleming 2005, 58

116   Sands 1878, 189

117   Mathieson 1928a, 130; Ordnance Survey 1928

118   Williamson and Boyd 1960, 104, 105; see also Williamson and Boyd 1963, 166–8

119   Martin 1749, 10–11; Martin and Monro 1999, 243; **9657**

120   Macaulay 1764, 48

121   Kennedy and Thomas 1875, 704, 709

122   Wilson 1842, 2, 4–5

123   Sands 1878, 189–90

124   Mathieson 1928a, 131

125   **303033, 303038, 303039**

126   RCAHMS H85189 PO (1953) and B356/1/5/34738–46 (1977); **346673**

Chapter Four

1   Harding and Gilmour 2000; Parker Pearson and Sharples 1999; **4100**; **9825**

2   Armit 1996, 162–78; Crawford and Switsur 1977, 130; Parker Pearson *et al* 2004, 106–14; **4009**; **4130**; **10319**

3   Armit 1996, 180; Parker Pearson *et al* 2004, 115

4   Ashmore 2002b, 153; Parker Pearson *et al* 2004, 117–21; http://canmore.org.uk/c14sample/AA-48605; **4357**; **139163**

5   Downes and Badcock 1998, 101; **140108**

6   Fisher 2001, 12, 26, 106, 108–9; RCAHMS 1928, 104, 126, Nos. 356, 438; **10189**; **21384**

7   Fisher 2001, 106; **21384**

8   Fisher 2001, x

9   Fisher 2001, 113, 116; Lawson 1997; **3993**; **167335**

10   Fisher 2001, 2 and notes; **21649**

11   Fisher 2001, 2 and notes; **23100**

12   Fisher 2001, 2–3; **10766**; **22158**

13   Fisher 2001, 136; RCAHMS 1984, 170–82, No. 354; **22361**

14   RCAHMS 1928, 165–6, No. 535; **11187**

15   Fisher 2001, 101; Gannon and Halliday 2002; RCAHMS 1928, 217, No. 679; RCAHMS 1999; **10766**

16   RCAHMS 1928, 3–4, No. 9; re-surveyed by RCAHMS in 2009; **1472**

17   Thacker (forthcoming, a)

18   Fisher 2001, 3; Robson 2005, 12

19   Fisher 2001, 13–14, 114; Harman 1979b; Stell and Harman 1988, 17–18; **9644**; **9645**; **319501**

20   Gannon and Parker 2012, 37; RCAHMS 2009, 195

21   Sands 1878, 186

22   Kennedy and Thomas 1875, 705; Mathieson 1928a, 130; **3966**

23   Robson 2005, 26

24   Macaulay 1764, 71–2

25   Whitelock (ed) 1961, 35

26   Whitelock (ed) 1961, 36

27   Anderson 1990, 255–6, 258

28   Andersen 1990, 133

29   Armit 1996, 186; Branigan and Foster 2002, 104; Parker Pearson *et al* 2004, 127

30   Armit 1996, 188; Barber 1985, 70

31   Parker Pearson *et al* 2004, 130–42; Sharples (ed) 2005, 6; information from MacDonald and McHardy 2007, cited in **334212**

32   Armit 1996, 192; **334732**

33   Neighbour and Burgess 1996; **4130**

34   Armit 1996, 191–2; Crawford 1975; Crawford and Switsur 1977, 124–36; **10319**

35   MacLaren 1974; **9945**

36   Sharples 2005; **108290**

37   Parker Pearson 2012, 418

38   Anderson 1875, 555; **9715**

39   *Ibid*; **10515**

40   *Proc Soc Antiq Scot* 9 1873, 446; **9893**

41   MacLeod 1916, 184; *Proc Soc Antiq Scot* 68 1934, 97; **4001**

42   Dunwell *et al* 1995; Welander *et al* 1988; **4007**

43   Taylor 1969, 120–3

44   Taylor 1969

45   Hutchinson 2014, 36–45; Taylor 1969

46   Harman 1997, 71, 326; Taylor 1969, 126

47   Coates 1990; Harman 1997, 53, 71, 337; Taylor 1969, 127–9

48   Mackenzie 1905, 397; 1911, 3; **9660**

49   Kearton 1897, 13; *Proc Soc Antiq Scot* 31 (1896–7), 153–4; **9697**

50   'It now appears that only one was lost, and the other acquired for the National Museum of Copenhagen (acc. no. 10 521: 1848: 118)', information from Ordnance Survey 495 record card; Anderson 1875, 555–6; Worsaae 1872, 420; **9699**

51   Harman 1997, 69–70; *Scots Magazine* 29 (June 1767), 326

52   Emery 1996, 79, 102, 179; Emery and Morrison 1995, 41; **9686**

53   Macgregor 1960, 25; Williamson and Boyd 1960, 63–4; **9671**

54   Emery 1996, 107–44; Stell and Harman 1988, 19, 42–3

55   Harden and Lelong 2011, 29–33, 182; **302991**

56   Fleming 2005, 65–6

57   Dunbar 1978; Miers 2008; RCAHMS 1928 107, 126–8, 152–4, Nos. 369, 439, 504; **10130**; **10835**; **21390**

58   Miers 2008; RCAHMS 1928, 100, 108, 129, Nos. 342, 371, 440; **9880**; **9962**; **21394**

59   Armit 1996; Badcock (ed) 2008; RCAHMS 1928, 51–3, Nos. 171–2; **10294**; **10364**

60   RCAHMS 1928, 39, No. 119; **10474**

61   RCAHMS 1928, 32–7, No. 111; Steer and Bannerman 1977, 97–8; **10521**

62   Miers 2008, 386; RCAHMS 1928, 30–1, No. 107; **10380**

63   Miles 1989; RCAHMS 1928, 31–2, 37, Nos. 109–10, 112–3, 115; **10468**; **10470**; **10475**; **10527**; **10535**

64   Miles 1989, 166, 175; **10470**

65   Branigan and Foster 2002, 112

66   Parker Pearson *et al* 2004, 149–51; Sharples 2005, 153–5; eg http://canmore.org.uk/c14sample/OxA-10292; **108290**

67   Armit 1996, 208; Armit *et al* 2008, 53–6; **10069**

68   Armit *et al* 2008, 58

69   Armit 1997, 907; **10066**

70   Symonds 2012, 294, 302; **77962**

71   Branigan and Foster 2002, 105–6, 112–13; **337965**

72   Thomas 1862; **72083**; **75023**; **133726**; **313882**

73   Robson 2005, 19

74   Harman 1997, 68; Robson 2005, 26

75   Martin 1749, 43; Martin and Monro 1999, 264

76   Martin 1749, 43; Martin and Monro 1999, 265; the present burial ground is about 70m in circumference

77   Martin 1749, 45; Martin and Monro 1999, 266

78   Macaulay 1764, 69, 71

79   Mathieson 1928b, 81

80   Mathieson 1928a, 124

81   Ordnance Survey 1928; Sands 1878, 187; **9655**

82   Wilson 1842 (2), 38; the depiction of a ruinous chapel by Wilson (1842 (2), 35) suggests how it may have appeared in the earlier 19th century

83   Mackenzie (1911, 23) describes how they 'built a massive wall around the burial ground', and the level ground surface within the interior, much higher than the surrounding fields, owes its profile to the same phase of work; **139741**

84   Wilson 1842 (2), 38

85   Lelong and Harden 2011, 78–9; Mathieson 1928a, 124; **9641**

86   Lelong and Harden 2011, 70, 72, 77, 79; Macaulay 1764, 71

87   Mathieson 1928a, 124; 1928b 81; **9647**

88   Harden and Lelong 2011, 9; Ovenden 2007, 199

89   Macaulay (1764, 88–9) describes the plain and the sacred stone, now known as the Milking Stone, in some detail; Mathieson 1928a, 126–7; Ordnance Survey 1928; Robson 2005, 26; **9649**; **294773**

90   Kennedy and Thomas 1875, 705

91   Kennedy and Thomas 1875, 705; see also Robson 2005, 4, 28; the death of a 'Eupham MacCrimon' aged 88 was recorded on 31 May 1869 (NRS Statutory Registers, Deaths, 111/03 0033); **3966**

92   Mathieson 1928a, 130; the principal evidence for pilgrimage in the Outer Hebrides lies in the post-Reformation continuation of practices that are detailed in historical accounts (Thacker forthcoming, a, b); **3971**

93   Martin 1749, 13–14; Martin and Monro 1999, 245–6

94   Martin 1749, 13; **3962**

95   Macaulay 1764, 95–6; see end note Chapter 4, 92

96   Stell and Harman 1988, 54; **294895**

97   The well of the servant of the church; Harman 1997, 332; Ordnance Survey 1928; **294755**

98   Harman 1997, 332; Macaulay 1764, 101; **9659**

99   Harman 1997, 332; Macaulay 1764, 99

100   Ordnance Survey 1928; **9658**

101   Harman 1997, 332; Ordnance Survey 1928; this well head features in historic photographs eg NTS Photo Library 1002549

102   Martin 1749, 13–14; Ordnance Survey 1928

103   Mathieson 1928a, 124–5; **9651**

104   Ordnance Survey 1928; **310371**

105   Macaulay 1764, 83

106   Harman (1997, 74) suggests this stood on Mullach Geal; Macaulay 1764, 83

107   Macaulay 1764, 95; Martin 1749, 13; **3962**

108   Macaulay 1764, 95–6

109   Kennedy and Thomas 1875, 705; Mathieson 1928a, 130; Sands 1878, 189; **3966**; **9696**

110   Harman 1997, 74, plan; Mathieson 1928, 129; Sands 1878, 189; it is possible that the enclosure could represent the remains of one of the six or seven chapels of St Kilda, mentioned in the 18th century (see end note Chapter 4, 23); **3961**

111   Fisher 2001, 101; Somerville 1899; **10766**; **320027**

112   Martin and Monro 1999, 22–23

113   Evans 1966, 189–190; Gibbons 2014; see end note Chapter 4, 92

114   Macaulay 1764, 42; Williamson 1957, 2; **9661**

115   Geddes 2011a; Stell and Harman 1988, 44; **9700**

116 Williamson 1958; 1960; Williamson and Boyd 1960; 1963

117 Nimlin 1979, 69; Stell 1995, 30; Stell and Harman 1988, 15

118 Ordnance Survey 495 record card for site NF19NW 15 (desk based assessment by Beverley Roy Stallwood, field visit by Jimmy Davidson), held in RCAHMS archive; Davidson 1967; **9661**

119 Stell and Harman 1988, 21–3, 43–8; **9672**; **9677**; **9678**; **9680**; **9681**; **9682**

120 Quine 1988; Quine (ed) 2001; Wilson 1842

121 Fleming 2005, 134

122 Fleming 2003

123 **10384**; **10385**

124 Geddes 2011a; Sands 1878, 35; **9700**

125 Geddes 2011a; Williamson 1957

126 Kearton 1897, 45; Stell and Harman 1988, 46; Williamson and Boyd 1960, 59–60; **9677**

127 Mackie 2013

128 Stell and Harman 1988, 27

129 Geddes 2011b

130 Harman 1997, 77, 152; Martin 1749, 12

131 Geddes 2011b; Harman 1997, 326; Martin 1749, 12; for Seton, the Roman goddess Diana was a more appropriate translation (1878, 306)

132 Geddes 2011a, 15; Muir and Thomas 1862, 230

133 Martin 1749, 21–2

134 Geddes 2011b

135 Calder 1958; see Geddes (2011a, 2011b) for a detailed discussion of comparative material for Hirta's corbelled structures

136 Fleming 2005, 23, citing Parker Pearson *et al* 2004, 106–14; **4130**, **9825**

137 Miers 2008, 383

138 **4187**

139 Muir and Thomas 1862, 226–7

140 Thomas 1862, 135; 1870; Muir and Thomas 1862, 227

141 Thomas 1862, 127; a number of the 'beehive' sites recorded by Thomas and others have been revisited by RCAHMS in recent years eg **75023**, **313882**; see also Mackenzie 1904; RCAHMS 1928, xli; Geddes and Grant (forthcoming)

142 Stell and Harman 1988, 27

143 Martin 1749, 21–2

144 **3968**; **310324**; **315929**

145 Fleming 2005, 58; Kennedy and Thomas 1875, 705; Macaulay 1764, 54–5; Thomas 1870, 153–5

146 Gannon and Parker 2012; see also Halliday 2013

147 SASC MS38449/5/3

148 **315924**

Chapter Five

1 Martin and Monro 1999, 329; RCAHMS 1928, xxi, citing Monro 1884

2 MacLeod 1927, 2–8

3 Lawson 1994; MacLeod 1927, 28, 46, 61; RCAHMS 1928, 39, No. 119; **10474**

4 Harman 1997; RCAHMS 1928, 152–4, No. 504; Simpson 1938; **10835**

5 MacLeod 1939, 69

6 Dodghson 1998; Newton 2009

7 Dodgshon 1998, 8

8 MacLeod 1927, 70–1; located at NM 479 580

9 *NSA* 14, 329–30; see also the battle at Coire na Creiche in 1601; **10939**; **10940**; **11233**

10 Fleming 2005, 28, 66–71

11 Dodgshon 1998, 33; a tacksman was a landholder of intermediate legal and social status in Scottish Highland society

12 MacKinnon and Morrison 1968a, 24; 1970, 201–2

13 MacLeod 1939, 71

14 Dodghson 1998, 75–6; MacLeod 1938, 145–61

15 Dodghson 1998, 75

16 *Ibid*

17 RCAHMS 1928 152–4, No. 504; Simpson 1938; **10835**

18 Miers 2008, 235; **100546**

19 This was perhaps used by Charles Robertson, the MacLeods' factor from 1772–1811; **100547**

20 Simpson 1938, xxv

21 MacLeod 1939, 114–15

22 MacLeod 1939, 94

23 RCAHMS 1928, 37, No. 114; **10493**

24 RCAHMS 1993, 11; **71351**

25 An example was recorded at Balranald on North Uist in 2012; **318499**

26 RCAHMS 1993, 5; the population of Pabbay in the early 19th century reached 323 (Lawson 2002, 88)

27 Harman 1997, 125

28 These totals were reached by undertaking a search in the Canmore database

29 Canon MacLeod (1852–1934) was the youngest son of the 25th chief of MacLeod, and author of three texts on the history of the family published in 1927, 1938 and 1939; MacLeod 1939, 79–86

30 Mary Harman's photographs taken in 1976 have been lodged with RCAHMS; field visits by Ordnance Survey 1965 and RCAHMS 2011 are recorded in individual Canmore entries; see also The Papar Project, Pabbay, www.paparproject.org.uk (page consulted 9 June 2015)

31 The Pabbay townships are recorded as **10384**; **10385**; **75706**; two candidates for tacksman's houses are located at NF 88956 86993 and NF 90404 88163 respectively

32 Centred NF 8936 8782; **318635**

33 Lawson 1994; **75706**

34 Lawson 1994, 15–6; 2002, 83

35 *Stat. Acct.* 10, 350–7

36 **318668**; **318776**

37 **318630**; **318637**

38 Bald 1829

39 **312646**; **312657**; **313282**; **318620**

40 RCAHMS 1993; **10914**; **711154**

41 RCAHMS 1993, 5, 9, citing Ordnance Survey 6-inch (1880; 1904)

42 RCAHMS 1993; **71214**

43 RCAHMS 1993, 9

44 Baldwin 1974; *NSA* 2, 321–2

45 Visits to North Rona, Sula Sgeir and the Flannan Isles have begun to improve the record of structures on these islands that are associated with fowling

46 Islands Book Trust 2004

47 Murray 2008

48 Martin and Monro 1999, 22

49 The mapping of the archaeological landscape of Mingulay by RCAHMS in 2003 recovered no evidence for structures associated with fowling, although the practice there is well attested (Buxton 1995, 79–83)

50 Tait 2012, 272–9

51 Emery 1996, 102; Low 1879, 28–9; **9423**; **9454**

52 Martin 1749, 7

53 Fleming 2003, 377; Quine (ed) 2001, 42; Turner 1999

54 Devon County Council Archive 1148M/23/F/19; Fleming 2003, 381–4; 2005, 135–6; Quine 1988, 11; Stell and Harman 1988, 3

55 Fleming 2003, 380, illus 3

56 Fleming 2003; Stell and Harman 1988; the final 1:1,000 ink drawing undertaken as part of the 1983–6 RCAHMS survey is available as a digital image RCAHMS DP209309; the twelve pencil drawings that formed the original 1:500 survey are available as digital images RCAHMS SC1451120–1, SC1451147–56

57 Harden and Lelong 2011, 118, 120, 130–1, 137; Will *et al* 2005, 145–6; 2006, 174

58 Macaulay 2009, 111; Stell and Harman 1988 45–6, No. 17; **9676**

59 90% of the population of Foula died from smallpox in 1720 (Harman 1997, 90); North Rona's population was wiped out in 1695 or thereabout, ostensibly by starvation caused by rodents eating all the grain (Robson 1991, 28–31)

60 Robson 2005, 140 citing Macaulay, NRS General Assembly papers, CH1/5/52, 255, 265, 338–41

61 Harman 1997, 97; Morrison 1969, 66–7

62 Stell and Harman 1988, 32, citing Lawson MS (unlocated), cf Lawson 1993

63 Harman 1997, 91–2; Macaulay 1764, 42–4

64 Mackie 2013

65 Holden *et al* 2001

66 Robson 2005, 116

67 Harman 1997, 67; Macaulay 1764, 69–72

68 Emery 1996, 137; Martin 1749, 52

69 Buchan 1818, 11; Martin 1749, 10; Sharbau 1860; **347919**

70 Harman 1997, 198; Martin 1749, 15–16, 49

71 Macaulay 1764, 30

72 Perhaps the best example of an enclosure which predates the system of crofts, but is reconstructed and continued in use, is located at NF 1028 9937; another, showing the same pattern of reconstruction, is located at NF 1008 9951

73 Fleming and Edmonds 1999, 140–6

74 Fleming and Edmonds 1999, 146

75 *Ibid*

76 Macaulay 1764, 27

77 **296522**

78 Harman 1997, 96–7; Macaulay 1764, 39–41

79 Harman 1997, 92

80 Harden and Lelong 2011, 75–87

81 Harden and Lelong 2011, 86

82 Harden and Lelong 2011, 87–96; Stell and Harman 1988, 23

83 Harman 1997, 192–3

84 Fleming 2005, 65

85 Williamson and Boyd 1960, 74, 105–6; **315925**

86 It has been suggested that the long tradition of transhumance finally ended as a result of the smallpox epidemic when the population had to be quickly rebuilt from elsewhere, but there is no confirmation that this was so (Harman 1997, 152; Stell and Harman 1988, 32). Macaulay (1764) does not appear to describe the practice

87 Martin 1749, 12

88 Thomas 1869, 176

89 Cottam 1979; Davidson 1967; Harman 1997, 152–5; Stell and Harman 1988, 27–8, Nos. 25–7, 29; Williamson 1958

90 Thomas 1869, 176

91 Thomas 1869, 176, fig 25

92 Harden and Lelong 2011, 33

93 Gillies 2010, 112–13

94 **10154**; **21948**; **75023**; **314273**

95 Harman 1997, 155; **3970**

96 Mackenzie 1911, 12

97 **301253**

98 **302248**

99 Geddes 2011b, 19

100 This idea was first mooted in Geddes 2011b, 19

101 Fleming 2005, 51–3; Fleming and Edmonds 1999, 148

102 Fleming and Edmonds 1999, 148

103 **301432**; **301433**, **301435**; **301438**

104 **298391**

105 This structure was photographed by Roy Ritchie in 1957, RCAHMS SC1463215; **301433**

106 **301438**

107 Geddes 2009a; Harman's photographs are held at RCAHMS B356/1/1/106/12 etc

108 It continued in use as a hunting ground into the 20th century (Gillies 2010, 108)

109 Geddes and Watterson 2013, 108; Harman 1997, 211; **296518**

110 Harman 1997, 155–9

111 Martin 1749, 20, 23; **3967**; **347920**

112 Harman 1997, 156–7 (Soay Nos. 29, 33); Sands 1876, 188–9; Harman's photographs are held at RCAHMS B356/1/2; **347921**; **347922**

113 Kearton 1897, 55; Sands 1878, 188; **3965**

114 Harman 1997, 157; **303016**; **303023**

115 **301066**; **303001**; **303018**; **303025**; **303033**; **303038**;

116 **320837**

117 **310338**

118 **310337**

119 **310344**

120 **310312**

121 **296509**

122 **302060**; **302063**; **317311**; **317313**

123 A recent summary is provided by Geddes and Watterson 2013

124 Martin 1749, 22

125 Macaulay 1764, 48

126 Fleming 2005, 94–5; Harman 1997, 164–6; Macaulay 1764, 128; Martin 1749, 15

127 **296516**; **296524**

128 Located at NF 0979 9950 and NF 1044 9969

129 This is particularly clear in the area centred NF 0979 9950 and encompassed by Cleitean 104, 114, 892 and 894

130 Photograph RCAHMS SC1483255, 1989

131 **9664**; **296524**

132 Davidson 1967; see reinterpretation in Harden and Lelong 2011, 166

133 **9664**

134 eg **310352**; **315908**

135 **315899**

136 Macaulay mentions the storage of 'peats, eggs and wildfowl' in cleitean (1764, 48)

137 Geddes and Watterson 2013

Chapter Six

1 The MacNeils of Barra succumbed to debt in 1840 and the island was sold to the soldier and politician Lieutenant Colonel Gordon of Cluny, Aberdeenshire (Branigan and Foster 2002, 138–9). Gordon had purchased South Uist and Benbecula only three years earlier from Reginald George MacDonald, 'an Eton and Oxford educated spendthrift' (Stewart 1999, 208). The Mackenzie island of Lewis was sold in 1844 to Sir James Matheson who built Lews Castle, and North Uist was sold by the MacDonalds of Sleat to Sir John Powlett Orde in 1855 (Miers 2008, 263, 321)

2 Dodgshon 1998; MacLeod 1939, 12, 71

3 At the outbreak of the American War of Independence in 1775, Alexander MacLeod, St Kilda's former tacksman (who had been born on Pabbay), took up arms for Britain and played a part as a Captain in the disastrous Battle of Moore's Creek in 1776, when two of his brothers were killed. After imprisonment, he joined The Earl Cornwallis 'and suffered more hardships from which he died at Charlestown in January 1782', at only 54 years of age; MacKinnon and Morrison 1970, 229–30; see also Hunter 2010

4 MacLeod 1939, 13, 97–8, 132–3

5 MacKinnon and Morrison 1968b, 51–5

6 Knox 1787, 158–65; MacKinnon and Morrison 1968b, 55–65, 73–4

7 MacKinnon and Morrison 1968b, 55–8; **104485**

8 **10522**

9 Bumsted 2005; MacKinnon and Morrison 1968b, 73–4

10 Buchanan 1997, 18; Hunter 2000, 49–71; MacKinnon and Morrison 1968b, 94–5; MacLeod 1939, 115–18; Parker Pearson *et al* 2004, 173

11 MacKinnon and Morrison 1968b, 75–6

12 MacKinnon and Morrison 1968b, 75

13 Harman 1997, 99; MacKinnon and Morrison 1968b, 75; Donald MacLeod died in Edinburgh on 22 April 1813. Something of his biography can be gleaned from a petition by him to the East India Company in 1793 in which his career and circumstances are set out at some length, including a note that he took part in 'nineteen sieges and eight general actions and was thrice wounded' (MacLeod 1796)

14 Carlyle 2015

15 MacLeod 1939, 132–3

16 Harman 1997, 98

17 Fleming 2005, 123

18 Harman 1997, 101

19 *NSA* 15, 114; Robson 2005, 343

20 McNeill 1851, Appendix A, 44

21 Lawson 2002, xii

22 Lawson 2002, 8, citing the notebook of Alexander Carmichael, 1870; University of Edinburgh Special Collections Coll–97/CW116/53

23 Fleming 2005, 142–3; Richards 1992; the Disruption of 1843 was a nationwide schism within the established Church of Scotland, which had a great impact upon the St Kildans

24 Hunter 2000, 205–28

25 Royal Commission of Inquiry into the Condition of Crofters and Cottars in the Highlands and Islands; see Cameron 1986

26 The Congested Districts Board was established in 1897; Geddes 2009b

27 **123236**; **318630**; **318631**; **318637**

28   **10384**

29   RCAHMS 1993; **71351**

30   Macaulay 1764, 39–41

31   Geddes (forthcoming)

32   Campbell 2005; Fleming 2005, 123–124; *NSA* Parish of Urquhart and Logie

33   Harden 2008; Stell and Harman 1988, 35–6, No. 2

34   **21382**; **36215**; **118898**

35   Miers 2008, 105–6, 302, 319, 325; **69531**; **171132**; **238220**

36   Robson 2005, 305

37   Harman 1997, 67; Macaulay 1764, 69–72

38   Mackenzie 1911, 23; **139741**

39   Robson 2005, 320

40   Mackenzie, referring to the discovery of antiquities, described how 'in clearing the glebe, I removed a mound' and 'in clearing for agricultural purposes a small park near the centre of the glebe, … I came upon a flat stone' (1911, 5, 7)

41   Mackenzie 1911, 21

42   Sharbau 1860

43   Mackenzie 1911, 21; Robson 2005, 340

44   Mackenzie 1911, 21; the saw pit stands immediately south-east of Cleit 1; Cleit 2 is known as the 'Coffin Cleit'

45   Fleming 2005, 128–31

46   Stell and Harman 1988, 7

47   Geddes and Watterson 2013, 105

48   Sharbau 1860; Stell and Harman 1988, 39–40; **9688**; **300979**

49   Emery 1996, 39–105; T A Quine 1983; D A Quine 1988; **9686**; **300989**

50   Harman 1997, 163–4; Hay 1978

51   Mackenzie 1911, 21; Robson 2005, 340

52   Sharbau 1860; **300986**; **300987**

53   Mackie 2013; Stell and Harman 1988, 21; Blackhouses D, F, G, K, Q, S and V

54   Mackenzie 1911, 21; Robson 2005, 343–4; Thomas 1869, 158

55   Mackenzie 1911, 21–2

56   Sharbau 1860; there are midden pits associated with Blackhouses A, B, G, O, P and T

57   Geddes and Grant (forthcoming)

58   Blackhouse A plan; **139442**

59   Stell and Harman 1988, No. 11, 42–3; **9671**

60   Lawson 1993, 15; Sharbau 1860; **139392**; **300977**

61   Williamson and Boyd 1960, 63–4; see also Macgregor 1960, 25

62   Emery 1996, 107–44, ; Stell and Harman 1988, No. 11, 42–3; the report by Norman Emery provides a useful summary of comparable structures in the Hebrides

63   Harman 1997, 150

64   Geddes and Grant (forthcoming); Robson 2005, 442–6

65   Harman 1997, 150; the quality of the masonry is variable, suggesting that most were constructed by the St Kildans themselves

66   Houses 5–7, 10–11, 13–14 appear to have yards constructed in the 1860s

67   These benches are not shown in the photo on page 92

68   Stell and Harman 1988, 39–9, 40–1; House 8 has an internal area of 35m²; Blackhouse G has an total internal area of 29m² including the northern unit and the byre; **9686**; **9689**

69   For a description of wool processing, including the production of tweed, see Harman 1997, 176–80

70   NTS St Kilda Sites and Monuments Record, RCAHMS DT000166

71   **140730**

72   Fleming 2005, 148; Harman 1997, 109; Johnstone 1998, 21; Sharbau 1860; **139390**; **300973**

73   RCAHMS 1928, 46; eg **171848**

74   **347919**

75   Sharbau 1860; Stell and Harman 1988, 41–2, No. 9; **9691**

76   Stell and Harman 1988, 35–6, No. 2

77   Robson 2005, 671

78   Miers 2008, 383–4, 388–9; **115561**; **122257**; **171925**

79   Stell and Harman 1988, 37, No. 3, 37; Harman 1997, 188–9; there are numerous records relating to the Board of Agriculture supply of bulls held at NRS. In relation to St Kilda, these include AF42/5247, AF42/6310, AF42/6483, AF42/8484, dating from 1908–11

80   Stell and Harman 1988, No. 3, 10, 37; **9685**

81   **331648**; **331666**

82   Letter from St Kildans to Col. Gore-Booth of the Scottish Office (NRS AF42/933); **287149**

83   The quay was lengthened and widened by the military during 1969–70 (Geddes 2009b, 10)

84   Harman 1997, 279–80; the concrete holdfasts for the masts were recorded by RCAHMS immediately south-east of the ablutions block, and 20m north-west of Cleit 18

85   Geddes 2008, 15

86   Geddes 2008, 15; Cleit 1203, but the location of the other is unknown; **303124**

87   Geddes 2008, 19; Morris 2013

88   Geddes 2009b; **214734**

89   Geddes 2009b, 10; **145532**

90   Geddes 2008; **133660**

91   Little survives of the boundaries that marked out the crofts within the area north-east and south-west of the factor's house

92   Mackenzie 1911, 22–3

93   The head dyke is up to 2m high, 1m thick and about 1.8km long; the Street measures over 700m in length; while the revetment of the Abhainn Ilishgil extends for about 150m

94   Sharbau's plan of 1860 shows the fields here with the annotation 'R.G.' for Rachel Gillies, the occupant of a nearby blackhouse (Z)

95   Mackenzie 1911, 105

96   Examples are recorded in Canmore, but only one other has been noted outside the Northern Isles and this was recorded during a watching brief in Gleann Da-Eig, Perthshire (Lewis 2010; **314704**)

97   The plots, described as turf cutting by Fleming (2005, 138), are visible in photograph C7186 in particular, University of Aberdeen Special Collections, George Washington Wilson. They are also shown in photographs taken by the RAF in 1957, RCAHMS SC1453627

98   *Stat. Acct.* 10, 350–7

99   MacDiarmid 1878, 244

100   Mackenzie 1911, 12

101   Mackenzie 1911, 14–15

102   Harman 1997, 188–9

103   Harman 1997, 191, Table 11

104   Mackenzie 1911, 15

105   MacDiarmid 1878, 245–6; Mackenzie 1911, 15

106   **320837**

107   Harman 1997, 100, 102; see also Robson 2005, 247

108   *Ibid*

109   Baldwin 1974, 96

110   Kearton 1897; Shrubb 2013, 140–1

111   *NSA* 2, 322

112   Harman 1997, 100

113   Lawson 1994

114   **310315**; **310316**; **310322**

115   Martin 1749, 59

Chapter Seven

1   Miers 2008, 311; **4075**

2   See p 173

3   Kinchin and Kinchin 1988; **44398**

4   Barry 1980; Mackay 2002, 53–7; Morris 2013, 67–72; Spackman 1982, 10–12; the remains of the aircraft are covered by the Protection of Military Remains Act; see also Pomeroy 1990; **303070**; **331485**; **331488**

5   St Kilda Could be Inhabited, *Glasgow Herald*, 15 December 1945; NRS AF57/48; Alexander Gillies Ferguson was a native of St Kilda and a regular visitor to the island; see p 163

6   Boyd became Scottish Director of the Nature Conservancy Council; Nicholson founded the World Wildlife Fund; while Lack made major contributions to evolutionary theory; Anderson 2013; Boyd 1999; Lack 1931

7   Bute was following the example of his father, who had left his houses at Charlotte Square in Edinburgh to the NTS in 1947; Love 2009, 305–6

8   Spackman 1982, 13

9   Between 1948 and 1966, the Air Construction Branch also operated in the Seychelles, Maldives, Thailand, Sarawak, Borneo, Aden and Cyprus (Walpole 2009); 5004 Squadron was based at RAF Wellesbourne, Warwickshire; see Mackenzie 1957 for a satire

10   Memorandum by Air Ministry, February 1957 (RCAHMS MS7273/27); NRS DD12/2012

11   See p 14, 22, 49–50

12   This summary is produced in the main from Roy Ritchie's Ministry of Works file on the Inter-Services Guided Weapons Range, St Kilda (RCAHMS MS7273)

13   'St Kilda Expedition – Personnel' (RCAHMS MS7273)

14   See location plan RCAHMS DP161740, 30 August 1956

15   RCAHMS DP161740; *Glasgow Herald* 7 November 1956; *The Scotsman*, 7 November 1956 (RCAHMS MS7273/27); **9645**

16   In this instance, the monitoring of construction works by an archaeologist; memorandum by P R Ritchie, 4 July 1957 (RCAHMS MS7273/44)

17   Note of meeting held St Andrew's House, Edinburgh, 17 January 1957 (RCAHMS MS7273/42)

18   The Air Ministry were required to consult the Ministry of Transport in relation to the renovation of the quay, while the Council were to be consulted on the 'layout and design of the buildings' (RCAHMS MS7273/27); see p 122

19   RCAHMS MS7273/27

20   St Kilda, Hebrides Range, Memorandum produced by S13, 13 February 1957 (RCAHMS MS7273/27); see also NRS DD27/1017; Rocket-tracking Base on St Kilda, *The Scotsman*, 4 February 1957

21   The purpose of the Advance Party was 'to prepare a slipway across the storm beach for the landing of future stores, the erection of tentage for the next party and to survey the proposed road lines and

building sites' (NA AIR20/10020, Operation 'Hard rock' 1957, Civil Engineering Report, Appendix C, 18)

22 Telegram from Williamson, Boyd (both Nature Conservancy) and Hillcoat (NTS) to Air Ministry, 19 April 1957 (NRS DD12/3231)

23 Reply from Air Ministry to Hardrock Detachment 26 April 1957 (NRS DD12/3231); there is a description of the final 'watching brief' phase of development in Williamson and Boyd (1960, 32–4), cited in Fleming (2005, 3); see also Harden and Lelong 2011, 9; Roy Ritchie noted that 'the Nature Conservancy … were of the opinion that the road proposals hitherto put forward would cause unnecessary disturbance to bird life' and, furthermore, that the 'Task Commander considered them unsuitable since his own preliminary surveys showed another route as likely to require less work and cost', Memorandum (RCAHMS MS7273/43)

24 Ritchie did not record the position of these lengths of wall in his memorandum (RCAHMS MS7273), but they are presumed to lie at NF 0982 9920 and, possibly, NF 0988 9919, to the north and north-east of the supposed location (Ordnance Survey 1928) of St Columba's chapel; **9647**

25 **294770**

26 Fleming 2005, 42–3, fig 25, citing Fisher 1948

27 RCAHMS SC1453627–8

28 Drawing KCE 27, 22 August 1957, viewed at the NTS, Balnain House, Inverness

29 Operations Record Book (NA AIR 28/1487); **139848**; **301792**; **302741**; no attempt has been made to relocate the survey stations depicted by Mathieson on his survey of 1927 (Ordnance Survey 1928); Weir 1982

30 NA AIR 28/1487

31 The drawings are dated July 1958; NRS DD12/3232

32 The original southern screening radar was located at NF 0945 9845

33 Spackman 1982, 17

34 The missile was fired at 16:25 on 23 June 1959; Spackman 1982, 17

35 Warwick 1977; 1984, 47; 1987; 2008

36 Information from NTS, St Kilda Sites and Monuments Record (RCAHMS DT000116); House 1 was re-roofed in 1966, 2 and 4 in 1967 and 3 in 1981; see also *St Kilda Mail* for additional details; Johnstone 1998; **139438**; **139439**; **139440**; **139441**

37 NA CM25/6; Spackman 1982, 25

38 Spackman 1982, 21

39 Compare plans dated September 1957 and May 1968 (NRS DD27/3231)

40 Spackman 1982, 28, 29

41 Spackman 1982, 20

42 The general and particular specifications, detailing the costs, materials etc, for this project are held in NA CM 25/16

43 A 1968 plan details the layout of the base before this project (NRS DD27/3231); the 1969–70 project budget was estimated at £540,000 but came to £980,000 (NA CM 25/26)

44 Spackman 1982, 31, 36–7

45 The gymnasium is depicted on a vertical aerial photograph taken on 25 May 1977 (RCAHMS SC1484568)

46 **347812**

47 Castro 1983; the museum was one of the first of a small number to be established in the Outer Hebrides and it was revamped with financial support from the St Kilda Club in 2003

48 Geddes (forthcoming); Johnstone 1999; RCAHMS DT000116

49 Turner 1995

50 Bain 2011; Harden 2008; **9679**

51 Walsh and Bain 2013

Conclusion

1   Martin 1698

2   See MacDonald 2001

3   eg Rackwitz 2007, 270–2; Williamson and Boyd 1960, 67–75

4   Geddes and Watterson 2013

5   Moray 1678; Martin 1698

6   Rowley-Conwy 2007

7   Rowley-Conwy 2007, 50–4, 138–40; Worsaae 1849

8   Thomas 1852

9   Wilson 1851

10   Dalglish 2002, 477–81; Geddes and Grant (forthcoming)

11   Mitchell 1880, 76–80

12   Thomas 1869, 161–2; now known as Airighean Tigh Duastal; **71052**

13   Mitchell 1880, 6

14   RCAHMS 1928; Wheeler 1929, 379–81

Landscape

1   Hiemstra *et al* 2015; Scottish Executive 2003, 42

2   Scottish Executive 2003, 47; UK averages for 1981–2010 were 3.7°C and 14.3°C respectively, www.metoffice.gov.uk/climate/uk/summaries (page consulted 26 May 2015)

3   Robson 1991, 28–30

4   Love 2009, 110 citing Mitchell *et al* 2004

5   Harman 1997, 38–55

6   Atkinson 1949, 368

7   Quine 1989, xi

St Kildans

1   Lawson 1993, 16; NRA Statutory Registers, Marriages, 111/04 0003; Quine 1988, 246–8

2   1749, Title page

3   Robson 2005, 432, see note 69; for plans of Betty Scott's House, see Thomas (1869) and Stell and Harman (1988, 41); NMS, Society of Antiquaries Collection, MS468

4   Betty Scott's death certificate, NRS Statutory Registers, Deaths, 111/03 0012; the 1841 census indicates that a 45-year-old Rachel Campbell was then living at Baddidarroch, NRS Census, 1841, 044/00 004/00 005

5   Seton 1878, 61; NRS Old Parish Registers, Marriages, 111/00 0020 0011

6   Seton 1878, 61

7   Seton 1878, 59

8   Robson 2005, 448, citing John Hall Maxwell; a photograph of Betty is published in Robson (2005, 433)

9   Mitchell 1999; NRS Statutory Registers, Births, 113/03 0008

10 Letter from Finlay MacQueen to Rev. Nicolson, Plockton, 1931 (NRS AF57/36)

11 NRS Statutory Registers, Deaths, 458/0B 0021

12 Mackay 2002, 53

13 Quine 1988, 253–8

14 Kearton 1897, 85–6

15 Quine 1988, 267

16 RCAHMS MS7273

17 NRS Statutory Registers, Deaths, 501/00 0335

18 Lawson 1993, 21; NRS Statutory Registers, Births, 111/03 0013; NRS Statutory Registers, Deaths, 458/0B 0024; Quine 1988, 259

19 Lawson 1993, 20

20 Kerr 2013, 51, 77

21 Lawson 1993, 17–8; information from NTS image database (SKA 509); Quine 1988, 148–84

22 Atkinson 1949, 259; Buchanan 1983, 53; Harman 1997, 111–12; MacGregor 1931, 274

23 The Book of Inverness 1914, 39, www.ambaile.org.uk (page consulted July 2015); Robson 2005, 570–1, 590–1

Seasons

1   Mackenzie 1911, 8

2   Harman 1997, 201; Wilson 1842, vol 2, 22

3   Macaulay 1764, 142

4   Quine 1989, 129

5   Harman 1997, 210

6   Macaulay 1764, 37

7   Mackenzie 1911, 43–4

8   Maclean 1839, 329

9   Mackenzie 1911, 43–4

10 MacCulloch 1824, 195

11 Quine 1988, 99–100; 1989, 106, 126

12 Quine 1988, 63, 84

13 Harman 1997, 186, 210

14 Quine 1989, 127

15 Harman 1997, 176–80; Quine 1988, 103

16 Harman 1997, 210–1; Lawson 1993, 16

17 Atkinson 1949, 260; Harman 1997, 210, 216

18 Buchanan 1983, 54; Harman 1997, 186; Quine 1988, 109–47

19 Harman 1997, 186; Love 2009, 227–8

20 Harman 1997, 100

21 Harman 1997, 176–80

22 Quine 1988, 86, 141–2; www.fleetwood-trawlers.info (page consulted 1 July 2015)

23 Quine 1988, 80–1, 129

24 Hutchinson 2014, 1–10; Quine 1988, 33

Tourism

1 Harman 1997, 91

2 Macaulay 1764, 184–5

3 Bray 1996

4 Johnson 1775; Pennant 1790

5 Robson 2005, 338 citing T J Torrie, EUL, General 1996/8/8

6 Robson 2005, 337–42; Acland (1787–1871) is well-known to students of St Kilda history as a benefactor and artist – thirteen of his watercolours describing St Kilda are held in the archives of Devon County Council 1148M/23/F/19

7 Robson 2005, 339

8 Robson 2005, 340 citing Neil Mackenzie's journal, 23 September 1834

9 Mitchell 1880

10 Robson 2005, 540

11 Heathcote 1900; Kearton 1897; Mackay 2006, 75, 78

12 Mackay 2006, 116–23

13 SSA 0418; 0431; see also SSA 0940; http://ssa.nls.uk/

14 SSA 2572; SSA 3615 (colour); Atkinson 1949, 222

15 RCAHMS 1928, 46

16 Kearton 1898, 78, 110; MacGregor 1931, 259

17 Martin 1749, 62

18 Fleming 2005, 103; Martin 1749, 18; Moray 1678, 928

Evacuation

1 MacGregor 1931, 297–8

2 Kearton 1897, 44; Stride 2011, 227

3 Fleming 2005, 4

4 NRS DD15/4/8

5 Geddes 1960; Mackay 2006, 184–5; NRS AF81/78; AF83/1486

6 Robson 2005, 400–11

7 Quine 1988, 253, 259; the role of ground officer and senior St Kildan was inherited by Alexander's brother Neil (b 1876)

8 Quine 1988, 43

9 Quine 1988, 45, 164–5

10 Quine 1988, 142–3

11 Lawson 1993

12 Letter from D Milne to R Rosenberg, 31 July 1930 (NRS AF57/32); Tom Johnston was a notable Scottish socialist

13 Letter from W W Walker to 'Secretary for Scotland', 25 July 1930 (NRS AF57/32)

14 Letters from Christina MacQueen to Secretary for Scotland, 7 August 1930, and to Under-Secretary for Scotland, 15 August 1930 (NRS AF57/32)

15 *Ibid,* 15 August 1930; her attitude received little sympathy from Tom Steel, who suggested that this was an 'ignorant accusation' (2011, 211)

16 Newspaper cuttings from *The Oban Times* 21 June and 12 July 1930 (NRS AF57/48)

17 MacGregor 1931

18 MacGregor 1931, 303

19 Anderson 2013, 17–19, 70, 73; Lack 1931; Roy Ritchie's fieldwork in 1956 was the first by a professional archaeologist and the first with an entirely archaeological focus

20 Quine 1988, 143

21 Of his 18 children, 10 died in infancy (Lawson 1993, 26)

22 Miers 2008, 84; Quine 1988, 35

23 Lawson 1993, 32

Military

1 Operations Record Book (NA AIR 28/1487)

2 *Ibid*, May 1957, 3

3 *Ibid*, August 1958, 1

4 *Ibid*, July 1957, 3

5 *Ibid*, June 1957, 3

6 'Far flung pub calls last orders', 9 August 2005, http://news.bbc.co.uk/1/hi/scotland/4134938.stm (page consulted 8 July 2015)

7 Described in detail in Chapter 7

8 Williamson and Boyd 1960, 41

9 Boddington 2010; 2011; Love 2009, 248, 311; Mackay 2002; 2006

10 Love 2009, 249

11 Spackman 1982, 27

12 Spackman 1982, 26

13 Spackman 1982, 33

14 Dalyell 1994; Love 2009, 308

Expeditions

1 Robson 1991, 28–31

2 Quine 1988, 105

3 Lack 1931; Love 2009, 65

4 Atkinson 1949, 23; see also Rutherford 1945

5 SASC MS38449/5/1

6 Warwick 1977, 2

7 Wood 1977, 3

8 Love 2009, xiv

9 Dunbar 1992, 6

10 RCAHMS 1924, No. 26, 15–16; 1928; **56636**

11 Murray 2009, 12, 15

Bibliography

Andersen, S 1990
Norse settlement in the Hebrides: what happened to the natives and what happened to the Norse immigrants? in Wood & Lund (eds) 1990, 131–47

Anderson, A 1990
Early Sources of Scottish History, AD 500 to 1286, vol 1, reprinted Stamford: Paul Watkins

Anderson, J 1875
Notes on the relics of the Viking period of the Northmen in Scotland, illustrated by specimens in the museum, *Proc Soc Antiq Scot* 10 (1872–4), 555

Anderson, T R 2013
The Life of David Lack: Father of Evolutionary Ecology, Oxford: Oxford University Press

Anon 1904
Obituary: Henry Sharbau, *Geographical Journal* 24 (1), 106–7

Armit, I 1996
The Archaeology of Skye and the Western Isles, Edinburgh: Edinburgh University Press

Armit, I 1997
Excavation of a post-medieval settlement at Druim nan Dearcag and related sites around Loch Olabhat, North Uist, *Proc Soc Antiq Scot* 127, 899–919

Armit, I 2006
Anatomy of an Iron Age Roundhouse, the Cnip Wheelhouse Excavations, Lewis, Edinburgh: Society of Antiquaries of Scotland

Armit, I, Campbell, E & Dunwell, A 2008
Excavation of an Iron Age, Early Historic and medieval settlement and metalworking site at Eilean Olabhat, North Uist, *Proc Soc Antiq Scot* 138, 27–104

Ashmore, P 1981
Callanish, *Discovery Excavation Scot 1981,* 49–50

Ashmore, P 2002a
Callanais, The Standing Stones, revised edn, Inverness: Historic Scotland

Ashmore, P 2002b
A List of Archaeological Radiocarbon Dates, *Discovery Excavation Scot 2002,* 142–53

Atkinson, R 1949
Island Going, 1995 edn, Edinburgh: Birlinn

Badcock, A (ed) 2008
Ancient Uists, Exploring the Archaeology of the Outer Hebrides, Stornoway: Comhairle nan Eilean Siar

Bain, S 2011
The Manse – St Kilda, *St Kilda Mail* 35, 27–8

Bald, W 1829
Map of Harris, the Property of Alexander Hume Esq., Surveyed by William Bald, assistant to Mr Ainslie 1804–5, Edinburgh: Ballantyne

Baldwin, J 1974
Sea bird fowling in Scotland and Faroe, *Folk Life* 12, 60–103

Ballin Smith, B & Banks, I (eds) 2002
In the Shadow of the Brochs: the Iron Age in Scotland, Stroud: Tempus

Barber, J 1985
Insegall, Edinburgh: John Donald

Barry, J 1980
Aircraft wrecks of St Kilda, *After the Battle* 30, 28–43

Bellenden, J (trans) 1821
The History and Chronicles of Scotland, written in Latin by Hector Boece, Canon of Aberdeen; and translated by John Bellenden, Archdean of Moray, and Canon of Ross, vol 1, Edinburgh: Tait

Benjamin, J, Bicket, A, Anderson, D & Hale, A 2014
A multi-disciplinary approach to researching the intertidal and marine archaeology in the Outer Hebrides, Scotland, *Journal of Island and Coastal Archaeology* 9, 400–24

Beveridge, E 1911
North Uist: its Archaeology and Topography, with Notes apon the Early History of the Outer Hebrides, Edinburgh: William Brown

Bishop, R R, Church M J & Rowley-Conwy, P A 2011
Northton: survey and sampling, *Discovery Excavation Scot 2011,* 185–6

Bishop, R R, Church, M J , Clegg, C, Johnson, L, Piper, S, Rowley-Conwy, P A & Snape-Kennedy, L 2013
Tràigh na Beirigh 2: excavation, *Discovery Excavation Scot 2013,* 198

Boece, H 1527
Scotorum historiae prima gentis origine, etc, Paris: Iodicus Badicus Ascanius

Boddington, D 2010
St Kilda Diary: A Record of the Early Re-occupation of St Kilda, Isle of Lewis: Islands Book Trust

Boddington, D 2011
A St Kilda diary, in Chambers (ed) 2011, 202–5

Boyd, J M 1952
St Kilda in 1952, *Scottish Field,* October, 28–30

Boyd, J M 1957
Animals and humans at St Kilda, *Discovery,* 344–8

Boyd, J M 1999
The Song of the Sandpiper: Memoir of a Scottish Naturalist, Grantown-on-Spey: Colin Baxter

Branigan, K (ed) 2005
From Clan to Clearance: History and Archaeology on the Isle of Barra c.850–1850 AD, Oxford: Oxbow Books

Branigan, K & Foster, P 2002
Barra and the Bishop's Isles: Living on the Margin, Stroud: Tempus

Bray, E 1996
The Discovery of the Hebrides, Voyages to the Western Isles 1745–1883, 2nd edn, Edinburgh: Birlinn

Buchan, A 1818
A Description of Saint Kilda by the Rev. Mr. Alex. Buchan, late minister there, rev edn, Glasgow: Robert Chapman

Buchanan, J L 1997
Travels in the Western Hebrides from 1782 to 1790, Waternish, Isle of Skye: Maclean Press

Buchanan, M 1983
St Kilda: a photographic album, Edinburgh: Blackwood

Buchanan, M (ed) 1995
St Kilda – the Continuing Story of the Islands, Edinburgh: Her Majesty's Stationery Office

Bumsted, J M 2005
The rise and fall of the kelping industry in the Western Isles, in Branigan (ed) 2005, 123–38

Burgess, C & Miket, R (eds) 1976
Settlement and Economy in the Third and Second millennia B.C., British Archaeological Reports 33, Oxford: BAR

Buxton, B 1995
Mingulay: An Island and its People, Edinburgh: Birlinn

Calder, C S T 1958
Report on the discovery of numerous Stone Age house-sites in Shetland, *Proc Soc Antiq Scot* 89 (1955–6), 340–97

Cameron, A D 1986
Go Listen to the Crofters, the Napier Commission and Crofting a Century Ago, Stornoway: Acair

Campbell, E 1991
Excavation of a wheelhouse and other Iron Age structures at Sollas, North Uist, by R J C Atkinson in 1957, *Proc Soc Antiq Scot* 121, 117–73

Campbell, I D 2005
Rev John Macdonald, Ferintosh (1779–1849), article dated 28 July 2005, https://banneroftruth.org/uk/resources/articles/, Page Consulted 23 June 2015

Campbell, J L 2002
Canna: The Story of a Hebridean Island, 4th edn, Edinburgh: Birlinn

Carlyle, E I 2015
MacLeod, Sir John Macpherson (1792–1881), 2004 edn, *Oxford Dictionary of National Biography,* Oxford: Oxford University Press, http://www.oxforddnb.com/view/article/17674, Page Consulted 18 June 2015

Carmichael, A (ed)1900
Carmina Gadelica, 2 vols, Edinburgh: T and A Constable

Castro, R 1983
The Restoration of Cottage No. 3, *St Kilda Mail* 7, 18–19

Celoria, F 1966
St Kilda, Keele University Expedition. Unpublished manuscript, NTS archive

Chambers, B (ed) 2011
Rewriting St Kilda, new views on old ideas, South Lochs: Island Books Trust

Church, M J, Bishop, R R, Blake, E, Nesbitt, C, Perri, A, Piper, S, Rowley-Conwy, P A, & Snape-Kennedy, L 2012a
Temple Bay: excavation, *Discovery Excavation Scot 2012,* 186

Church, M J, Bishop, R R, Blake, E, Nesbitt, C, Perri, A, Piper, S, Rowley-Conwy, P A, Snape-Kennedy, L, & Walker, J 2012b
Tràigh na Beirigh [NB 1002 3628]: excavation, *Discovery Excavation Scot 2012,* 190

Church, M J, Bishop, R R, Blake, E, Nesbitt, C, Perri, A, Piper, S, Rowley-Conwy, P A, Snape-Kennedy, L, & Walker, J 2012c
Tràigh na Beirigh [NB 1003 3633]: excavation, *Discovery Excavation Scot 2012,* 190

Clarke, A 1992
Artefacts of coarse stone from Neolithic Orkney, in Sharples & Sheridan (eds) 1992, 244–58

Clarke, A 2006
Stone Tools and the Prehistory of the Northern Isles, British Archaeological Reports 406, Oxford: Archaeopress

Close-Brooks, J 1978
Valtos: cairn, *Discovery Excavation Scot 1978,* 34

Close-Brooks, J 1995
Excavation of a cairn at Cnip, Uig, Isle of Lewis, *Proc Soc Antiq Scot* 125, 253–77

Coates, R 1990
The place-names of St Kilda: Nomina Hirtensia (Celtic studies), Lampeter: Edwin Mellen Press

Cottam, M B 1973
St Kilda Archaeological Survey I, Unpublished report, RCAHMS MS 7393/1

Cottam, M B 1974
St Kilda Archaeological Survey II, Unpublished report, RCAHMS MS 7393/1

Cottam, M B 1979
Archaeology, in Small (ed) 1979, 36–61

Cowie, T G 1987
Barvas Sands: structure, middens, inhumations, *Discovery Excavation Scot 1987*, 62

Crawford, I A 1964
Rossinish, Benbecula, *Discovery Excavation Scot 1964*, 33

Crawford, I A 1975
Excavations at Coileagan an Udail, North Uist, Unpublished report, RCAHMS Library

Crawford I A 1979
A corbelled Bronze Age burial chamber and Beaker evidence from the Rosinish machair, Benbecula, *Proc Soc Antiq Scot* 108 (1976–7), 94–107

Crawford, I A 1980
Excavations and Research at Coilegan an Udail, North Uist. Unpublished report, RCAHMS Library

Crawford, I A 1981
Excavations and Research at Coilegan an Udail, North Uist. Unpublished report, RCAHMS Library

Crawford, I A 1983
Excavations and Research at the Udal. Unpublished report, RCAHMS Library

Crawford, I A 1984
An t-Udal. Unpublished report, RCAHMS Library

Crawford, I A 1986
The Udal Project. Unpublished report, RCAHMS Library

Crawford, I A & Selkirk, A 1996
The Udal, *Current Archaeology* 147, 84–94

Crawford, I A & Switsur, R 1977
Sandscaping and C14: the Udal, N Uist, *Antiquity 51,* 124–36

Crone, A, Armit, I, Boardman, S, Finlayson, B, MacSween, A & Mills, C 1993
Excavation and survey of sub-peat features of Neolithic, Bronze and Iron Age date at Bharpa Carinish, North Uist, Scotland, *Proc Prehist Soc* 59, 361–82

Curtis, M R 2010
Boreray, St Kilda, Western Isles: stone circle (possible), *Discovery Excavation Scot 2010*, 176

Curtis, M R & Curtis, G R 2007
Gleann Mor, Hirta, St Kilda: survey of prehistoric circular stone setting, *Discovery Excavation Scot 2007,* 198–9

Curtis, M R & Curtis, G R 2008
Gleann Mor, Hirta, St Kilda, Western Isles (Harris parish): plans and photographs of prehistoric stone circle, *Discovery Excavation Scot 2008, 178*

Dalglish, C 2002
Highland rural settlement studies: a critical history, *Proc Soc Antiq Scot* 132, 475–97

Dalyell, T 1994
Obituary: Joe Eggeling, *Independent*, 15 February 1994

Davidson, J 1967
Some Further Discoveries on St Kilda. Unpublished report, RCAHMS MS 7272/1

Donaldson, M P, Edwards, K J, Meharg, A A, Deacon, C & Davidson, D A 2009
Land use history of Village Bay, Hirta, St Kilda World Heritage Site: A palynological investigation of plaggen soils, *Review of Paleobotany and Palynology,* 153 (1–2), 46–61

Dodgshon, R 1998
From Chiefs to Landlords: Social and Economic Change in the Western Highlands and Islands, c.1493–1820, Edinburgh: Edinburgh University Press

Downes, J & Badcock, A 1998
Berneray Causeway: Neolithic settlement; burial cairns; post-medieval cultivation. *Discovery Excavation Scot 1998*, 101

Dunbar, J G 1978
Kisimul Castle, Isle of Barra, *Glasgow Archaeol J* 5, 25–43

Dunbar, J G 1992
The Royal Commission on the Ancient and Historical Monuments of Scotland: the first eighty years, *Trans Ancient Monuments Soc* 36, 13–77

Dunwell, A J, Neighbour T & Cowie, T G 1995
A cist burial adjacent to the Bronze Age cairn at Cnip, Uig, Isle of Lewis, *Proc Soc Antiq Scot* 125, 279–88

Edwards, K 1996
A Mesolithic of the Western and Northern Isles of Scotland? Evidence from pollen and charcoal, in Pollard & Morrison (eds) 1996, 23–38

Emery, N 1988
Excavations on Hirta 1987, *St Kilda Mail* 12, 9–10

Emery, N 1990
Excavations on Hirta – 1989, *St Kilda Mail* 14, 19–21

Emery, N 1991
Excavations on Hirta – 1990, *St Kilda Mail* 15, 18–19

Emery, N 1996
The Archaeology and Ethnology of St Kilda No 1: The Archaeological Excavations on Hirta 1983–1990, Edinburgh: Her Majesty's Stationery Office

Emery, N & Morrison, A 1995
The archaeology of St Kilda, in Buchanan (ed) 1995, 39–59

EUL
University of Edinburgh Library, Special Collections

Evans, E 1966
Prehistoric and Early Christian Ireland, London: Batsford

Fairhurst, H 1969
Rosal: a deserted township in Strath Naver, Sutherland, *Proc Soc Antiq Scot* 100 (1967–8), 135–69

Fairhurst, H 1971
The wheelhouse site at A' Cheardach Bheag on Drimore Machair, South Uist, *Glasgow Archaeol J* 2, 72–106

Feachem, R W 1964
St Kilda. Unpublished manuscript, RCAHMS Batch 359/462/7

Fisher, I 2001
Early Medieval sculpture in the West Highlands and Islands, RCAHMS/ Society of Antiquaries of Scotland monograph series 1, Edinburgh: RCAHMS

Fisher, J 1948
St Kilda: a natural experiment, *New Naturalist* 1, 91–104

Fleming, A 1994
Clash na Bearnaich: stone quarries and stone working areas, *Discovery Excavation Scot 1994*, 95

Fleming, A 1995
The stone quarries of Clash na Bearnaich, *St Kilda Mail* 19, 16–17

Fleming, A 1997
The stone hoe-blades of Hirta, *St Kilda Mail* 21, 18–20

Fleming, A 2003
St Kilda: the pre-Improvement clachan, *Proc Soc Antiq Scot* 133, 375–89

Fleming, A 2005
St Kilda and the Wider World: Tales of an Iconic Island, Macclesfield: Windgather Press

Fleming, A & Edmonds, M 1995
Clash na Bearnaich, Hirta, St Kilda: stone implements and mauls, *Discovery Excavation Scot 1995*, 106

Fleming, A & Edmonds, M 1996
Village Bay, St Kilda (Harris parish): field wall, Neolithic pottery, *Discovery Excavation Scot 1996*, 105

Fleming, A & Edmonds, M 1998
Village Bay, St Kilda: stone quarries, field wall, *Discovery Excavation Scot 1998*, 100

Fleming, A & Edmonds, M 1999
St Kilda: Quarries, Fields and prehistoric agriculture, *Proc Soc Antiq Scot* 129, 119–59

Fojut, N 1982
Towards a geography of Shetland brochs, *Glasgow Archaeol J* 9, 38–59

Fox, C 1928
Review, Royal Commission on the Ancient and Historical Monuments and Constructions of Scotland, Ninth report with inventory of monuments and constructions in the Outer Hebrides, Skye and the Small Isles, *Antiq J* 8, 536–8

Frodsham, P, Topping, P & Cowley, D (eds) 1999
'We were always chasing time'. Papers presented to Keith Blood. *Northern Archaeology* Special Edition, 17–18, Newcastle-upon-Tyne: Northumberland Archaeological Group

Gannon, A R (forthcoming)
Movement and Mobility in the Hebridean Neolithic in Leary, J (ed) forthcoming

Gannon, A R & Halliday, S P 2002
The archaeology of Canna and Sanday, in Campbell 2002, xxii–xxix

Gannon, A & Parker, I 2012
Surveying St Kilda, *Current Archaeology* 263, 36–41

Geddes, G 2008
The Magazine and Gun Emplacement, St Kilda: a Conservation Statement. Unpublished manuscript, RCAHMS MS 6961/WP 003151

Geddes, G 2009a
Remote archaeological recording on Hirta, *St Kilda Mail* 33, 28–30

Geddes, G 2009b
The Pier, St Kilda: a Conservation Statement. Unpublished manuscript, RCAHMS MS 6962/WP003548

Geddes, G 2011a
Calum Mor's House, Hirta, St Kilda: a Conservation Statement. Unpublished manuscript, RCAHMS MS 6339/WP 000657

Geddes, G 2011b
The Amazon's House, Hirta, St Kilda: a Conservation Statement. Unpublished manuscript, RCAHMS MS 6341/WP 000658

Geddes, G F 2014
RCAHMS Archaeological Survey, North and South Uist, 2012–3, Edinburgh: RCAHMS

Geddes, G F (forthcoming)
The Storehouse, St Kilda: a Conservation Statement. Unpublished report for the NTS

Geddes, G F & Grant, K 2015
The plan and the *Porcupine*: dynamism and complexity on St Kilda, *Landscapes* 16 (2), 1–19

Geddes, G F & Watterson, A 2013
'A Prodigious Number of Little Cells'– Cleitean and the St Kilda World Heritage Site, *Architectural Heritage* 24, 103–18

Geddes, T 1960
Hebridean Sharker, 2012 edn, Edinburgh: Birlinn

Gibbons, M 2014
Croagh Patrick and prehistoric mountain pilgrimage in Ireland: modern myth or ancient reality? in Moran and Muraile (eds) 2014, 45–65

Gibson, E (ed) 1695
Camden's Britannia, Newly Translated into English: with Large Additions and Improvements, London: A Swalle and J Churchil

Gillies, D J 2010
The Truth about St Kilda: An Islander's Memoir, Edinburgh: Birlinn

Graham-Campbell, J 2008
Viking Age and Late Norse gold and silver from Scotland: an update, *Proc Soc Antiq Scot* 138, 193–204

Grillo, O & Venora, G (eds) 2011
Biodiversity Loss in a Changing Planet, Rijeka: InTech

Halliday, S 2013
I Walked, I Saw, I Surveyed, but what did I see? … and what did I survey?, in Opitz & Cowley (eds) 2013, 63–75

Harden, J 2008
The St Kilda Manse, a review of its development circa 1820–today, for the National Trust for Scotland and Historic Scotland. Unpublished manuscript, RCAHMS MS 6959/WP 003550

Harden, J & Lelong, O 2011
Winds of Change: The Living Landscapes of Hirta, St Kilda, Edinburgh: Society of Antiquaries of Scotland

Harding, D W & Dixon, T N 2000
Dun Bharabhat, Cnip, an Iron Age Settlement in West Lewis. Edinburgh: University of Edinburgh Department of Archaeology

Harding, D W & Gilmour, S M D 2000
The Iron Age Settlement at Beirgh, Riof, Isle of Lewis, Excavations 1985–1995. Volume 1 – The Structures and Stratigraphy. Edinburgh: University of Edinburgh Department of Archaeology

Hardy, K & Wickham–Jones, C R 2000
Scotland's First Settlers: Data Structure Report. Edinburgh: Centre for Field Archaeology

Harman 1977
National Trust for Scotland Cleit Survey, St Kilda, interim report. Unpublished manuscript, RCAHMS Library

Harman 1978
National Trust for Scotland Cleit Survey, St Kilda, second interim report. Unpublished manuscript, RCAHMS Library

Harman, M 1979a
Cleits – a running commentary, *St Kilda Mail* 3, 16–17

Harman, M 1979b
An incised cross on Hirt, Harris, *Proc Soc Antiq Scot* 108 (1976–77), 254–8

Harman, M 1982
A visit to Stac an Armin, *St Kilda Mail* 6, 27–8

Harman, M 1992
Robert Atkinson's photographs of the Hebrides, *St Kilda Mail* 16, 22–32

Harman, M 1997
An Isle called Hirte: History and Culture of the St Kildans to 1930, Waternish, Isle of Skye: Maclean Press

Hay, G D 1978
Scottish wooden tumbler locks, *Post-medieval Archaeol* 12, 125–7

Heathcote, N 1900
St Kilda, London: Longmans, Green and Co.

Henshall 1972
The Chambered Tombs of Scotland, vol 2, Edinburgh: Edinburgh University Press

Hetherington, T 1984
Cleits – another theory, *St Kilda Mail* 8, 32

Hetherington, T 1985
Another community on St Kilda? *St Kilda Mail* 9, 27

Hiemstra, J F, Shakesby, R A & Vieli, A 2015
Late Quaternary glaciation in the Hebrides sector of the continental shelf: was St Kilda overrun by the British–Irish Ice Sheet? *Boreas* 44, 178–96

Holden, T, Dalland, M, Burgess, C & Walker, B 2001
No. 39 Arnol: the excavation of a Lewis blackhouse, *Scot Archaeol J* 23 (1), 15–32

Holderness, H 2007
A865 / A867 Road Improvement Scheme, North Uist, Western Isles: watching brief and excavation, *Discovery Excavation Scot 2007*, 202

Hunter, J 2000
The Making of the Crofting Community, rev edn, Edinburgh: John Donald

Hunter, J 2010
A Dance Called America: The Scottish Highlands, The United States and Canada, rev edn, Edinburgh: Birlinn

Hutchinson, R 2014
St Kilda: A People's History, Edinburgh: Birlinn

Islands Book Trust 2004
Traditions of Sea-bird Fowling in the North Atlantic Region, Port of Ness, Isle of Lewis: Islands Book Trust

Jamie, K 2012
Sightlines: A Conversation with the Natural World, London: Sort Of

Johnson, S 1775
A Journey to the Western Islands of Scotland, London: Cadell

Johnstone, L 1998
The Ruinous Dwellings of St Kilda, GUARD 362.2. Unpublished report for the NTS, RCAHMS MS 725/267

Johnstone, L 1999
Archaeological assessment on the Renovated and/or Restored Mortared structures of St Kilda, GUARD 362. Unpublished report for the NTS, RCAHMS MS 725/247

Kearton, R 1897
With Nature and a Camera: Being the Adventures and Observations of a Field Naturalist and an Animal Photographer, 1899 edn, London: Cassell and Company

Kennedy, A & Thomas, F W L 1875
Letter from St Kilda with notes by F W L Thomas, *Proc Soc Antiq Scot* 10 (1872–4), 702–11

Kerr, M 2013
George Murray: a schoolteacher for St Kilda, 1886–7, Isle of Lewis: Islands Book Trust

Kinchin, P & Kinchin, J 1988
Glasgow's Great Exhibitions: 1888, 1901, 1911, 1938, 1988, Bicester: White Cockade

Knox, J 1787
The Highlands and Hebrides in 1786, 1975 edn, Edinburgh: James Thin

Lack, D 1931
The effect of the exodus from St Kilda upon the island's fauna and flora: interesting changes observed during a recent visit, *Illustrated London News*, 26 December 1931, 1054–5

Lawson, B 1993
Croft History; Isle of St Kilda, Northton, Harris: Bill Lawson Publications

Lawson, B 1994
The Teampull on the Isle of Pabbay: a Harris Church in its Historical Setting Northton, Harris: Bill Lawson Publications

Lawson, B 1997
The Isle of Taransay: a Harris Island in its Historical Setting, Northton, Harris: Bill Lawson Publications

Lawson, B 2002
Harris in History and Legend, 2011 edn, Edinburgh: Birlinn

Leary, J (ed) forthcoming
Movement and Mobility, Neolithic Studies Group seminar papers, Oxford: Oxbow

Lewis, J 2010
Roromore Hydro Scheme, Perth and Kinross (Fortingall parish): watching brief, *Discovery Excav Scot 2010*, 143

Love, J A 2009
A Natural History of St Kilda, Edinburgh: Birlinn

Low, G 1879
A Tour through the islands of Orkney and Schetland, containing hints relating to their ancient, modern and natural history, collected in 1774, Kirkwall: W Peace & Son

Macaulay, C 2011
Voices from St Kilda in the School of Scottish Studies Archives, in Chambers (ed) 2011, 35–63

Macaulay, K 1764
The History of St Kilda, 1974 facsimile edn, Edinburgh: James Thin

Macaulay 2009
The Prisoner of St Kilda, Edinburgh: Luath

MacCulloch, J 1824
The Highlands and Western Isles of Scotland, vol 3, London: Longman

MacDiarmid, J 1878
St Kilda and its inhabitants, *Trans Highland Agricultural Soc* 10, 232–54

MacDonald, F 2001
St Kilda and the sublime, *Ecumene* 8 (2), 151–74

MacDonald, F 2011
Doomsday fieldwork, or, how to rescue Gaelic culture? The salvage paradigm in geography, archaeology, and folklore, 1955–62, *Environment and Planning D: Society and Space* 29, 309–35

Macgregor, A A 1931
A Last Voyage to St Kilda, London: Cassell and Company

MacGregor, D R 1960
The island of St Kilda – a survey of its character and occupance, *Scottish Studies* 4, 1–48

MacGregor, D R 1989
An expedition in 1957, *St Kilda Mail* 13, 18–25

Mackay, J A 1959
Report on Tigh Calum Mor, St Kilda. Unpublished report, RCAHMS MS7641/2

Mackay, J 2002
Soldiering on St Kilda, Honiton, Devon: Token Publishing Ltd

Mackay, J 2006
The St Kilda Steamers: A History of McCallum, Orme & Co, Stroud: Tempus

Mackenzie, C 1957
Rockets Galore, London: Chatto and Windus

Mackenzie, J B 1905
Antiquities and old customs in St Kilda, compiled from notes by Rev Neil Mackenzie, Minister of St Kilda, 1829–48, *Proc Soc Antiq Scot* 39 (1904–5), 397–402

Mackenzie, J B (ed) 1911
Episode in the Life of the Rev. Neil Mackenzie at St Kilda from 1829 to 1843, Aberfeldy: Privately printed

Mackenzie, W M 1904
Notes on certain structures of archaic type in the Island of Lewis – beehive houses, duns and stone circles, *Proc Soc Antiq Scot* 38 (1903–4), 179–82

Mackie, C 2013
The bed-alcove tradition in Ireland and Scotland: reappraising the evidence, *Proc Royal Irish Academy* 113C, 1–32

Mackinnon, D & Morrison, A 1968a
The MacLeods – The Genealogy of a Clan, Section 1, MacLeod Chiefs of Harris and Dunvegan, Edinburgh: The Clan MacLeod Society (see also www.macleodgenealogy.org)

Mackinnon, D & Morrison, A 1968b
The MacLeods – The Genealogy of a Clan, Section 2, The MacLeods of Talisker, Berneray, Orbost, Luskintyre, Hamer, Greshornish, Ulinish and Dalvey, Edinburgh: The Clan MacLeod Society (see also www.macleodgenealogy.org)

Mackinnon, D & Morrison, A 1970
The MacLeods – The Genealogy of a Clan, Section 3, MacLeod Cadet Families, Edinburgh: The Clan MacLeod Society (see also www.macleodgenealogy.org)

MacLaren, A 1974
A Norse house on Drimore Machair, South Uist', *Glasgow Archaeol J* 3, 9–18

MacLean, L 1839
Sketches of the Island Saint Kilda, *The Calcutta Christian Observer* 8, 326–37

MacLean, C 1996
Island on the Edge of the World: The Story of St Kilda, rev edn, Edinburgh: Canongate

MacLeod, D 1796
The Case of Lieut. Col. Donald MacLeod, of the Honourable East India Company's Service, London

MacLeod, D J 1916
An account of a find of ornaments of the Viking time from Valtos, Uig, in the Island of Lewis, *Proc Soc Antiq Scot* 50 (1915–16), 184

MacLeod, F T 1915
Notes on Dun an Iardhard, a broch near Dunvegan, excavated by Countess Vincent Baillet de Latour, Uiginish, Skye, *Proc Soc Antiq Scot* 49 (1914–15), 57–70

MacLeod, R C 1927
The MacLeods of Dunvegan from the time of Leod to the end of the seventeenth century, Edinburgh: privately printed for the Clan MacLeod Society

MacLeod, R C 1938
The Book of Dunvegan, being the documents from the muniment room of the MacLeods of MacLeod at Dunvegan Castle, Isle of Skye, volume first, 1340–1700, Aberdeen: Third Spalding Club

MacLeod, R C 1939
The Book of Dunvegan, being the documents from the muniment room of the MacLeods of MacLeod at Dunvegan Castle, Isle of Skye, volume second, 1700–1920, Aberdeen: Third Spalding Club

McNeill, J 1851
Report to the Board of Supervision by Sir John M'Neil, G.C.B., on the Western Highlands and Islands, Edinburgh: Her Majesty's Stationary Office

Manville, H E 1993
Additions and Corrections to Thompson's Inventory and Brown and Dolley's Coin Hoards, *British Numismatic Journal* 63, 91–113

Martin, M 1698
A Late Voyage to St Kilda, 1986 edn, Edinburgh: Mercat Press

Martin, M 1749
A Voyage to St Kilda, London: R Griffith

Martin, M & Monro, D 1999
A Description of the Western Isles of Scotland ca 1695 and A Late Voyage to St Kilda [with] *Description of the occidental i.e. western islands of Scotland*, Edinburgh: Birlinn

Mathieson, J 1925
Earth-house or galleried building near Durness, Sutherland, *Proc Soc Antiq Scot* 59 (1924–25), 221–3

Mathieson, J 1928a
The antiquities of the St Kilda Group of Islands, *Proc Soc Antiq Scot* 62 (1927–28), 123–32

Mathieson, J 1928b
St Kilda, *Scottish Geographical Magazine* 44 (2), 65–90

Mathieson, J 1932
The story of Antarctic exploration, 1716–1931: With a map showing the tracks and discoveries of recent explorers, *Scottish Geographical Magazine* 48 (6), 321–9

Meharg, A A, Deacon, C, Edwards, K J, Donaldson, M, Davidson, D A, Spring, C, Scrimgeour, C M, Feldmann, J, & Rabb, A 2006
Ancient manuring practices pollute arable soils at the St Kilda World Heritage Site, Scottish North Atlantic, *Chemosphere* 64, 1818–28

Miers, M 2008
The Western Seaboard: an Illustrated Architectural Guide, Edinburgh: Rutland Press

Miket, R 2002
The souterrains of Skye, in Ballin Smith and Banks (eds) 2002, 77–110

Miles, A E W 1989
An Early Christian Chapel and Burial Ground on the Isle of Ensay, Outer Hebrides, Scotland with a Study of the Skeletal Remains, British Archaeological Reports 212, Oxford: BAR

Mitchell, A 1880
The Past in the Present: What is Civilisation? Edinburgh: David Douglas

Mitchell, W R 1999
Finlay Macqueen of St Kilda, 2nd edn, Argyll: House of Lochar

Mitchell, I, Newton, S F, Ratcliffe, N & Dunn, T E 2004
Seabird Populations of Britain and Ireland, London: Poyser

Monro, D 1884
Description of the Western Isles of Scotland called Hybrides with the Genealogies of the Chief Clans of the Isles [1549], Glasgow

Moran, G & Muraile, N O 2014
Mayo, History and Society: Interdisciplinary Essays on the History of an Irish County, Dublin: Geography Publications

Moray, R 1678
A description of the Island Hirta, *Trans Royal Soc* 12, 927–9

Morris, C & Emery, N 1987
The 1986 Archaeological Expedition, *St Kilda Mail* 11, 5–8

Morris, R 2013
Defending St Kilda, Isle of Lewis: Islands Book Trust

Morrison, A 1969
Harris Estate Papers, 1724–1754, *Trans Gaelic Soc Inverness* 45 (1967–8), 33–97

Muir, T S 1885
Ecclesiological Notes on Some of the Islands of Scotland, Edinburgh: David Douglas

Muir, T S & Thomas, F W L 1862
Notice of a beehive house in the Island of St Kilda, *Proc Soc Antiq Scot* 3 (1857–9), 225–32

Murray, D 2008
The Guga Hunters, Edinburgh: Birlinn

Murray, S 2009
Dun Dare, *Scottish Island Explorer* 10, 10–15

NA
The National Archives, Kew, London

Neighbour, T & Burgess, C 1996
Traigh Bostadh (Uig Parish): 1st millennium AD settlement, *Discovery Excavation Scot 1996*, 113–14

Newton, M 2009
Warriors of the Word: The World of the Scottish Highlanders, Edinburgh: Birlinn

Nimlin, J 1979
Historical St Kilda, in Small (ed) 1979, 69–75

NMS
National Museum of Scotland

NRS
National Records of Scotland

NSA 1834–45
The New Statistical Account of Scotland, 15 vols, Edinburgh: Blackwood

Opitz, R S & Cowley, D C (eds) 2013
Interpreting Archaeological Topography, 3D Data, Visualisation and Observation, Oxford: Oxbow

Ordnance Survey 1928
Map of St Kilda or Hirta and Adjacent Islands and Stacs, Southampton: Ordnance Survey

Ovenden, S 2007
St Kilda, *Discovery Excavation Scot 2007*, 199

Parker Pearson, M 2012
Settlement, agriculture and society in South Uist before the Clearances, in Parker Pearson (ed) 2012, 401–25

Parker Pearson, M (ed) 2012
From Machair to Mountains: Archaeological Survey and Excavation in South Uist, Oxford: Oxbow

Parker Pearson, M & Sharples, N 1999
Between Land and Sea: Excavations at Dun Vulan, South Uist, Sheffield: Sheffield Academic Press

Parker Pearson, M, Sharples, N & Symonds, J 2004
South Uist: Archaeology and History of a Hebridean Island, Stroud: Tempus

Pennant, T 1790
A Tour of Scotland, and Voyage to the Hebrides, 2 vols, London: printed for Benj. White

Pollard, T & Morrison, A (eds) 1996
The Early Prehistory of Scotland, Dalrymple monograph no. 3, Edinburgh: Edinburgh University Press

Pomeroy, C A 1990
Wreck recovery wartime style, *After the Battle* 68, 6–11

Poore, M E D, Robertson, V C & Godwin, H 1949
The vegetation of St Kilda in 1948, *Journal of Ecology* 37 (1), 82–99

Quine, D A 1988
St Kilda Portraits, Frome: Dowland Press

Quine, D A 1989
St Kilda Revisited, 3rd edn, Frome: Dowland Press

Quine, D A (ed) 2001
Expeditions to the Hebrides by George Clayton Atkinson in 1831 and 1833, Isle of Skye: Maclean Press

Quine, T A 1983
Excavations in Village Street, Hirta, St Kilda, 1983, Glasgow: University of Strathclyde

Rackwitz, M 2007
Travels to Terra Incognita: The Scottish Highlands and Hebrides in early modern travellers' accounts c. 1600 to 1800, New York: Waxmann Munster

RCAHMS 1924
Eighth Report with Inventory of Monuments and Constructions in the County of East Lothian, Edinburgh: His Majesty's Stationary Office

RCAHMS 1928
Ninth Report with Inventory of Monuments and Constructions in the Outer Hebrides, Skye and the Small Isles, Edinburgh: His Majesty's Stationary Office

RCAHMS 1984
Argyll: an Inventory of the Monuments Volume 5: Islay, Jura, Colonsay and Oronsay, Edinburgh: Her Majesty's Stationary Office

RCAHMS 1990
North-east Perth: An Archaeological Landscape, Edinburgh: Her Majesty's Stationary Office

RCAHMS 1993
Waternish, Skye and Lochalsh District, Highland Region: An Archaeological Survey, Edinburgh: RCAHMS

RCAHMS 1995
RCAHMS Broadsheet 1: Muirkirk, Ayrshire: An Industrial Landscape, Edinburgh: RCAHMS

RCAHMS 1997
Eastern Dumfriesshire: An Archaeological Landscape, Edinburgh, RCAHMS

RCAHMS 1998
RCAHMS Broadsheet 4: St Kilda, Settlement and Structures on Hirta, Edinburgh: RCAHMS

RCAHMS 1999
RCAHMS Broadsheet 5: Canna, the Archaeology of a Hebridean landscape, Edinburgh: RCAHMS and NTS

RCAHMS 2003
RCAHMS Broadsheet 12: Eigg, the Archaeology of a Hebridean landscape, Edinburgh: RCAHMS

RCAHMS 2007
In the Shadow of Bennachie: A Field Archaeology of Donside, Aberdeenshire, Edinburgh, RCAHMS and Society of Antiquaries of Scotland

RCAHMS 2009
St Kilda, Discovery Excavation Scot 2009, 195

RCAHMS 2010
Mingulay: Archaeology and Architecture, Edinburgh: RCAHMS and NTS

Richards, E 1992
St Kilda and Australia: emigrants at peril, 1852–3, *Scot Hist Rev* 71, 129–55

Robson, M 1991
Rona, the Distant Island, Stornoway: Acair

Robson, M 2005
St Kilda: Church, Visitors and 'Natives', Isle of Lewis: Islands Book Trust

Rowley-Conwy, P 2007
From Genesis to Prehistory: The Archaeological Three Age System and its Contested Reception in Denmark, Britain and Ireland, Oxford: Oxford University Press

Rutherford, I W 1945
At the Tiller, London and Glasgow: Blackie and Son

Sands, J 1876
Out of the World; or, Life in St Kilda, Edinburgh: Maclachan and Stewart

Sands, J 1878
Notes on the antiquities of the island of St Kilda, *Proc Soc Antiq Scot* 12 (1876–8), 186–92

Sands, J 1882
Notes on the antiquities of the island of Tiree, *Proc Soc Antiq Scot* 16 (1881–2), 459–63

SASC
University of St Andrews Special Collections

Saville, A 1994
A decorated Skaill knife from Skara Brae, Orkney, *Proc Soc Antiq Scot* 124, 103–11

Secretary of State for Scotland 1985
Nomination of St Kilda for inclusion in the World Heritage List, Edinburgh

Scott, W L 1935
The chambered cairn of Clettraval, North Uist, *Proc Soc Antiq Scot* 69 (1934–5), 480–536

Scottish Executive 2003
Revised Nomination of St Kilda for inclusion in the World Heritage Site List, Edinburgh

SDD
Scottish Development Department

Seton, G 1878
St Kilda: Past and Present, Edinburgh

Sharbau, H 1860
Plan of Village Bay, St Kilda, NMS, Society of Antiquaries of Scotland Collection, MS 158

Sharkey, J & Payne, K 1986
The Road Through the Isles, Aldershot: Wildwood House

Sharples, N 1983
Dalmore: early bronze age settlement, *Discovery Excavation Scot 1983*, 81

Sharples, N 1984
Dalmore, *Current Archaeology* 91, 230–5

Sharples, N 1998
Silgenach, Cill Donnain: multi-period settlement, *Discovery Excavation Scot 1998*, 104–5

Sharples, N (ed) 2005
A Norse Farmstead in the Outer Hebrides: Excavations at Mound 3, South Uist, Oxford: Oxbow

Sharples, N (ed) 2012
A Late Iron Age Farmstead in the Outer Hebrides: Excavations at Mound 1, Bornais, South Uist, Oxford: Oxbow

Sharples, N & Sheridan, A (eds) 1992
Vessels for the Ancestors: Essays on the Neolithic of Britain and Ireland, Edinburgh: Edinburgh University Press

Shepherd, I A G & Tuckwell, A N 1976
Benbecula, Rosinish, *Discovery Excavation Scot 1976*, 35–6

Shepherd, I A G & Tuckwell, A N 1977
Benbecula, Rosinish, *Discovery Excavation Scot 1977*, 18

Sheridan, A 1992
Scottish stone axeheads: Some new work and recent discoveries, in Sharples & Sheridan (eds) 1992, 194–212

Shrubb, M 2013
Feasting, Fowling and Feathers: A History of the Exploitation of Wild Birds, London: Poyser

Simpson, D 1966
A Neolithic settlement in the Outer Hebrides, *Antiquity* 40, 137–9

Simpson, D D A 1976
The later neolithic and beaker settlement at Northton, Isle of Harris, in Burgess and Miket (eds) 1976, 221–6

Simpson, D A, Murphy, E M & Gregory, R A 2006
Excavations at Northton, Isle of Harris, British Archaeological Reports 408, Oxford: Archaeopress

Simpson, W D 1938
The Saga of Dunvegan, in MacLeod 1938, xiii–xxxiv

Small, A (ed) 1979
St Kilda Handbook, Edinburgh: National Trust for Scotland

Snape-Kennedy, L, Church, M J, Bishop, R R, Clegg, C, Johnson, L, Piper, S, & Rowley-Conwy, P A 2013
Tràigh na Beirigh 9: excavation, *Discovery Excavation Scot 2013*, 199

Somerville, J E 1899
Notice of an ancient structure called 'The Altar' in the Island of Canna, *Proc Soc Antiq Scot* 33 (1898–9), 133–40

Spackman, R A 1982
Soldiers on St Kilda: A Chronicle of Military Involvement on the Island of St Kilda, the Farthest Hebrides, Benbecula: Uist Community Press

SSA
Scottish Screen Archive

Stat. Acct. 1791–9
The Statistical Account of Scotland, Edinburgh: William Creech

Steel, T 2011
The Life and Death of St Kilda, rev edn, London: Harper Press

Steer, K A & Bannerman, J W M 1977
Late Medieval Monumental Sculpture in the West Highlands, Edinburgh: RCAHMS

Stell, G P 1995
The study of buildings, in Buchanan (ed) 1995, 24–38

Stell, G P & Harman, M 1988
Buildings of St Kilda, Edinburgh: RCAHMS

Stewart, J A 1999
The jaws of sheep: The 1851 Hebridean Clearances of Gordon of Cluny, *Proc Harvard Celtic Colloquium* 18/19, 205–226

Stride, P 2011
Limited bio-diversity and other defects of the immune system in the inhabitants of the Islands of St Kilda, Scotland, in Grillo & Venora (eds) 2011, 221–40

Stukeley, W 1740
Stonehenge: A Temple Restor'd to the British Druids, London: W Innys & R Manby

Symonds 2012
Excavations at Medieval Gearraidh Bhailteas, in Parker Pearson (ed) 2012, 294–307

Tait, I 2012
Shetland's Vernacular Buildings, 1600–1900, Lerwick: The Shetland Times

Taylor, A B 1969
The Norsemen in St Kilda, *Saga Book of the Viking Society for Northern Research* 17 (1966–9), Viking Society, 116–44, London: University College

Thacker, M in prep (a)
The Norse Church in the Northern Hebrides: A Reassessment of the Chapel on North Rona

Thacker, M in prep (b)
The quick and the dead, PhD (Archaeology) Thesis, University of Edinburgh

Thomas, F W L 1852
An account of some Celtic antiquities of Orkney, including the stones of Stenness, tumuli, Picts houses &c., with plans, *Archaeologia* 34

Thomas, F W L 1862
Notice of beehive houses in Harris and Lewis; with traditions of the 'Each-uisge', or water-horse, connected therewith, *Proc Soc Antiq Scot* 3 (1857–59*)*, 127–44

Thomas, F W L 1869
On the primitive dwellings and hypogea of the Outer Hebrides, *Proc Soc Antiq Scot* 7 (1) (1866–7), 153–95

Toland, J D 1814
A New Edition of Toland's History of the Druids: with An Abstract of His Life and Writings; and A Copious Appendix Containing Notes Critical, Philological, and Explanatory, ed. E Huddleston, Montrose: James Watt

Turner, R 1995
NTS St Kilda Report, *St Kilda Mail* 19, 39–41

Turner, R 1996
Excavations at the Gap, St Kilda, *St Kilda Mail* 20, 2–3

Turner, R 1999
Locating the old village in Village Bay, *St Kilda Mail* 23, 30

Walker, M J C 1984
A pollen diagram from St Kilda, Outer Hebrides, Scotland, *New Phytologist* 97, 99–113

Walpole, N 2009
Built to Endure: The Story of the RAF Airfield Construction Branch in the Cold War, Cowbit, Lincolnshire: Old Forge Publishing

Walsh, A & Bain, S 2013
The Factor's House, *St Kilda Mail* 37, 15–17

Warwick, A 1977
The beginning, *St Kilda Mail* 1, 1–2

Warwick, A 1984
St Kilda in Trust: The Early Days, *St Kilda Mail* 8, 46–8

Warwick, A 1987
The beginning, *St Kilda Mail* 11, 53

Warwick, A 2008
St Kilda work parties 1958, facsimile, *St Kilda Mail* 32, 5

Weir, T 1982
'My Month', *Scots Magazine* September 1982, 625–31

Welander, R, Batey, C & Cowie, T 1988
A Viking burial from Kneep, Uig, Isle of Lewis, *Proc Soc Antiq Scot* 117, 149–74

Wheeler, R E M 1929
Review, Royal Commission on the Ancient and Historical Monuments and Constructions of Scotland, Ninth report with inventory of monuments and constructions in the Outer Hebrides, Skye and the Small Isles, *Antiquity* 3, 379–81

Whitelock, D (ed) 1961
The Anglo-Saxon Chronicle: A Revised Translation, London: Eyre and Spottiswoode

Wickham-Jones, C R 1990
Rhum: Mesolithic and Later Sites at Kinloch: Excavations 1984–86, Edinburgh: Society of Antiquaries

Wickham-Jones, C R & Hardy, K 2004
Camas Daraich: a Mesolithic site at the Point of Sleat, Skye, *Scottish Archaeological Internet Reports* 12, Edinburgh: Society of Antiquaries of Scotland, www.sair.org.uk/sair12/index.html, Page Consulted 28 May 2015

Will, R, Shearer, I & Maguire, D 2005
The Village, Hirta, St Kilda: 19th century crofting village; prehistoric remains, *Discovery Excavation Scot 2005*, 145–6

Will, R, McLellan, K, & Maguire, D 2006
The Village, Hirta, St Kilda: geophysical survey, trial trenching, *Discovery Excavation Scot 2006*, 174

Williamson, K 1946
The horizontal water-mills of the Faroe Islands, *Antiquity* 20, 83–91

Williamson, K nd
The Gleann Mor settlement, St Kilda. Unpublished report, RCAHMS MS7641/2

Williamson, K 1957
The Medieval Village at St Kilda, Unpublished report, RCAHMS MS7641/1

Williamson, K 1958
Ancient St Kilda, *Scottish Field* 105, 46–9

Williamson, K 1960
From cleit to cottage, *Countryman* 57 (3), 505–10

Williamson, K & Boyd, J M 1960
St Kilda Summer, London: Hutchison

Williamson, K & Boyd, J M 1963
A Mosaic of Islands Edinburgh: Oliver and Boyd

Wilson, D 1851
The Archaeology and Prehistoric Annals of Scotland, Edinburgh: Sutherland and Knox

Wilson, J 1842
A Voyage Round the Coasts of Scotland and the Isles, 2 vols, Edinburgh

Withers, C 1999
Introduction, in Martin and Monro 1999, 1–11

Wood, G 1977
Opening time 1976, *St Kilda Mail* 1, 2–4

Wood, I & Lund, N (eds) 1990
People and Places in Northern Europe 500–1600: Essays in Honour of Peter Hayes Sawyer, Woodbridge: Boydell

Worsaae, J J A 1849
The Primeval Antiquities of Denmark, trans W J Thoms, London: John Henry Parker

Worsaae, J J A 1872
Ruslands og det Skandinaviske Nordens bebyggelse og aeldste kulturforhold, *Aarbøger for nordisk Oldkyndighed og Historie*, 309–430

Young, A 1955
An aisled farmhouse at the Allasdale, Isle of Barra, *Proc Soc Antiq Scot* 87 (1952–3), 80–105

Young, A & Richardson, K M 1962
A Cheardach Mhor, Drimore, South Uist, *Proc Soc Antiq Scot* 93 (1959–60), 135–73

Acknowledgements

This study of St Kilda is founded upon the results of a survey undertaken between 2007 and 2009 by RCAHMS, in partnership with the NTS, with additional forays made in later years. The Commissioners and the Chief Executive, Diana Murray, have been wholly supportive throughout its gestation, while the project would never have been realised without the enthusiasm and commitment of Robin Turner, initially Head of Archaeology at the NTS, and Jack Stevenson, Head of Survey and Recording at RCAHMS. Both were instrumental in ensuring the successful implementation, co-ordination and completion of the field survey. Robin, in particular, has made a major contribution to the management, understanding and interpretation of St Kilda over many years. He played a key role in the successful bid to extend St Kilda's WHS status to include the cultural heritage and he has also taken an interest in promoting research on the islands and its prompt publication. His appointment as Head of Survey and Recording at RCAHMS in 2010, in succession to Jack, ensured his unwavering support.

The study also draws upon information obtained by RCAHMS during an earlier survey of Village Bay and Gleann Mòr carried out in 1983–6 and first published as *Buildings of St Kilda* (1988). That expedition, which was led by architectural historian Geoffrey Stell, included three surveyors, Alan Leith, Ian Parker and Sam Scott, and the photographer John Keggie. Some of their original work is included here without emendation. The team also included Mary Harman, whose fieldwork up to 1983 provided a firm footing for the study. Indeed, her numbering system for recording the structures on the islands, together with the accompanying maps and photographs, are the foundation upon which both of the surveys were based; and more than 2,200 of her photographs are now held within the RCAHMS Collection.

Ian Parker was the project manager of the second expedition, which was undertaken as part of the NTS work party programme. His good humour, care and attention to detail were a great asset; and his sterling efforts to prepare numerous illustrations for this book before his well-earned retirement in 2014 is very much appreciated. His team included Georgina Brown, Dave Easton, Angela Gannon, Alex Hale, Strat Halliday, James Hepher, John Sherriff, Adam Welfare and the photographer Steve Wallace, while a link between the two expeditions was provided by Alan Leith, and by Mary Harman, who offered a great deal of valuable advice, not to mention an exquisite reading of the story of 'Roderick the Imposter' over one evening. The field team also included three representatives of the NTS – Jill Harden, Regional Archaeologist (North); Samantha Dennis, St Kilda Archaeologist; and George Geddes, who followed Sam in that post before being appointed as field investigator at RCAHMS.

Everyone on the 2007–9 expedition benefited from the fine accommodation and friendly atmosphere offered by the restored houses and the company of our fellow travellers. These included Annette Hepburn and Christine McPherson, who were responsible for the catering, David Ackroyd, who later kindly provided us with a complete set of the *St Kilda Mail*, Hannah Dinneen, John Duncan, Penny Franklin, Ian McPherson, Andy Robinson, Iain Small, Glyn Young and John Wills. In addition, we were joined by the freelance journalist Claire Black, the watercolour artist Claire Harkess, and the poet Kathleen Jamie, who wrote so evocatively about St Kilda in her memoir *Sightlines* (2012). Especial thanks must also be extended to Susan Bain, the NTS Western Isles Manager, who oversaw the logistical arrangements for each field trip, while Alison Andrew and Johanna Moffat provided administrative support from Inverness. Other small kindnesses were shown by NTS staff, including Derek Alexander, Alexander Bennett and Daniel Rhodes.

The additional campaigns after 2009 were made under the guidance of Stuart Murray, whose extensive knowledge of the islands and stacks is unparalleled. He led an expedition to Boreray in 2010, with Strat

Halliday, Jill Harden, Ian Parker and Sarah Wanless; another to Soay in 2011, with Jill Harden and Ian McHardy of the NTS; and following a failed attempt to reach Stac an Àrmainn, he made a trip to Dun with George Geddes, Jill Harden and Strat Halliday in 2013. A final expedition to Hirta was undertaken in 2014, when the team included George Geddes, Alison McCaig and Joe McAllister of RCAHMS, Kevin Grant of the NTS, and also Cathy MacIver.

The smooth progress of the field work on Hirta was aided by the staff of QinetiQ who provided accommodation and support when required, sometimes at extremely short notice. In addition, they proffered medical care, communication facilities, a constant power supply to recharge batteries, as well as the occasional lift to the top of the hill.

In practice, reaching St Kilda is far from straightforward and we are grateful to Angus Campbell and his crew at *Kilda Cruises*, who always ensured the safe landing and collection of the teams with their equipment. A small number of helicopter trips were also provided thanks to the courtesy of the NTS, QinetiQ and PDG Helicopters of Inverness, while accommodation at the beginning and end of each trip was provided by Ruari Beaton at Am Bothan, Leverburgh.

We also owe a great debt of gratitude to our colleagues at RCAHMS who have contributed in one way or another directly or indirectly to the production of this book. We are especially grateful to John Sherriff, who has offered encouragement and guidance whenever necessary and summarily delayed other calls on our time, allowing us the space to concentrate upon the work in hand; while the reader will readily understand our indebtedness to John Borland, Georgina Brown and Alison McCaig. John created the fine illustration of the recently discovered cross-incised stone, Georgina prepared the attractive maps, while Alison produced many of the excellent line drawings and the plan of Village Bay on the large map. We also owe a considerable debt to

Derek Smart, who took particular responsibility for the preparation of some 300 photographs for the book, often wresting a remarkably powerful image from a well-worn print in a dusty envelope. Indeed, Derek and everyone else in the photographic section, including Tahra Duncan-Clark, Zoe Gibson and Anne Martin, have been of enormous help to us. They have digitised the many hundreds of drawings and photographs collected during the 1983–6 expedition and made these available to view online. In addition, they have helped us ensure that the great majority of the material resulting from the fieldwork undertaken by RCAHMS in preparation for the *Ninth Report and Inventory of Monuments and Constructions in the Outer Hebrides, Skye and the Small Isles* (1928) has also been catalogued, digitised and made available online. The combined resource runs to more than 1,000 images.

St Kilda was omitted from the Aerial Survey programme of the 1980s, not least because it required the use of an aeroplane with a greater range than normally available, but David Cowley made good this deficiency by undertaking sorties in 2012 and 2013, capturing roughly 150 oblique views of the islands. Aerial images taken by his colleague Robert Adam in the Outer Hebrides have also been used. In addition, unpublished aerial photographs in the National Collection of Aerial Photography curated by RCAHMS were identified and digitised by David Buice, Ruta Gauld and Kevin McLaren; while Susan Casey, Leanne McCafferty and Peter McKeague provided much valued advice and assistance with the Oracle database the engine underlying the Canmore website.

The book has been designed with great care by Oliver Brookes at RCAHMS (with assistance from Alasdair Burns), whose experienced eye for detail has fashioned the final layout. The essential roles of proof reader and indexer were fulfilled by Mairi Sutherland and Linda Sutherland, respectively; while comments on sections of the text were provided by Mary Harman, Geoffrey Stell and Mark Thacker. Robin Turner read and commented on the whole text. Kirsty MacDonald of

Historic Scotland checked Gaelic spellings throughout the volume. Jamie Crawford, RCAHMS Publications Manager, has exercised his experience to advise us on the creation of a book that will appeal to a wide audience.

Jamie and Oliver's judgement has greatly helped us with the sifting of thousands of historic photographs. Although our own staff created many of these (some as long ago as 1914), others have been drawn from collections donated to RCAHMS, including those by Stuart Murray, who was kind enough to bring in the originals for copying and provide additional material. Our colleagues in the educational charity, SCRAN (Scottish Cultural Resources Access Network), have also made available images held in their collection. Special thanks in this regard are due to Joe McAllister and Neil Fraser of RCAHMS, who were exceedingly efficient in the provision of SCRAN imagery. The originals are courtesy of Newsquest (Herald and Times), the Scotsman, the NMS and the NTS. The majority of Norman MacLeod's photographs of St Kilda taken in 1886 are now held at the University of Aberdeen within the George Washington Wilson collection. Our thanks go to Kim Downie for providing the copies presented here. Those images taken by Robert Atkinson between the 1930s and the 1950s are now held in the School of Scottish Studies at the University of Edinburgh. These are reproduced by kind permission of his family and we are grateful to the School's archivist, Cathlin Macaulay, and her colleague, Colin Gateley, for making these available. Other pictures from the Society of Antiquaries of Scotland, Alasdair Alpin MacGregor and Alexander Cockburn were sourced from the NMS with the help of Dorothy Kidd and Margaret Wilson; while Iain Banks, following enquiries to Olivia Lelong and Jill Harden, provided an image from the archive of GUARD. Douglas Wilcox supplied the striking image from a kayaking expedition, and Benjamin Dürig the wonderful distant view of Hirta. Sir Thomas Dyke Acland's watercolours which also form the book's endpapers are included thanks to the generosity of his family and Stuart Tyler, archivist at the Devon Heritage Centre, and Jenny Liddle of the National Trust. The front cover design was produced with the help of Dr Lyn Wilson, Historic Scotland.

Despite these riches, perhaps our greatest debt for the imagery included in these pages is to the NTS, who have allowed us free access to their extensive collection. In permitting this, they have provided us with a unique opportunity to frame the archaeology and history of St Kilda in a more human and personal light. The identification of date and subject was undertaken by one of the authors (GG), with the aid of the previously published work of Meg Buchanan and David Quine, in addition to a database curated by the NTS St Kilda Archaeologist. We are especially grateful to Marcin Klimek and Ian Riches, who facilitated the supply of numerous images from the collection. We should also add that we offer our sincere apologies if we have perpetrated any errors in identifying the subjects and dates of any of the illustrations, or incorrectly attributing their copyright.

Many institutions hold fascinating archives relating to St Kilda – reading the original papers is a thrilling experience and we would encourage any reader to do this. Some of the research underpinning the narrative in this book was undertaken by one of the authors (GG) while working for the NTS under Susan Bain and Jill Harden between 2008 and 2011. It was during this period that research on the quay and gun emplacement in Village Bay was undertaken at the National Records of Scotland and at The National Archives at Kew. Morton Boyd's archive has also been consulted at the Special Collection Centre at the University of St Andrews, while documentation relating to the military base has been examined at the offices of the NTS at Inverness through the kindness of Susan Bain. The administrative files of RCAHMS have allowed us to fill out the story of our own work on St Kilda and in the Outer Hebrides over the years, while early editions or obscure texts have been accessed through Edinburgh City Libraries, the National Library of Scotland, and at the University of Edinburgh's Libraries.

Numerous professional colleagues and friends have also given freely of their time and material. Ian Whittaker contributed details regarding the context and results of his work on St Kilda in 1957 and Cathlin Macaulay produced a commentary on the involvement of the School of Scottish Studies on St Kilda between 1957 and 1958. Further assistance in relation to the biographies of Donald Macgregor and Roy Ritchie was provided by colleagues in Historic Scotland and at the Universities of Dundee and Edinburgh. Rosemary Cramp volunteered information clarifying the Durham University research projects on Hirta in the late 1980s and early 1990s, while Mike Copper, Mark Edmonds,

Andrew Fleming, Ann MacSween and Alison Sheridan all helped locate and verify the identification of the two sherds of Neolithic Hebridean pottery found in Village Bay. Niels Andersen of Moesgaard Museum and Peter Pentz from the National Museum of Denmark helpfully checked the origins of a Viking brooch which had been mistakenly attributed to St Kilda. They also provided the image of Jens Worsaae's drawing of the genuine find from a Danish journal published in 1872, while further assistance in this enquiry was provided by Anne Cameron, Katinka Dalglish and Fraser Hunter. Strat Halliday, Jill Harden and Isabel Henderson answered a query relating to analogies for the recently discovered cross-incised stone, while Mark Thacker took time to discuss several aspects of Early Christian and medieval St Kilda. We are also grateful to Helen Bradley for providing us with information relating to the archaeology of the fowling economy on Foula; to David Kear for bringing to our attention a recent paper on the late quaternary glaciation of the islands, to Peter Lack for information about his father and the Oxford and Cambridge expedition of 1931; to David Hosking for consulting his father's photographic collection; and to Simon Welfare for checking various newspaper references.

Finally, there are two individuals who above all are deserving of our greatest and most heartfelt gratitude – our editors, Jill Harden and Adam Welfare. Jill has been ever present on nearly every field trip, providing critique and counsel from a wealth of experience on the island. There are few archaeologists who can claim to have as thorough a knowledge of St Kilda as her and we were therefore delighted when she agreed to act as our external editor. In this capacity she has been rigorous and thorough, submitting pointed questions and comments that have signally helped to form both the final structure and the content of the book. Adam accepted the equally demanding task of editing this volume which he has accomplished meticulously and with supreme tact. He has chopped, changed and challenged the text, questioned the legitimacy of interpretations and at all times insisted that these are grounded in the available evidence. His unwavering attention to detail has been exercised throughout and he has helped us create a fully integrated and well-structured volume where text, illustrations and captions all help inform the narrative. Jill and Adam share an infectious enthusiasm for archaeology with a wealth of experience. Their energy and positive approach has proved a great inspiration.

Editorial Notes

Editorial conventions follow the guidelines of RCAHMS which were updated most recently in 2009. Placenames on St Kilda include examples derived from English, Gaelic and Norse, but we have generally used the name that is most commonly found in the archaeological literature, supplying the Gaelic equivalent where necessary on the first occasion that each arises. Translations have only been provided where strictly necessary. Each archaeological site has been classified in accordance with the RCAHMS thesaurus: www.canmore.org.uk/thesaurus.

References

Every chapter or image section includes a series of end notes which refer to primary and secondary sources. These are fully expanded in a bibliography at the rear of the volume and abbreviations not expanded in the text have been included within this. Recourse has also been had to material that is usually not publically available within the administrative archive of RCAHMS, but applications to view these items can be made to John Sinclair House. The bibliography contains only those entries that are relevant to the text, as an extensive bibliography for St Kilda was published by the Scottish Executive in 2003. This is available on the St Kilda website administered by the National Trust for Scotland: www.kilda.org.uk

The end notes also include the unique reference number of each of the sites mentioned in the text in bold type. By entering this number as a search, it is possible to access specific information from Canmore, the online catalogue of Scotland's archaeology, buildings, industrial and maritime heritage: www. canmore.org.uk.

Canmore holds descriptive notes prepared by archaeologists of the Ordnance Survey Archaeology Division and RCAHMS investigators during more than a century of recording, as well as information derived from a wide range of other organisations and individuals. It also provides access to material held within the RCAHMS Collection, including manuscripts, drawings and photographs. While every effort has been made to ensure that all of the RCAHMS images used in this publication are available in a digital format and online, the original items can also be consulted in the public search room at John Sinclair House.

Photographs

Each photograph is accompanied by a caption that includes the following information when known: the name of the photographer, the collection from which the image is sourced, a unique identification number and the date. Items held in the RCAHMS Collection can be identified by the prefixes DP (digital photograph) and SC (scanned image). The selection from RCAHMS includes images taken by the staff photographers John Keggie in 1986 and Steve Wallace in 2008, as well as those taken by the field staff during the course of the survey. The ranging-poles included in some of the photographs for scale are of metric type, with each division measuring 0.5m.

Numbering

RCAHMS has adopted several long-standing sequences of numbers and letters to identify the structural remains on each island. In line with a long accepted practice, the lime-mortared houses of the inhabitants are numbered in a sequence running from east to west from House 1 to 16, while the early to mid 19th century drystone blackhouses and similar buildings are assigned a corresponding sequence of letters from A to Z. Cleitean and other structures, such as peat-stands, huts and bothies, have been included within a single series of numbers originating from those initially assigned to village cleitean and their like by Morton Boyd and Peter Jewell in the early 1960s. Newly recognised structures have continued their sequence. The numbering of structures on the outer islands follows the same pattern, but builds on the work of Mary Harman from 1977. An exception has been made with the shieling huts and gathering folds situated in Gleann Mòr. Here we have used the existing sequence of letters developed by Kenneth Williamson and Morton Boyd in the late 1950s. Some buildings are unnumbered and these include unique structures such as the church, the manse, the storehouse and the burial ground etc, as well as those forming part of the military base constructed after 1957.

Copyright
Unless otherwise specified, the contents of this volume are Crown Copyright. Copies of RCAHMS photographs, maps and plans (individually identifiable by the catalogue number at the end of the caption) are available to view and purchase online at www.canmore.org.uk. Vertical aerial sorties can be viewed and purchased through the National Collection of Aerial Photography (www.ncap.org.uk). In addition, a wide range of historic images from a variety of collections can be viewed at www.scran.ac.uk.

Further Information
Information about Scotland's archaeological, architectural and maritime heritage can be found in Canmore, the national database, and can be consulted at www.canmore.org.uk

The archipelago of St Kilda is owned by the National Trust for Scotland. Information on visiting the islands can be gathered from the NTS St Kilda website www.kilda.org.uk or from their office at Balnain House, Inverness.

Notes on Maps and Plans

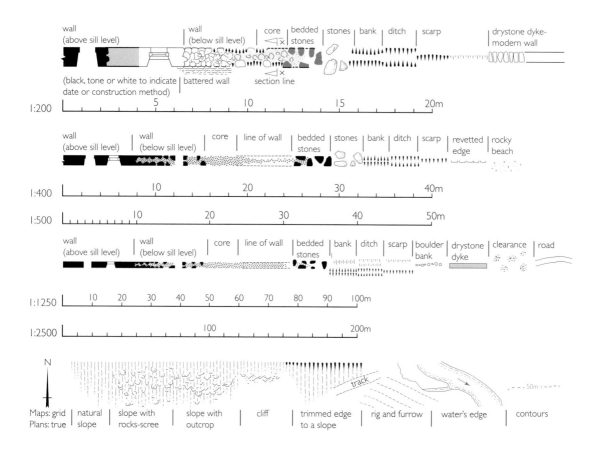

Conventional representations on maps and plans

Maps

The mapping of St Kilda in 2007–9 was undertaken with a Leica GPS1200 High performance GNSS system to an accuracy of a few centimetres in relation to the National Grid. This dataset was supplemented by information from handheld GPS units, plane-table surveys and linework taken from ortho-rectified aerial photographs. Additional material was drawn from plane-table surveys prepared by GUARD and tape-and-offset surveys by Mary Harman. The survey data is available as RCAHMS collection item TM000078. The pull-out map of the archipelago is presented at a scale of 1:10,000 from the final survey dataset.

Chapters 3–7 include two series of maps which locate the sites mentioned in the text, whether in the wider context of the Western Isles, or on the archipelago itself. Both make use of symbols, the first in conjunction with an alphabetically arranged numerical list, the second with a key derived from site classifications. Each is aligned to Grid North, and the National Grid is marked along the margin. All maps are based on information derived from the Ordnance Survey and are reproduced with their permission © Crown Copyright 2015 License Number 100020548.

Plans

Area surveys in 1983–6 and 2007–9 were taken with Wild self-reducing alidades and plane-tables at a scale of 1:500. They are reproduced through the volume at reduced scales varying from 1:1000 to 1:2500. Individual buildings on St Kilda were surveyed at 1:100 and the plans are reproduced here at 1:200. The ink drawings prepared for the 1988 publication have been reproduced with minor changes to labels, and a modern scale and north arrow. All of the original drawings are available to view at the office, and on the Canmore website.

The pull-out map includes on one side the survey of Village Bay undertaken by RCAHMS in 1983–4, revised and amended in 2007–9. It is reproduced here at 1:1250, in order to facilitate comparison with the previous published version.

Index

Page numbers in italics refer to captions and illustrations, those suffixed (n) indicate notes.

gun emplacement 108, *109*, 235

Halistra, Skye 73
Halliday, Strat 47
hammers 29, 38
hand-milling machine 106, *106*
harbour facilities, Village Bay *198*
    breakwater 106, 107
    naust 77
    quay 97, 104, 107, *108*, 115, 129, *161,* 235, *260*
    slipway 232, 235
    see also landing craft
harbours, Rodel 95, *95*
Harden, Jill 23, 40, 43, 73, 249
Harebell, HMS 7, *212*
Harman, Mary
    An Lag Bhon Tuath stone settings 35
    Boreray terraces 63
    cleitean 15, 16, 22–3, 89
    committee member 266(n)
    Dun wall 43
    fowling structures 88–9
    Gleann Mor dyke 82
    Soay peat and turf cuttings 89
    survey work 8, 15, 16, *22*, 23, 249
Harris 7, 20
    agriculture 69, 112
    Berneray causeway 117
    Both a' Chlair Bheag 53
    brochs *27*, 35
    Bunavoneader 119, *191*
    Ceapabhal 49
    chapels *27*, 52
    churches 52, *52*, 95, 99
    clearances 97
    crosses on stones 45
    forts 19
    gathering folds 82
    Greabhal 49
    harbours 95, *95*
    Horgabost 49
    Leverburgh 7, 119, 249
    Loch Steisebhat 49
    MacDonalds' move to 214
    MacLeod clan 67, 69, 70, 93, 95, *95*
    Norse place-names 49
    Northton 25, 27, *27*, 31, 35, 97, 119
    pilgrimages to St Kilda 55, *55*
    Rodel 52, *52*, 95, *95*, 112
    see also McNeil family, Rodel
    sale of 93, *95*
    Scarista (Sgarasta) 49, *94*, 99
    shielings 17, 53, 62
    Sròn Smearasmal 53
    tourism 198
    townships 70, 113, 119
    transportation from 95
    whaling 119, *191*
    see also Pabbay
Harris, Dr Mike 246, *255*
Harris tweed *see* weaving
harvest 178, 181, *195*
head dykes
    Boreray 63
    Pabbay 71
    Village Bay 51, 57, 79, *79*, 80, *80*, 110, 122, *192*
        dimensions 273(n)
Heathcote, Norman 20, 201
Hebrides 198, 201, 214, 217
Herlofsen, Karl *191*
    see also whaling
Hetherington, Tom 22
Highland and Agricultural Society of Scotland
    (HASS) 104, 106, 107
Hinba 47
Hiort 7
Hirta 7, 19–20, *25*, *136*, 138, *145*, *155*
    arable ground 80
    bothies *72*, *88*, 89, 113
    Carn Mòr *87*, 88, 89, 141, *172*
    cattle 82, *112*, 178
    chapels 21, 53–4, *99*
    church 99, *99*
    cists 19, 33, 35
    cleitean 22, *87*, 89, *111*, 141
    conservation work *250*
    Fleming, Andrew, *St Kilda and the Wider*
        World 132–3
    manse 19, 77, 99, *99*
    military use 7–8, *117*, 122, *123*, *124*, 126, 232, 235
    Norse and 50
    peat stands 89
    peat and turf 54, 89, 113, 141
    pilgrimages 55, *56*
    place-names 50
    plane crashes 121, *121*
    sheep 113, 178, *188*, *217*, 222
    soils 23